Alternatives to Capitalism in the 21st Century

Series Editors: **Lara Monticelli**, Copenhagen Business School, and **Torsten Geelan**, University of Copenhagen

---

Debates about the future of capitalism demonstrate the urgent need to envision and enact alternatives that can help tackle the multiple intertwined crises that societies are currently facing. This ground-breaking new series advances the international, comparative and interdisciplinary study of capitalism and its alternatives in the 21st Century.

Forthcoming in the series:

Capital to Commons
Hannes Gerhardt

Money Commons:
Remaking Money for an Inclusive and Sustainable Future
Ester Barinaga

Out now in the series:

The Future is Now:
An Introduction to Prefigurative Politics
Edited by **Lara Monticelli**

Find out more at

bristoluniversitypress.co.uk/
alternatives-to-capitalism-in-the-21st-century

Alternatives to Capitalism in the 21st Century

Series Editors: **Lara Monticelli**, Copenhagen Business School, and **Torsten Geelan**, University of Copenhagen

---

Advisory board:

Wendy Harcourt, Erasmus University Rotterdam, Netherlands
Vasna Ramasar, Lund University, Sweden
Tom Malleson, King's University College, Canada
Silvia Federici, Hofstra University, US
Richard D. Wolff, The New School for Social Research, US
Nancy Fraser, The New School for Social Research, US
Luke Martell, University of Sussex, UK
Laura Basu, openDemocracy and University of Utrecht, Netherlands
Juliet Schor, Boston College, US
Isabelle Ferreras, Université Catholique de Louvain, Belgium
Göran Therborn, University of Cambridge, UK
Gar Alperovitz, The Democracy Collective and the Next System Project, US
Francesca Forno, University of Trento, Italy
Flor Avelino, Erasmus University Rotterdam, Dutch Research Institute for Transitions, Netherlands
Emanuele Leonardi, University of Parma, Italy
David Bailey, University of Birmingham, UK
Ashish Kothari, Global Tapestry of Alternatives, India
Aris Komporozos-Athanasiou, University College London, UK
Arturo Escobar, University of North Carolina, US
Albena Azmanova, Brussels School of International Studies, Belgium

Find out more at
bristoluniversitypress.co.uk/
alternatives-to-capitalism-in-the-21st-century

POLITICS OF THE GIFT

Towards a Convivial Society

Frank Adloff

Translated by Björn Bosserhoff

Originally published in German by Edition Nautilus in 2018 as
Politik der Gabe: Für ein anderes Zusammenleben

Originally published in German by Edition Nautilus, Hamburg as
Politik der Gabe: Für ein anderes Zusammenleben (2018)

English language edition published in Great Britain in 2024 by

Bristol University Press
University of Bristol
1-9 Old Park Hill
Bristol
BS2 8BB
UK
t: +44 (0)117 374 6645
e: bup-info@bristol.ac.uk

Details of international sales and distribution partners are available at bristoluniversitypress.co.uk

© Bristol University Press 2024

British Library Cataloguing in Publication Data
A catalogue record for this book is available from the British Library

ISBN 978-1-5292-2622-5 hardcover
ISBN 978-1-5292-2623-2 paperback
ISBN 978-1-5292-2624-9 ePub
ISBN 978-1-5292-2625-6 ePdf

The right of Frank Adloff to be identified as author of this work has been asserted by him in accordance with the Copyright, Designs and Patents Act 1988.

All rights reserved: no part of this publication may be reproduced, stored in a retrieval system, or transmitted in any form or by any means, electronic, mechanical, photocopying, recording, or otherwise without the prior permission of Bristol University Press.

Every reasonable effort has been made to obtain permission to reproduce copyrighted material. If, however, anyone knows of an oversight, please contact the publisher.

The statements and opinions contained within this publication are solely those of the author and not of the University of Bristol or Bristol University Press. The University of Bristol and Bristol University Press disclaim responsibility for any injury to persons or property resulting from any material published in this publication.

Bristol University Press works to counter discrimination on grounds of gender, race, disability, age and sexuality.

Cover design: Liam Roberts
Front cover image: "Exit through the gift" by Zualidro

Contents

Introduction: From Capitalism's Crises to a Convivial Society ... 1

PART I An Anthropology of Giving
1 Self-interest, Altruism, and the Gift ... 13
2 Mauss' Gift ... 25
3 *Homo Donator*: A Different Anthropology ... 38

PART II Society's Gifts
4 Locating the Gift in Society ... 55
5 The Gift between Socialism and Capitalism ... 70
6 Commodities, Values, Money, Gifts ... 81

PART III Crossing the Borders
7 Science and Technology, Nature and Conviviality ... 99
8 Gifts of Nature ... 108
9 Civil Society, Conviviality, Utopia ... 119

PART IV Worlds of Conviviality
10 Aesthetic Freedom, or The Gift of Art ... 131
11 Pluriversalism: Towards a European and Global Politics of Conviviality ... 141

Conclusion ... 154

Notes ... 159
References ... 161
Index ... 182

Introduction: From Capitalism's Crises to a Convivial Society

Humans are living longer, healthier, wealthier, safer, and more peaceful lives than ever—not just in the Global North but in many regions around the world. And yet many feel that we are living in an era of crisis. The war in Syria and the millions of refugees it produced brought home to us that armed conflicts and material human suffering are not a thing of the past but affect even "us" in the North quite directly. In Germany and elsewhere, right-wingers intent on protecting their people from *Überfremdung* and "replacement" tried to use this situation to their advantage. Meanwhile, international cooperation, crucial for effectively fighting global warming, has been stagnating for years, and the effects of climate change are becoming more and more apparent as natural disasters proliferate. Large parts of Africa have been shattered by wars, corruption, hunger, and forced displacement. Social inequality is rising dramatically in many countries, and the economic, financial, and debt crisis is far from over. According to Oxfam, in 2018, the wealth of the 42 richest individuals on earth equaled that of the poorest 3.7 billion. And the gap continues to grow: the top 1 percent now rank in more than 80 percent of the global economic growth, and the number of billionaires is higher than ever before. Perhaps worst of all, democracy is under attack in many places, with authoritarian leaders trampling on liberal values and human rights, and corporations shamelessly exploiting the fragility of once strong democratic institutions and processes. On top of all that, in 2020 the globe was hit by one of the deadliest pandemics in modern history, which has further aggravated the social inequalities both within our societies and globally.

This is the dire state we are in 30 years after the Cold War ended. The end of history? Think again. Little wonder, then, that calls for a radical transformation are becoming louder, voices that demand that we finally move beyond neoliberal financial capitalism, confront inequality, overcome stereotyping and isolationism, and develop new, sustainable forms of living on earth. Which is exactly what I, too, call for in this book. In what follows, I try to lay the foundations for an understanding of new forms of human cooperation and institutional orders. In doing so, I will make ample use of the concept of convivialism (from Latin *con-vivere*: living together), which is based on another sociological concept that is the focal point of my argument: the gift. Starting out with everyday varieties of gift giving, I will work my way towards the global scale and examine different shapes that a "politics of the gift" could take, a politics that aspires to change the ways we treat each other and the world in which we live.

In this endeavor, I was inspired by a small volume published in 2013 by a group of 64 mostly French academics, the *Convivialist Manifesto*. Intended to make plain that "[a] different kind of world is not just possible" but "a crucial and urgent necessity" (Les Convivialistes, 2014: 38), the manifesto was signed by intellectuals of various political convictions who nonetheless agreed on the two main causes for today's societal crises: the primacy of utilitarian, self-interested behavior, and a persistent belief in the blissful effects of economic growth. The convivialists' response to this diagnosis is a fundamentally different vision of the good life. What matters most, they insist, is that we become more mindful of the quality of social relationships and of humanity's relationship with nature: for our "living together" to succeed, we must first realize that our lives are based on a cycle of giving, receiving, and reciprocating (see also Adloff, 2014; Adloff and Heins, 2014a, 2014b). A second *Convivialist Manifesto* was published in 2020 and has already been translated into various languages. Reacting to current political developments, such as the worldwide renaissance of illiberal regimes, it makes more concrete policy suggestions than its predecessor; and since it grew out of a broader collective discussion, the second manifesto is also more international in character: almost 300 academics and intellectuals from 33 countries ended up signing it (see Convivialist International, 2020).

The idea for the first manifesto was born at a colloquium in Japan in 2010. This was followed by a proceedings volume and by Alain Caillé's *Pour un manifeste du convivialisme* (Caillé, 2011a; Caillé et al, 2011). The debate on conviviality and convivialism was initially focused on the work of Ivan Illich (1926–2002), an Austrian American theologian and philosopher who was a radical critic of modern technology and an early proponent of degrowth. His book *Tools for Conviviality* was popularized in France by André Gorz and received much critical attention around the world. Like his friend Erich Fromm (1976), Illich believed that it was time to once again prioritize "being" over "having": a truly convivial society would limit its use of technology, which otherwise may take on a life of its own and cause more problems than it solves (Illich, 1973).

A second, much older, and perhaps surprising source of the conviviality concept is the book *The Physiology of Taste* (1825), in which the French gastronome Jean Anthelme Brillat-Savarin described the "spirit of conviviality" as that which "brings together from day to day differing kinds of people, melts them into a whole, animates their conversation, and softens the sharp corners of the conventional inequalities of position and breeding" (Brillat-Savarin, [1825] 2009: 160–1). In both the French and English languages, "conviviality" is still commonly used to denote friendly social intercourse—and this could be expanded to include people's relations with "things" (such as artifacts, infrastructures, technologies, or institutions).

There are two more strands of thought that have influenced the convivialist vision: the anti-utilitarianism of Caillé and critiques of growthism as voiced by Patrick Viveret and Serge Latouche. The philosopher Viveret (2011) identifies the structural exorbitance of modern productivism, in both its capitalist and socialist versions, as the root of our current crisis. The fixation on economic growth, he holds, ought to be replaced by other criteria of wealth and the good life—and the measure of the gross domestic project in particular be reconsidered. Latouche, an economist, is the most prominent proponent of degrowth theory or *décroissance*. He champions a society of "frugal abundance" (2014) and, like Viveret, calls for a new conception of wealth that goes beyond its monetary aspects. In Latouche's view, a convivial society must radically question the idea of growth; it must limit itself. New forms of economic activity are needed which put an end to the permanent creation of ever more (potentially unlimited) pseudo-needs. Latouche sees growth for growth's sake as the maxim of a religion of the economy that, along with the ideal of the *homo oeconomicus*, we should finally get rid of.

Currently, ideas of growth and material wealth serve as a screen onto which people project all sorts of hopes and fears. To be sure, hopes for individual future prosperity hold societies together, even though they usually remain unrealized. But what happens when the time of high growth comes to an end (as already appears to be the case, at least in Western societies), when unemployment can no longer be minimized by growth, when incomes are not enough to get by on any more, when social inequality keeps rising? For the convivialists, the answer is clear: our ideals of a good life must be decoupled from material wealth, and democracy and conviviality acknowledged as ends in themselves. Such an adoption of completely new ideals to guide the lives of individuals and whole societies would amount to nothing less than a political and ethical revolution.

Degrowth theory has its origins in earlier debates on the ecological crisis and "post-development." Adherents of the latter concept, also drawing on Illich, are highly critical of a modernization of the Global South along the lines of Western/Northern notions of economic growth (see Chapter 11). For Latouche and others, in light of the current social and ecological double crisis caused by capitalist hegemony, future human self-limitation is imperative. In capitalism, the economy must keep growing, so as to keep competition between companies and the eternal struggle for profits running. Many now come to realize, however, that this mode of economic activity is just not sustainable, since it relies on energy prerequisites that soon will no longer be available: we are consuming and destroying livelihoods to an extent that makes it impossible for the earth to replenish them.

Capitalism thus not only produces social inequality and exploitation on a massive scale; it also uses up humanity's very livelihood. Modern capitalist society is simply too expansive. It needs to be fettered. While it is undeniable that during the last 200 years or so, mass consumption made possible an emancipation from material straits for many, it is important to realize that this was accomplished at the expense of others: of nature and the Global South (to say nothing of the extreme inequalities *within* Northern societies). Stephan Lessenich (2019) calls ours an "externalization society" by which he means that the freedom and prosperity Europeans and North Americans enjoy today were achieved by colonizing and destroying the worlds of others. The North has been living beyond the means of the South; its well-being is dependent on sacrifices made elsewhere. What is more, the substandard working conditions in many countries of the South (one thinks of the notorious Bangladeshi garment worker) and the massive environmental destructions (for example on mega-plantations contaminated with pesticides) go hand in hand with ostracism and social devaluation. Meanwhile, Northerners continue to celebrate their own superiority and berate the South for its "underdevelopment" and alleged lack of efforts. Lessenich contends that this is a case of a repression or denial of one's own guilt, instead projecting it onto others. What results is an "imperial mode of living" (Brand and Wissen, 2017), the "habitual practice ... of *externalizing* the costs of [our] way of life to others while at the same time *blanking out* this structural connection from [our] daily lives" (Lessenich, 2019: 42). To sustain itself, capitalism is appropriating more and more areas of life, subjecting them to its monetary ideology and robbing them of profit. Just think of the privatization of water (Nestlé), of biopiracy (Monsanto resp. Bayer AG), or of the destruction of smallholding structures in whole regions of Latin America, Africa, and Asia to produce biofuel for the EU. Rosa Luxemburg ([1913] 2003) and Hannah Arendt (1951) already knew about capitalism's proclivity for appropriation (*Landnahme*), and their analyses are now more topical than ever.

All this goes to show that there are no isolated societies (left) on this globe, and no dividing line between nature and culture either: the effects of climate change—floods, droughts, and so on—are directly linked to poverty, displacement, and armed conflicts. All human and nonhuman lifeforms are thus interconnected and interdependent. But this global interdependence is extremely asymmetrical, with some managing to generate profits and externalize their costs, be they of an economic, a cultural, a social, or an ecological nature. For instance, millions of Brazilian peasants were displaced to make room for vast soy plantations that produce exports for the newly health-conscious Global North (Altieri and Bravo, 2009). Some are always just taking, others just giving. Convivialism, by contrast, aims at a solidary exchange. It is not for nothing that the first *Convivialist Manifesto*'s subtitle reads "A Declaration of Interdependence."

But what is the alternative to the pursuit of profit, to growthism and consumerism? Which social logic could economic self-limitation be based on? Which logic of action lends itself to the transformation into a convivial society that champions cooperation, no longer externalizes its costs, and acknowledges the interdependence of everyone and everything? These are questions addressed by the sociologist and economist Alain Caillé, the driving force behind the *Convivialist Manifestos*, who has transferred ideas of conviviality into convivial*ism*—the political concept, the theory, the movement. For Caillé, it all comes down to one question: how can we live together without any compulsion to conform—and without butchering each other? He glimpses an answer to that question in the work of Marcel Mauss (1872–1950), and in particular in the Maussian paradigm of the gift which he, Caillé, has substantially advanced over the last decades. Mauss, a sociologist and anthropologist, described how reciprocal giving creates a bond between groups, though without dissolving their principal "agonality," their combative attitude towards each other ([1925] 1990: 4–5; see also Adloff, 2016: 24ff.). In the mode of gift giving, people truly recognize each other and assure one another of their esteem. Convivialism takes up this idea and argues that the simple acknowledgment of a common humanity could lead to worldwide conviviality (Caillé, 2011a: 21). A radical and universal equality, then, grounded in the logic of the gift, is the precondition of convivial coexistence.

In this book, I follow Caillé's gift paradigm and inquire how our self-conceptions and ways of living together might change once we realize that humans are not just selfish takers but also inclined to give (Caillé, 2020). As Mauss cautioned, modern social relations increasingly conform to the model of the market. We are in danger of actually becoming the *homines oeconomici* that economists have long assumed us to be. Mainstream economic theory continues to insist that humans act rationally—in a very narrow sense: only those who strive to optimize their profits are considered rational. Competitiveness in markets is good for us all, so the theory goes, because it results in an optimized supply of goods and services. During the last decades, this belief in "the market" as a great regulator has proved very influential, and economics has become a master discipline of sorts whose reach goes far beyond the economy to include questions of how to best organize human coexistence more generally. Its success is not least due to the field's rigorous self-discipline: the economic curriculum is extremely standardized, with the same texts and econometric methods being studied around the world and the same old basic premises being used to build ever new mathematical models. The problem is that these models capture only a tiny segment of social reality. And yet, alternative schools, such as "real-world" or "post-autistic" economics, are regularly rejected as crude aberrations from neoclassical orthodoxy.

This unity within the discipline ensures its hegemonial influence on economic practice. Even the financial crisis of 2007–08 failed to harm economics, notwithstanding the alarming naivete of its response to that crisis: economists were unswerving in their belief that financial markets are essentially efficient and that the overall economy always returns to a state of equilibrium (Herrmann, 2017). Much has been written about the fact that economics abides by these unrealistic assumptions—with the unfortunate result that its evaluations of economic reality are often plainly wrong. What matters to me in this context is the self-fulfilling prophecy effect of such assumptions, the question whether that which economic theory purports to only describe, the individual's eternal pursuit of further gains, is not instead created by it in the first place. Since a view of humans as ultimately egoistical beings has been propagated for decades, it is no wonder that this has become our default cultural self-conception. And yet, this conception fails to recognize one simple fact: that being human does not generally amount to separation and selfishness, that bonds, interdependencies, and relations based on taking and giving shape our lives in elemental ways.

In 1985, the sociologist Robert Bellah published a seminal study of American society, *Habits of the Heart*. He showed that members of the US middle class tend to think of themselves as rationally pursuing their self-interest, with even relationships being strategically chosen to enhance their own well-being; behind this was the belief that normative obligations served as just another means of self-realization (Bellah et al, 1985). It is easy to detect here the neoliberal, individualistic rhetoric of the Reagan years. However, the actual lives of those interviewed by Bellah and his colleagues did not exactly match their self-descriptions: they did have strong bonds and commitments, they did feel responsible for others, and they were part of all sorts of communities—they were merely unable to adequately articulate these bonds, commitments, obligations, and attachments. Bellah concluded that a rhetoric of competition and isolation had indeed become pervasive in 1980s United States, obscuring traditional practices of care. It does matter, therefore, how we describe both ourselves and the conduct of others. In sociology, the so-called Thomas theorem states that "[i]f men define situations as real, they are real in their consequences" (Thomas and Thomas, 1928: 572). It follows that we would be well-advised to return to a language of giving, of care and solidarity, which corresponds to people's real needs and behaviors and is bound to have productive effects if many people adopt it. A language that no longer conceives of man as "wolf to man" (Hobbes) but espouses a more positive anthropology. To be sure, over the whole course of history, humans have engaged in harming, oppressing, and killing each other, as well as other creatures. Yet it would be wrong to naturalize evil and regard it as "human nature." Once we leave behind the capitalist logic of utility maximization and start taking serious viable alternatives, both in the economy and in our everyday lives, we will prove capable of cooperation for the benefit of all.

This book is intended as a contribution to this desirable development. I will introduce the concept of the *homo donator* (see Chapter 3) as an alternative to the *homo oeconomicus*—which was never more than a fiction to begin with. Ontologically speaking, interactions, interdependencies, and bonds come prior to separation and independence. The giving human being is a sociable creature; it has little to do with the liberal illusion of a (male) subject that exists autonomously from others and is free of vulnerabilities. Such a view ignores that independence is in fact dependent on others—usually on women who care for their husbands and families, but also on nature as giver of life per se. The gifts bestowed upon others in these relationships tend to be overlooked, trivialized, or consciously concealed. As of late, for White middle-class women this may no longer be as true as it once was. But it still is for female workers in the Global South, for migrant domestics, nannies, and so on. The problem is not that there are no gifts in our societies but that these gifts are not appropriately acknowledged. Be it employees in precarious jobs, the economies of former colonies, or various ecosystems: we must recognize what "subalterns" give us and dispose of the extreme asymmetry inherent in these kinds of relations. That would be truly convivial.

What is needed, then, is a world of equality, a world in which all are recognized as givers. My project of advancing an anthropology and politics of giving amounts to a challenge: it is meant to prompt readers to join in the search for "real utopias" (Wright, 2010) which help us to overcome utilitarianism and the fixation on growth and develop an attractive new vision of coexistence on earth, a vision that will not scare people off because everybody benefits from it. All are called upon to creatively partake in this transformation, to experiment with new forms of conviviality and establish the gift as a leading paradigm. This no doubt sounds naive to some. But as the Italian philosopher and convivialist Elena Pulcini pointed out at a conference some years ago, in that very naivete lies the radicality and power of the convivialist project.

★

In the following, I want to briefly explain the book's structure. But first a pointer for those who have little time or are unwilling to follow the more intricate sociological and theoretical deliberations: if you skim or skip Chapters 1, 3, and 4, you will still be able to grasp the book's sociopolitical thrust.

Chapter 1 examines how sociologists normally respond to one key question: what motivates us to give to others or to reciprocate a gift? I argue that the two established approaches—utilitarianism and normativism—are problematic and fall short in explicating this phenomenon. This is because they both wrongly assume that taking comes more naturally to us than giving. They are simply too individualistic in outlook and thus fail to account for social interactions.

An alternative theoretical framework is provided by Marcel Mauss whose [1925] 1990 essay *The Gift* is the main focus of Chapter 2. Mauss made us understand the seminal role that gifts and reciprocity played in past societies, and still play today. His as well as Caillé's work makes evident that gifts comprise an element of freedom and unconditionality. They cannot be reduced to either self-interest or obligation; rather, giving, receiving, and reciprocating are intrinsically linked to forms of mutual recognition.

In Chapter 3 we temporarily leave the Maussian gift and make some detours, leading us towards the alternative anthropology of the *homo donator*. In particular, Mauss' approach will be contrasted with the classical pragmatism of John Dewey and George Herbert Mead. A model of human action is here developed that breaks with utilitarianism and the Western idea of a subject–object dualism. Moreover, it integrates affects and affective valuations into the action model, and addresses the problems of intersubjectivity, empathy, cooperation, and prosociality, drawing conclusions for normative democratic theory.

Chapter 4 focuses on the question regarding which kinds of gifts exist in society and on which levels of sociality they are located. I will introduce the distinction between ordinary and extraordinary gifts, in which trust and reciprocity play quite different roles. Then, I will illustrate that gifts may be found not just on a micro-sociological level: we can conceive of them as a medium of symbolic communication that circulates in society as a whole, and constitutes a background mechanism for cooperation of all kinds.

Chapter 5 revisits Mauss and recalls his political activism. A socialist who championed individual freedoms and democracy, his political arguments have lost none of their relevance. They are of value especially to current concepts of post-growth and a solidarity economy, which defy the traditional dichotomy of capitalism vs. state socialism. While the principle of the gift is of utmost importance in interpersonal relationships, it can have just as much impact in the realm of the economy.

Whoever speaks of the gift cannot remain silent about value, commodity, and money, the interconnections of which are the subject of Chapter 6. Following Mauss and Karl Polanyi, I will demonstrate that non-capitalistic gifts foster the capitalist economic process. No economy can do without gifts given for free; in fact, it is the non-symmetry and non-equivalence inherent to the gift that form the very basis of our coexistence. Even money contains aspects of gift giving, and it is these aspects that would become more important in a reformed money system.

Chapter 7 deals with our relationship with nature, in particular as it gets mediated through science and technology. The roots of our instrumental view of nature lie in the Western naturalist tradition which assumes a categorical difference between human culture on the one hand and nature on the other. However, this worldview is not incontestable: experiences of nature as an equal have always been a part of modernity, and even technology can be shaped in such a way as to be convivial—as already imagined by Illich in the 1970s.

As I argue in Chapter 8, nature does not have to be regarded as mere material, as a passive "resource" that is at the disposal of humanity. The new materialism, as well as some novel approaches within the sciences, already transcend this traditional view, and in the era of the Anthropocene it indeed makes sense to talk about the gifts of nature. Once we conceive of nonhuman beings as quasi-subjects, we will be able to forge alliances with "Gaia," and a new politics of the gift can come into being.

The project of a politics of the gift points to the domain of civil society, the subject-matter of Chapter 9. Practices of conviviality are mostly self-organized, emerge beyond the grasp of markets and state, and are frequently utopian in character. Such utopian practices may best be put to the test, and eventually realized, in social experiments.

In Chapter 10, I discuss the relationship between art and the gift. I argue that aesthetic experiences can lead us to more freedom and self-determination. Without freedom, alterity, and imagination there can be neither gift relationships nor aesthetic experiences. Art, too, ultimately builds on the aesthetic dimensions inherent to the gift. And in some projects, such as those pursued by the Invisible Committee, the poetics and politics of the gift merge.

Chapter 11 is about Europe's role in the world. When we embark on a collective quest for new forms of human coexistence, it is imperative that Europe bids farewell to nationalism and colonialist structures of exploitation for good. Because in order to develop positive visions for living together convivially, we have to look beyond the borders of Europe. The concept of "development" and simplistic notions of a universal morality must finally be scrutinized. Only when the pluriversalism of different cosmologies is acknowledged, can we create pluralistic models of the good life and true equality between the Global North and South.

Finally, in my conclusion, I respond to current developments like the COVID-19 pandemic, which were unforeseeable when this book was published in German in 2018. While a convivialist transformation of society is badly needed, it will doubtless take some time to accomplish it—time that we have almost run out of. Therefore, our mission must be to fight for a cultural and political change that is as broad and swift as possible, and that includes positive visions for a new, convivial society.

PART I

An Anthropology of Giving

1

Self-interest, Altruism, and the Gift

Why do we give things to others? Why do we pay attention to, help and forgive them? Are gifts a normal part of everyday life or rather an exception to the rule of self-interest? Gift giving is frequently linked to the principle of exchange: person A gives something of value to person B and receives something else that is of similar value. The exchange is beneficial to both since each desires that which the other owns more than what they own themselves. For Adam Smith, the "father of modern economics," "the propensity to truck, barter, and exchange one thing for another" is a part of "human nature" and distinguishes us from other animals. After all, "[n]obody ever saw a dog make a fair and deliberate exchange of one bone for another with another dog" (Smith, [1776] 1957: 10).

In exchanges it is usually clear which goods change hands at what time, as persons A and B have agreed on certain conditions. However, there are situations in which material or immaterial goods are given without an exchange taking place: person A gives something to person B but does *not* expect something in return. Perhaps person B will return the favor at a later point, and perhaps they won't; it is entirely up to them to decide if and when to reciprocate person A's gift.

Whereas exchanges, with their overtly self-interested motives, require no further explanation, acts of gift giving do. Scholarship on this issue tends to proceed along one of three paths: first, one can try to show that behind seemingly disinterested acts of giving there are in fact self-interested motives; second, one accepts that people give but assumes that this is merely due to the values and norms they have internalized during socialization; or third, one insists that people are indeed capable of acting altruistically, of making sacrifices. Since the altruism model often cannot be clearly separated from the internalization model, we are left with a simple dichotomy: theories of self-interest vs. theories that emphasize values, norms, and altruistic acts. Thus, sociological theories of rational choice focus on exchanges between self-interested individual agents while normative social theory is concerned with powerful supra-individual values and norms which individuals comply with.

On the one hand, then, there is the utilitarian model of the self-interested individual agent who engages with other individuals very selectively and briefly: you meet, exchange something to the mutual benefit of those involved, and move on. This is essentially the principle of the market, and it may include behaviors such as borrowing and paying off debts. On the other hand, there is the more holistic model that stresses ethical conduct based on obligations and internalized norms and values.

My contention is that this kind of dichotomy makes it impossible to adequately understand many forms of giving. Gifts are neither purely expressive of self-interest, nor can they be reduced to merely acting according to norms. There is a surplus of spontaneity, freedom, and sympathy manifest in gifts, which both rational-choice and normative theories are unable to capture.

Exchange and norms

A somewhat contradictory attempt at joining the two strands—norms vs. self-interest—may be found in Georg Simmel's (1858–1918) essay on "Faithfulness and Gratitude." Simmel here analyzes how feelings of social obligation are formed which contribute to the continuation of social relationships far beyond the duration of the initial motivations for entering them. Such relations, he argues, are stabilized by feelings of gratitude and a bond based on reciprocity: without a permanent process of giving and receiving "society could simply not exist" ([1908] 1950: 379). According to Simmel, social relationships are often marked by a lasting personal indebtedness—in contrast to market relationships, in which the exchange of goods and services of equal value precludes the accrual of obligations. The subjective response of gratitude is effective beyond the acts of giving and receiving, and hence constitutive of a social relationship characterized by reciprocity. Yet, as Simmel further points out, because the initial gift was entirely voluntary, a counter-gift is always stained by the obligation to reciprocate and therefore can never amortize that personal debt. "[W]e *cannot* return a gift," Simmel writes, "for it has a freedom which the return gift, because it is *that*, cannot possibly possess" ([1908] 1950: 393). The original asymmetry cannot ever be overcome; the counter-gift is per definition inferior.

To be sure, Simmel is very insightful when it comes to the big role played by gratitude in social life. But generally, he regards modern society as an anonymous affair governed by other two mechanisms: money and the law. "The division that has appeared in the original unity of the subjective and the objective," he writes, "is, as it were, embodied in money" ([1900] 2011: 136). By liberating them from social obligations, money provides modern subjects with more personal freedom; at the same time, and for this very reason, it threatens to undermine the moral order and divide societies. It is the classic dichotomy all over again: gifts and gratitude in personal relationships vs. unpersonal money-mediated exchanges in public life.

Some 50 years after Simmel, the American sociologist Alvin Gouldner (1920–80) studied phenomena of reciprocity, in particular with regard to their function of securing personal relationships. Gouldner understood reciprocity as a universal norm that those engaged in social interactions will have internalized and feel obliged to fulfill. This "norm of reciprocity" consists of "two, interrelated, minimal demands: (1) people should help those who have helped them, and (2) people should not injure those who have helped them" (Gouldner, 1960: 171). Also, the norm of reciprocity can serve as a "starting mechanism," that is, "help to initiate social interaction" (1960: 176): since they may assume that the other person, too, is committed to it, the norm "provides some realistic grounds for confidence, in the one who first parts with his valuables, that he will be repaid" (1960: 177). The risk that accompanies giving is thus reduced.

But Gouldner also wanted to explore the limits of the norm of reciprocity, especially pertaining "the importance of something for nothing" (1973: 260ff.). Charitable behavior, for example, does not usually involve the expectation of getting something in return. When we give one Euro to a beggar, we know that he will not repay us later. As for our children, we can no longer assume that they will support us in old age, and yet we give to them all the time. Gouldner believed that such behavior is motivated by another norm, that of beneficence, which obliges us to give even to those who cannot reciprocate our gifts. It is important to distinguish between motives and effects in this respect: an act motivated by beneficence may still have the effect of provoking a return gift, albeit unintended—for instance, when we do our neighbors a favor.

Pierre Bourdieu (1930–2002), who developed one of the major theories of reciprocity, was very interested in that frequently muddled connection between motives for actions and their consequences. His work on the economy of symbolic goods repeatedly addresses the ambiguity inherent in practices of giving, for example in *La sens pratique* ([1980] 1990: 98ff.). While he appears to take the subjective perspective seriously—acknowledging that people believe to have disinterested motives for presenting each other with valuable things—Bourdieu is convinced that such gifting practices are actually exchanges, demanding a counter-gift. He contends that participants in the gift economy do in fact mostly have self-serving ulterior motives, but that the true nature of their practices is concealed (even to them) by the passing of time:

> [T]he functioning of gift exchange presupposes individual and collective misrecognition of the truth of the objective "mechanism" of

the exchange, a truth which an immediate response brutally exposes. The interval between gift and counter-gift is what allows a relation of exchange that is always liable to appear as irreversible, that is, both forced and self-interested, to be seen as reversible. (Bourdieu, [1980] 1990: 105)

Bourdieu here attempts to link subjective motive (disinterested gift) and objective effect (self-interested exchange) by attributing to givers a calculating non-calculation, as it were. Behind gift exchanges, he argues, there is an economic reality of exchange and profit which, like other objective structures, is unconsciously internalized in the habitus of subjects. That Bourdieu's gift theory is thus ultimately based on economic factors and self-interest is a little surprising in a thinker as fiercely anti-utilitarian as he was. While coherent, his theory is also one-sided and fails to do justice to the ambivalence and complexity of gifting practices. What is more, he places himself above the subjects of his analysis: the enlightened theoretician sees through their self-reported motives and knows more about their gifting practices than they do. This kind of attitude is problematic to say the least. It bespeaks a view of humans as immature beings unable to understand their own actions—a view we should surely aspire to leave behind.

Utilitarian approaches

Let us now turn to the venerable theoretical tradition of individualist utilitarianism. The concept of utilitarianism I employ here is a broad one and not restricted to the Benthamite school with its famous "greatest happiness" principle. Utilitarianism, as I understand it, proceeds from the assumption of self-interested actors' intent on reducing their costs and thus maximizing their benefits. In terms of a utilitarian sociology of reciprocity, the work of Peter Blau (1918–2002) is of special importance. Following Simmel, Blau saw social exchanges as the basis of all societies. He was convinced that humans have a primordial interest in other humans and can only accomplish certain individual goals by cooperating. A social exchange therefore always involves gratification; it is a voluntary act motivated by the anticipation of the other's reciprocation—that is, by self-interest. Gratifications need not be material but can take the form of recognition and reassurance as well. In this model, you give to others so as to receive something from them: *do ut des*. Acts of giving are reciprocated, obligations incurred, and a long-term cooperation develops—whereas non-reciprocal behaviors, such as ungrateful responses, usually result in a termination of the social exchange.

But Blau also conceived of reciprocity as a mechanism for creating power imbalances. Such imbalances arise whenever there are grave differences in terms of status or available resources between people engaging in a social exchange. If the recipient of benefits is unable to reciprocate, the exchange tends to become asymmetrical. Said beneficiary will then be forced to acknowledge the power imbalance and accept his inferior place in the social hierarchy; *that* is his reciprocation. Blau gives the example of a new employee in a company who depends on the advice of a more experienced colleague. All the newbie can do to reciprocate the favor is to acknowledge his colleague's higher status within the company (Blau, 1964: 131).

Over the last decades, social exchange theory has become an established research area in American sociology in particular: researchers investigate different versions of reciprocity and their repercussions on social cohesion, mostly by way of empirical studies. Some interesting discoveries have resulted from this—discoveries that in fact call into question the individualistic convictions underlying this approach. Take the basic assumption, common to all exchange theories, that subjects act self-interestedly, that is, strive for positive effects of actions and try to avoid negative ones (Molm 2003). As a number of experiments have shown (which usually involve college students and interconnected computers in a lab), the avoidance of risks or losses makes for a stronger motive than the anticipation of rewards. Also, participants in such experimental games appear to value their relationship, and thus the principle of reciprocity, for its own sake; they do not regard it as just a means to an end. This pattern can be observed in games in which the contributions of each player have not been agreed upon and are therefore uncertain to both. It does *not* occur in games based on bargaining, that is, games simulating real-life contractual agreements that define each partner's costs and benefits: in such contractual exchanges, participants tend to become more aware of their conflicting interests. By contrast, uncertain, risky exchanges tend to strengthen the relationship. As Linda Molm finds, risk "increases integrative bonds by promoting trust" (2010: 124) as well as "affective regard and solidarity" (2010: 129). Apparently, cooperation feels quite rewarding to actors—which casts some doubt on the model of individual utility maximization.

Rational-choice contributions to the field come to similar conclusions: to attain their goals, even those acting solely out of self-interest need to cooperate with others and build relations that are beneficial to both. In this context, then, giving per se means reciprocal giving, that is, exchanging. The risk inherent in such exchanges—a potential failure on the part of the other to fulfill the agreed-upon contract—can be reduced by building robust, trusting relationships.

Game theory approaches consider social learning to be of great importance in the creation of reciprocity. In his now-classic study of "the evolution of cooperation," Robert Axelrod (1984) attempted to determine which strategies were most successful in decision-making. He programmed computers to act according to different strategies in a virtual tournament—most radically, total cooperation and immediate defection—which corresponded to certain scores. The winning strategy was one called "Tit for tat," which consisted in acting cooperatively on the first move and reciprocating whatever the other player did on subsequent moves (that is, respond cooperatively to cooperative moves and uncooperatively to uncooperative moves). Once again it turned out that reciprocity, abiding by the rules, and demonstrations of trust have a stabilizing effect on cooperative relationships.

The question of how egoistical human actions really are has recently played a big role in experimental economics. To find out about this, a program was developed that simulates decision situations and tests participants' self-interestedness, often using real money to avoid measuring behavior that is merely hypothetical. A typical example is the so-called ultimatum game in which one of two players is endowed with money and the power to propose how to split it. The other player can either accept or reject that proposal, and only if they accept it will the proposed sums be paid out; if they reject both get nothing. Findings show that, in contrast to the assumptions of the model of utility maximization, proposers tend to act rather fairly, typically offering their counterpart between 40 and 50 percent of the total sum. Responders tend to reject offers of less than 30 percent, which results in no money being paid to either of them (Fehr and Schmidt, 1999). Similar patterns have been found in experiments around the world (Henrich et al, 2005). It seems that humans are universally inclined to reject an immoral offer and punish the one who proposed it. Only business students, conditioned for profit maximization, were ready to accept pathetically small sums rather than receiving nothing at all.

Even if it costs themselves, then, most people seem to be oriented towards norms of fairness. Economists call this kind of behavior conditional cooperation: people are willing to contribute to the production of collective goods as long as others do too. This includes a certain tolerance for imbalances and redistributions, such as providing benefits to those in need—unless they appear to make no real efforts to better their situation, in which case people tend to become rather critical rather quickly (Lessenich and Mau, 2005). History is full of examples of conditional cooperation. Apart from disdain for refugees and the unemployed, one may think of the derogatory term "welfare queens" which was used widely in political rhetoric during the 1980s and 1990s and usually referred to African American single mothers relying on social services. Such extreme demands for reciprocity are often taken up by the media, as well as by economists of a neoliberal persuasion.

Other economists, however, have been calling for an integration of economic and sociological perspectives, for a union, as it were, of *homo oeconomicus* (guided by self-interest) and *homo sociologicus* (guided by norms; see Dahrendorf, 1968). This is something sociologists have always heeded, but economists only recently discovered the concept of the internalization of social values and norms (Fehr and Gintis, 2007). In any case, such an integration of normative and utilitarian approaches would not solve the problem that the freedom, creativity, and riskiness involved in giving is not adequately addressed by either of the two. (More on this later.)

Nonetheless, a shift of perspective is taking place in parts of economics as well as political science, an increasing willingness to question the traditional view of humans as selfish utility maximizers. For what the aforementioned findings from experimental economics and exchange theory suggest is that prosociality and cooperation are as much part of the repertoire of human behaviors as is the self-interested pursuit of individual gains. This becomes especially apparent if we consider how much the focus has shifted from so-called public choice approaches to the examination of practices of commoning. In keeping with ecologist Garrett Hardin's famous dictum of the "tragedy of the commons," it was long taken for granted that without government regulation or private property rights, shared resources would be overused because nobody cared about their sustainability. According to Hardin (1915–2003), as soon as a resource (for example a pasture or a forest) is declared open to all, individuals will try to generate as much gain for themselves from it as they can. The "tragedy" begins once the resource in question is about to be depleted, that is, when too many utilize it. Then the long-term costs, which individuals had hitherto neglected in light of their short-term gains, have to be borne by the community at large (Hardin, 1968).

This view—that individuals are not capable of cooperative action, or rather, won't engage in it because it is not beneficial to (what they perceive to be) their own interests—has been challenged by many field studies since, not least those conducted by Nobel Prize laureate Elinor Ostrom (1933–2012). These studies have demonstrated that a sustainable use of commons—in fishing, logging, and so on—is possible after all. Around the world locals have self-organized to come up with their own regulations, monitor the use of resources, and enforce sanctions when needed (Ostrom, 2010). Studies like Ostrom's reveal how theories like that of the "tragedy of the commons" utterly fail to accurately describe empirical realities. The real tragedy is that such false models of human behavior are taken up by politicians, and that functioning practices of commoning are overlooked, or looked down upon, which in turn has the effect of legitimizing a further depletion of resources belonging to all.

Altruism or social capital?

Apart from the norm- and self-interest-oriented perspectives there is a third model of giving which is prevalent in social psychology in particular: altruism. This all but forgotten concept has of late received renewed attention since it has become clear that people who make generous donations do more than what conventions, norms, or the law require, that they make economic sacrifices. The selflessness of the altruist, a term and concept introduced by Auguste Comte in the mid-19th century, forms an antithesis to the self-interest of the egoist. Some decades later, Émile Durkheim's *solidarité* would have a very similar meaning as Comte's *altruisme*. An early critic of this kind of orientation in social science (and social reformism) was Friedrich Nietzsche ([1887] 2017) who thought that altruistic sentiment, like all of Christian morality, was born of *ressentiment*. Along with Hobbes and Freud, Nietzsche is one of the progenitors of a long tradition that wants to debunk altruism by showing that, in the end, it is motivated by nothing but self-interest. Since the 1970s, however, two strands of research have ushered in a renaissance of the altruism concept: work on the motives of those who rescued Jews from the Holocaust (Oliner and Oliner, 1988) and work on voluntary blood donations (Titmuss, 1970); the latter in particular had great influence on the investigation of donations in general.

To find out if and how some persons are more altruistic than others, you need to first come up with a viable definition of altruism—such as that submitted by Kristen Monroe who, following Comte, defines altruistic behavior as acts "intended to benefit another, even when doing so may risk or entail some sacrifice to the welfare of the actor" (1994: 862). In order to behave altruistically, then, you would have to be willing to relinquish something for the benefit of another person, to accept a potential diminution of your own welfare. By contrast, "[a]n act that improves both my own welfare and that of another person would not be altruistic" (1994: 863). Monroe further advises against "dichotomizing behavior," that is, assuming that it must be either selfish or altruistic. Rightly so, since there are in fact many behaviors that cannot be placed on either side of this dichotomy, such as sharing, giving, and cooperating.

Unfortunately, not much valuable knowledge can be gained from studying cognitive and social psychology approaches to altruism. Topics analyzed in these fields include the question whether there exists something like an "altruistic personality" (Rushton, 1984) or whether altruistic behavior is situational. As to the first question, it was established that there are indeed certain traits that distinguish altruists from non-altruists, but that these are not very distinct. Thus, Samuel and Pearl Oliner (1988) compared personality traits of "rescuers" to those of other Nazi-era persons with similar attributes regarding parameters like sex, age, level of education, social background, and so on. They found that rescuers had strong ethical values and shared a belief in the equality of all humans. But the main difference between them and non-rescuers was that they came from family backgrounds characterized by secure attachment and care. Also, they were asked for help directly, which was not the case with non-rescuers. Another study, from the late 1970s, found that kidney donors were different from non-donors in exactly one point: they had more trust in others. In addition, however, most of them were personally told about the need for a donation, from which fact researchers inferred that "being asked" is of major importance for altruistic behaviors. Finally, studies on sex differences highlighted that women are willing to help much sooner, whereas people tend to expect help from men in exceptional, non-routine situations only (see Piliavin and Charng, 1990). Generally, these social psychological studies thus seem to suggest that rather than with certain personality traits, altruistic behavior mainly correlates with specific kinds of interactions and situations.

Accordingly, the sociologist Kieran Healy (2000) opted for a different approach when he examined altruism from a comparative perspective. As a starting point he took the simple fact that some EU countries are able to solicit a much greater amount of blood donations than others: in the early 1990s, for example, 44 percent of the adult population of France donated blood while in Luxembourg that number was only 14 percent. Does this mean that the French are more altruistic than Luxembourgians (and Norwegians, Italians, and so on)? To prevent such a premature and fallacious conclusion, Healy explains that these countries vary regarding how practices of blood donation are institutionalized and which demographic groups are reached by which methods to activate the population's readiness to donate. He observed that it is not so much the motives of blood donors that differ from country to country but the institutional settings of campaigns and collections. In short, the more people are informed about the possibility of donating blood, the more actually donate. Those that do not are not necessarily less altruistic but in all likelihood were simply not asked. If we still do not have enough blood to satisfy the medical demand for it, then, this is not due to selfishness but to bad organization.

Healy comes to similar conclusions in another study, this time on organ donations. After comparing a number of US states, he was able to establish that the main reason behind the varying willingness to donate is that "the same practice is organized differently in different places" (2004: 401). Contrary to other forms of voluntary engagement, organ donations constitute "one-shot events" in that the altruistic act consists of only one occasion and does not occur regularly. And yet—just like volunteer work in clubs or associations—it is heavily institutionalized and relies on organization and PR. Healy shows that donation rates are dependent on the degree to which organ procurement organizations succeed in making contact with the relatives of a recently deceased person, primarily in hospitals. It follows that altruistic behavior is more than an individual affair; it is embedded in institutional and organizational contexts (Adloff and Sigmund, 2005). Organizations create spaces of potentiality for donations, and altruism emerges within interactions.

The reliance of prosocial behaviors on interactional contexts, and thus on social relationships, is also captured by another sociological concept, even though individualistic assumptions tend to creep in here as well. I am talking about social capital, a term that in its current usage goes back to Bourdieu (1986) and James Coleman (1988) and that is furthermore closely connected to Robert Putnam's work on the decline of social cohesion, especially in the US. In a series of essays and then in his much-discussed book *Bowling Alone* (2000), Putnam (b. 1941) analyzed and lamented the loss of social capital within American society. He had started this project, largely unnoticed, with a study on Italy, in which he stated that North Italy was more successful than the South (in both economic and political terms) because it commanded more social capital (Putnam, 1993). Social capital refers to phenomena like trust, norms, and networks, which make it easier to coordinate collective action. Loose forms of association in particular, as in clubs and initiatives, tend to generate a willingness to communicate and cooperate in their members. The more such attitudes prevail, Putnam argues, the easier it is for economic transactions as well as relations between the political apparatus and citizens to develop.

Social capital has both an individual and a collective side to it; it can be "simultaneously a 'private good' and a 'public good'" (Putnam, 2000: 20). To be sure, individuals affiliate with others when it serves their own interests—one thinks of the usefulness of "networking" in finding a job (2000: 20). But social capital also has effects on society as a whole, for example by increasing trust among its members. Social networks produce and reproduce mutual obligations and the norm of reciprocity. In fact, there is more than one such norm since the scope varies: while with a narrow norm of reciprocity, it is possible to specifically name the exchange partners and objects ("I'll help you pick apples if you help me assemble my new wardrobe"), a generalized norm of reciprocity proceeds on the assumption that if I help this person now, someone someday will give me something back. The so-called Golden Rule—Do unto others as you would have them do unto you—is an expression of such generalized reciprocity, and Putnam claims that in societies that value this principle, people are more willing to cooperate (2000: 21). However, social capital can have harmful effects as well. This is the case when it only works internally, increasing the *esprit de corps* within certain groups (like the mafia or the KKK) while doing harm to society at large. Putnam thus distinguishes between "bonding" social capital, which strengthens identity and homogeneity within certain groups, from its "bridging" counterpart which connects people across social differences, does not exclude anyone, and has positive effects on society as a whole; here he has the Civil Rights Movement or ecumenical religious organizations in mind (2000: 21ff.).

Putnam presents a plethora of data in *Bowling Alone* to document the decline in social capital in the US since the 1990s. His arguments have proved controversial, but what matters to me is the insight that social capital is unevenly distributed within societies: there are groups with more and groups with less of it. Whereas workers used to be firmly integrated in organizations associated with the labor movement or the Catholic Church, nowadays lower income groups and people with lower levels of education are underrepresented in such organizations, resulting in less social capital for them. The support system provided by traditional associations is largely a thing of the past; and other forms of organizations that emerged in their stead do not offer it to the same extent. What the new social movements or support groups require from their members are classic middle-class competencies: autonomy, self-reflection, the pursuit of individual fulfillment (Joas and Adloff, 2006). Social engagement has become a temporary affair. In Germany, there is the stereotype of a new type of affluent mother who gets involved in the parents' council of her children's schools, donates to Amnesty International or Greenpeace, organizes a block party in support of refugees—and she does all this in a most efficient and professional manner; after all, she was trained as a project manager. The poor and the uneducated, however, are largely excluded from participation in civil society today. Thus, the unequal distribution of income and wealth, education and management skills directly affects abilities to connect, to network, to get involved socially or politically, to trust—in short: to give without immediately profiting from it (Adloff, 2005).

On the preceding pages I provided a brief overview of different approaches to giving and reciprocity. We have seen that two main positions can be identified: reciprocity as an internalized social norm vs. reciprocity as an expression of long-term self-interest. But there are astonishing parallels. Except for overly simplistic self-interest models, both camps assume that norms of reciprocity are of vital importance; they also agree that reciprocity engenders social relationships and is dependent on trust. What they disagree about is how norms of reciprocity come into being and how closely related reciprocity is to market-style economic exchanges.

What is more, the two positions appear to increasingly converge: normative theories now factor in the individual and his/her interests, while utilitarian theories have come to acknowledge the limits of their rational choice and utility maximization models. And yet it is not enough to merely combine the two, for two reasons: first, because we have seen how good other theories, that is, those that focus on situational contexts (Healy, Putnam), are in explaining forms of giving and prosociality; and second, because both positions ultimately rely on a rather questionable view of human beings: they posit self-interest as "natural" and state that we need to confine it by teaching people to act according to values and norms.

But what if a human propensity for giving was just as "natural"? In my view, we should begin to systematically locate practices of giving beyond the spheres of self-interest and norms. What is needed is a theory that focuses not on the motives of individuals but on what comes to pass *between* individuals. In more technical terms: an interactionist theory of giving that is neither utilitarian nor normative. And it is such a theory that we find in the work of Marcel Mauss.

2

Mauss' Gift

When it comes to gift giving, scholars frequently argue in historical terms, claiming that the principle of the gift used to regulate all sorts of social relationships. Thus, while in medieval times people still owed each other support and deference (even though this was not explicitly defined in terms of a gift-based exchange), with the advent of modernity there occurred a split in what once was a unified principle, with the spheres of public economic exchanges and of private acts of giving or donating parting ways. We encounter this model, for example, in *Sociology of Giving* by Helmuth Berking ([1996] 1999) who, after investigating its conceptual history, concludes that the gift proper survives only in a residual sphere that is marginalized by market exchange and utilitarianism, namely, in the private practice of gifting. We are confronted with a dichotomy of exchange and self-interest as *signa* of modernity on the one hand versus the gift as something "premodern" and irrational on the other. The Hobbesian solution, assuming that the convergence of individual interests can under certain conditions lead to cooperation, and the Rousseauist solution, supposing that cooperation requires a common cultural background consisting of shared norms, values, and knowledges, are thus squarely juxtaposed. Attempts to bring the two views together again usually result in the widespread contention that for cooperation to work, you need to first teach people to behave prosocially—and use sanctions if they do not.

Marcel Mauss resisted this dichotomy and this antinomy, and he challenged many of the contract theoretical premises prevalent in political and economic theory, such as Adam Smith's belief in a human "propensity to exchange." In his [1925] 1990 seminal *Essai sur le don* (*The Gift*), Mauss rejects the assumption that exchanges and contracts form the basis of society. What he assumes instead is that all human institutions are based on practices of giving, practices that synthesize the polarities of freedom vs. obligation and self-interest vs. solidarity, be it in premodern or in modern societies (Hart, 2007). Mauss' goal is to establish a gift discourse for our own times. While Europeans had increasingly lost sight of gift relations during most of the

1800s, which were dominated by the emergence of capitalism, bureaucracy, and positivism, towards the end of the century the tables began to turn. This was the time when the first anthropologists brought back a multitude of materials from their colonial travels and drew attention to the importance still ascribed to practices of giving elsewhere (Liebersohn, 2011). Mauss carefully studied the ethnographic works of Boas, Malinowski, and Thurnwald, and he inferred that the practices depicted by them were but local instances of a universal phenomenon: a basic human tendency towards association, towards giving, which he hoped to revive. Moreover, his essay is the product of his search for a "third way" between economic liberalism and state socialism; it presents his idiosyncratic version of socialism, which builds upon principles of cooperation and conviviality.

Mauss' work was slow to find followers outside of France, but in recent years the paradigm associated with his name, gift giving, has been discussed widely in disciplines such as philosophy, theology, history, sociology, and cultural studies, to name just a few. Among his works, the most attention by far is being paid to *The Gift*, which is understandable given the colorful descriptions with which the text is replete and its reputed accessibility. On closer inspection, it becomes apparent though that one is never really finished with this work since interpretations shift with every reading. This is because, though Mauss avoids abstract and generalized conclusions, his essay hints at a multitude of theoretical ideas which sometimes appear to contradict one another.

Émile Durkheim (1858–1917), the founder of French sociology, was Mauss' uncle and teacher.[1] Like Durkheim, Mauss was born in Épinal, Eastern France, to a Jewish family. At the age of 18, he began his studies at the University of Bordeaux where—unlike his uncle, who became his tutor there—he quickly got involved in socialist circles. After graduating with a degree in philosophy, Mauss moved to Paris and continued his education at the prestigious École pratique des hautes études under Sylvain Lévi, a famed indologist who became another mentor and main influence on his work. In the late 1890s, both Durkheim and Mauss were major voices in the Dreyfus affair, fighting against antisemitism in French society. Mauss also helped Durkheim with the publication of his seminal work on *Suicide* ([1897] 1965). His own first publications were reviews of books on comparative religion in Durkheim's journal *L'Année sociologique* (which Mauss would, much later, continue). In 1899, he cooperated with his close friend and colleague Henri Hubert on a study of the nature and functions of sacrificial rites. Mauss considered the sacred to be of societal origin—again much like Durkheim whose important book *The Elementary Forms of the Religious Life* would appear in 1912. In 1901, Mauss was appointed to the Chair of Religions of Non-Civilized People at the École pratique, a designation he criticized in his inaugural address, stressing that there were no "non-civilized people," only different civilizations. His next books dealt with magical beliefs and rituals (Mauss and Hubert, [1902] 1975) and with "primitive classification." In the latter work, Mauss and Durkheim ([1901] 1963) examined how different systems of classification impact on the social organization of societies; they thus laid the foundation for a sociology of knowledge.

Mauss was known for his great erudition—as his Paris students would say: "Mauss sait tout." They knew this because, far from being an ivory-tower type of intellectual, he was very approachable; he would meet and debate with them, listen to their worries, even become their friend. In the course of his career, he managed to tear down the walls that Durkheim had erected between disciplines, for example between sociology and psychology, and build interdisciplinary bridges. His uncle, fond as he was of him, considered Mauss to be quite undisciplined and passed censure on his bohemian lifestyle. Mauss' political life properly began around the turn of the century when he met Jean Jaurès, became involved in the socialist movement, and developed a particular interest in cooperative forms of economic activity (see Chapter 5). Even though he was an internationalist and pacifist, he served as an interpreter for the French Army during World War I. Among the millions of casualties of that war were many of his friends and students, as well as his cousin André—an event Durkheim never recovered from, dying two years later at the age of 59.

Mauss now focused all his energy on the task of securing his uncle's legacy. He published Durkheim's previously unpublished works and revived *L'Année Sociologique*, the first new issue of which, in 1925, featured what would come to be considered his most influential text: *The Gift*. Mauss was personally very familiar with relationships informed by reciprocal giving: networks of relatives and friends were all-important for his life and work, with most of his publications being co-productions and the whole Durkheim school of sociology essentially being a cooperative affair. In addition to reviving that cooperative work after the war, *The Gift* also signaled Mauss' leadership. The first half of the 1920s saw a number of other political articles by him as well, published in various socialist papers and journals—such as those on the cooperative movement in *La vie socialiste*, in which he also critically discussed bolshevism. Finally, Mauss' projected magnum opus on the nation was begun in those years, but it remained a fragment. What Mauss was concerned with here was the question of how to secure peace between nations. He believed that their mutual social and economic dependencies would have to be gradually transferred into a normative international bond: from the socialist nation to the United States of Europe to, ultimately, a global civilization based on cooperation ([1920] 1969).

In 1925, the year *The Gift* came out, Mauss, Lucien Lévy-Bruhl, and Paul Rivet founded the Institut d'ethnologie de l'université de Paris. The lectures he gave there between 1926 and 1939 mostly drew on fieldwork done by his students, and they later would be published by one of them, Denise Paulme, in the *Manuel d'ethnographie* (Mauss, [1947] 2007). The 1930s were marked by the further institutionalization of Durkheimian sociology and anthropology, not least through Mauss' professorship at the Collège de France (1931–40), as well as by the rise of fascism. Mauss was disgusted by Europe's regression into primitivism under Hitler and Mussolini, joined the antifascist movement, and handed in his resignation as professor as soon as the Vichy regime assumed power. Two years later, Mauss had to abandon his apartment and start wearing the Star of David. Only his renowned and influential acquaintances saved his family from being deported, like many other French Jews, to internment and concentration camps. Soon after the war, his wife Marthe died, and Marcel Mauss, silenced and suffering from memory loss, followed her in 1950.

In *The Gift*, Mauss stresses that in all interactions between people, "things"—whether material or symbolic—are given and received: a cycle of reciprocity that is often fragile and risky because it depends on trust. He further points out that relationship-building based on reciprocity requires both voluntariness *and* the obligation to give, take, and reciprocate. He then highlights two varieties of premodern gifting ceremonies: the Melanesian *Kula* ring, as then recently described by Bronislaw Malinowski in *Argonauts of the Western Pacific* (1922), and the potlatches practiced by the Kwakiutl of Vancouver Island and other native tribes of the Pacific Northwest Coast.

The main distinction Mauss makes in this context, though somewhat implicitly, is between more vs. less "agonistic" gifts. Those gifts that could be called *weakly agonistic* create a sphere of approximate equivalences and mutual indebtedness, in which the focus is not primarily on the accumulation of wealth. Since gifts provoke counter-gifts, they permanently create obligations that can never be fully discharged. This is the case with the *Kula* ring, a gifting ritual in which the inhabitants of the Massim archipelago (off the southeast coast of New Guinea) exchange two kinds of valuables, necklaces and bracelets, along circular routes. Their acts of giving, receiving, and reciprocating serve the purpose of creating a cooperative atmosphere and securing a solidary relationship between the two groups involved—important prerequisites for the trading of consumer goods that usually follows (Mauss, [1925] 1990: 27ff.).[2] By contrast, strongly agonistic gifts signal a competition for renown. Thus, the North American potlatch ritual involves gifts that progressively increase in value. The ritual ends when one clan or chief needs to back off from that cycle of giving-ever-more. Only one party can win the potlatch—and their price is a gain in status. In other words: the (self-) attribution as either superior or inferior keeps alternating until one of the parties is no longer capable of reciprocating and gets permanently moved into the inferior position. As Mauss puts it: "It is a competition to see who is the richest and also the most madly extravagant. Everything is based upon the principles of antagonism and rivalry" (Mauss, [1925] 1990: 47).³

Mauss wonders what it is that makes us reciprocate gifts, "[w]hat power resides in the object given that causes its recipient to pay it back" ([1925] 1990: 4). He evokes the Maori concept of *hau*, that is, the spirit of the giver that is present in the gift and obligates the recipient to give something back; a force originating neither in the thing nor in the individual person, but in the collective at large ([1925] 1990: 14ff.). He also mentions the concept of *mana*, the "magical, religious, and spiritual force" ([1925] 1990: 13) inherent in all creatures, which amounts to their "authority" (1925] 1990: 11) or "honour" ([1925] 1990: 48). Like the sacred, *mana* is of societal origin, going back to collective affective states. Mauss here takes up ideas he and Durkheim had developed earlier. In *The Elementary Forms of the Religious Life* ([1912] 1965), the latter had explained that to the Aboriginal Australians the sacred was a thoroughly social affair, that the collective practice of worshipping in fact created the sacred to begin with. In totemism, the clan or tribe in effect worships itself since, as Durkheim writes, "religious force is nothing other than the collective ... force of the clan" ([1912] 1965: 221). This social/sacred power supports and energizes each individual member of the group, especially when in ritualistic gatherings, agitation is evoked through synchronized movement and sounds: in such moments of collective ecstasy, an external moral force takes possession of the group, a force of which "the totemic emblem is like the visible body" ([1912] 1965: 221).⁴

In the third section of *The Gift*, Mauss deals with "the survival of these principles in ancient systems of law and ancient economies" ([1925] 1990: 60). He observes that current societies tend to distinguish rigorously between the rights of things and the rights of persons. Such a distinction was not prevalent in older cultures, he states, and neither was that between gifts and paid services. He is very aware, however, that once these two distinctions are omitted, things will appear as animated and persons as solely material (Därmann, 2009), and it will become equally hard to differentiate between property and wealth. For instance, a group or individual may be entitled to the use of something, but nobody possesses the full right of disposition to it (see Mauss, [1925] 1990: 64). Clearly, Mauss is alluding here to socialism's efforts of overcoming private property. In his balanced view, gifts can also create or consolidate hierarchies, exclusions, and inequalities, namely when the parties involved have very different amounts of resources at their disposal. Three scenarios come to mind: first, privileged groups may not feel compelled to adequately reciprocate gifts they receive from others—as in the labor market where employers frequently exploit their power over employees by not paying them nearly enough for their work. Second, power asymmetries, debts, and dependencies tend to develop when people cannot reciprocate gifts because they are simply too poor to do so—as is the case with recipients of alms whose only contribution to the exchange is a demonstration of gratitude, an acknowledgment of the charitable giver's higher social status. And third, certain groups may be excluded from the circulation of (material and immaterial) goods, and thus from the exchange of gifts and recognition, altogether. In all three scenarios, there is no reciprocity between equals: either the exchange assumes a hierarchical character, or someone remains outright excluded from it.

In the fourth and final section of *The Gift*, Mauss provides some moral, political, and economic conclusions. It now becomes evident that his main concern throughout has been to reinforce a principle of giving that connects people "horizontally." For instance, he attacks the notion of charity because he feels that the poor are being degraded if they are not given the chance to reciprocate the gifts they receive—and this asymmetry also characterizes paternalistic social policies in modern welfare states. Consequently, Mauss wants to redefine social security as a *counter*-gift of society to its labor force. The wage the worker is paid, he thinks, is simply not enough to compensate him for his sacrifice, for his gift: "The state itself, representing the community, owes him, as do his employers ... a certain security in life, against unemployment, sickness, old age, and death" (Mauss, [1925] 1990: 86). In today's world, one way to achieve the Maussian ideal would perhaps be the universal basic income, which recognizes the contributions all of its members make to society, regardless of what form they take.

What Mauss does not really elaborate on in his essay is the non-agonistic variety of the gift—and I will get back to this later because it is in fact this variety of gifts that forms the very basis of our everyday lives. Mauss does mention such solidary, entirely non-combative acts of giving in his *Manuel d'ethnographie*, but merely as historical precursors to agonistic gifts. In *The Gift*, then, he focuses on agonistic gifts, which he positions between such primal non-agonistic gifts on the one hand and the individualistic, legal contracts of the modern world on the other. He is highly critical of this latter form of configuring societal life, and he censures both capitalism's utilitarian individualism and bolshevism's state centrism. The socialist Mauss favored a society shaped by the principles of solidarity and association, by reciprocal social relationships and obligations. He glimpsed instances of this in some of the historical societies he explored, not least in Germanic tribal law (Mauss, [1925] 1990: 77ff.). Acutely aware that modern social relations increasingly adhere to the rules of the market economy, he warned that the golden age of the *homo oeconomicus* was still ahead—because the more we base our institutions on the assumption that humans are essentially egoistic utility maximizers, the more this will actually become the case. Mauss wants to prevent this. The history of humankind, he insists, is not one of market-type exchanges but one of giving and reciprocity. If you present a gift to someone, you do not know whether, when, and how they will reciprocate it; these decisions are entirely up to the recipient. In exchanges, by contrast, both parties agree on the modalities beforehand, and goods flow accordingly.

Asymmetry, the agonistic, and the non-agonistic gift

As we have seen, social science research has closely linked the concept of the gift to that of reciprocity. If you give something, you usually get something back, thus the assumption goes, and Mauss is often (misleadingly) referenced in this context. Philosophical texts about gift giving, for instance by Derrida and Marion, are particularly concerned with the question whether or not there exists something like an unconditional gift, a disinterested act that involves no expectations of a reciprocation. In the following I will show that we need to take this philosophical debate seriously and acknowledge that, next to forms of exchange and reciprocity, there are unilateral gifts as well.

Definitions of gift giving ought not to include reciprocity because if a gift relied on being reciprocated, we would be dealing with an exchange. The obligation a gift *might* implicate is not mandatory, nor can it be legally claimed (see Caillé, 2000a; Adloff, 2016: 29ff.). Thus, in the few still existing hunter-gatherer cultures, such as that of the Nayaka of South India, "it is inconceivable not immediately to give someone whatever he asks for" (Descola, 2013: 316). In such societies, and this used to be the case in "primitive" cultures around the world, practices of giving and sharing are much more prevalent than practices of exchange, which require reciprocity. When everything belongs to everyone, there is simply no need to exchange (or distribute) things. Reciprocity, then, is only an option; it is not necessarily a part of gift giving. All societies know gift giving relationships as much as they know relationships characterized by hierarchy and exchange. If we acknowledged that the principle of non-agonistic gift giving exists, this would change our understanding of sociality quite drastically.

The French deconstructivist philosopher Jacques Derrida (1930–2004) distinguished gift giving from the mode of economic circulation. The gift, he writes in *Given Time*, is "that which interrupts economy ... [t]hat which opens the circle so as to defy reciprocity or symmetry. ... It must not circulate, it must not be exchanged" (1992: 7). Mauss' classic essay, Derrida charges, is about "everything but the gift: It deals with economy, exchange, contract (do et des)" (1992: 24). For Derrida, a gift can only exist in the total absence of calculation and circulation; only if spontaneously and disinterestedly given, it will manage to escape the logic of reciprocity and exchange. However, his critique of Mauss reveals that he fails to appreciate the all-important *social* (as opposed to the economic) function of gifts. Derrida's position is typical of modernity in that it disregards the middle ground between complete selflessness on the one hand and utter selfishness on the other (Parry, 1986). In effect, therefore, the gift emerges from his text as "the impossible" (*passim*).

Derrida's work on gift giving has been widely studied, including by theologians who, for instance, have connected it to Christian notions of divine grace (Caputo and Scanlon, 1999). As does Derrida himself, in *Donner le temps* and elsewhere, this strand of research builds on the phenomenological tradition of Husserl and Heidegger. An example would be Jean-Luc Marion's book *Being Given* ([1997] 2002) in which an irreducible "givenness" is proclaimed as a basic precondition for giving. Marion, too, regards gift and exchange as diametral opposites and, again like Derrida, claims that Mauss' essay does not "concern the gift" but "only exchange." The gift, Marion believes, per se "excludes ... reciprocity" and is "accomplished perfectly with the disappearance of one of its extremes (giver or givee)" ([1997] 2002: 113). As a sociologist, I am quite baffled by such statements because they do nothing to elucidate actual practices of giving. Gifts can only function as social binding agents when *someone* gives something to *someone else*. If we followed the phenomenologists, we would either have to declare all practices of gifting to be merely exchanges (because they do not conform to the ideal of the gift) or futilely search for gift phenomena that feature no giver or no recipient. The reflections of Derrida and Marion thus remain pure speculative adventures (see Waldenfels, 2012: 226). What we should keep in mind, however, is their warning that there is a tension between the concept of the gift on the one hand and reciprocity and exchange on the other.

Of more relevance in terms of a social science perspective is the work of French philosopher Paul Ricœur (1913–2005) whose interpretation of gift giving stresses the role of forgiveness—a term hailing from the religious sphere—in everyday life. Ricœur (2006) sees forgiveness as a form of active forgetting that makes new beginnings possible, as in the continuation of social relations after "sins" have been committed. In many languages, he observes, *for-giving* is semantically directly related to the concept of the (non-agonistic) gift: *pardonner*, *perdonar*, and so on. Indeed, like the gift, forgiving involves an asymmetry—no reciprocation is required of the recipient of forgiveness. Consequently, Ricœur considers forgiveness to be more closely associated with love than with justice: it does not conform to a logic of weighing and compensation but instead springs from a "superabundance" (1995: 300). This to him is most clearly expressed in the Christian commandment to love one's enemies, which he regards as a corrective to the "Golden Rule" (Do unto others as you would have them do unto you). Whereas the latter is based on a "logic of equivalence" and permanently runs the risk of lapsing into a utilitarian *do ut des*, forgiving means to break with the cycle of reciprocity (1995: 300). It is in this sense that forgiveness is a non-agonistic gift, a gift that consists in forgetting the impact of a past action on the present and future.

Ricœur elaborates on the subject of non-agonistic giving—or what he also calls *agape*—in his book *The Course of Recognition* (2005). Here, he counterposes the idea of an endless fight for recognition (as put forth by Hegel or Axel Honneth, for example) with states of peace in which that fight is put on hold. In the mode of "mutuality," Ricœur contends, there is no complete equivalence of giving and receiving between the two parties involved, that is, no reciprocity. In fact, the two movements that occur here both amount to acts of receiving: receiving the first gift and receiving the second or counter-gift. The reaction to the generosity with which the first gift is given is not a compensation, which actually would destroy the first gift, but rather a response to an offer. Therefore, the second gift is really a second first gift because the gratitude of the recipient goes along with a desire to be generous themselves (instead of just feeling obliged to give something back). In effect, the whole cycle of giving, receiving, and reciprocating is here dis- and then reassembled. In states of peace, then, the two parties give out of generosity, gratitude, and solidarity, their rivalry is at least temporarily suspended, and their gifts constitute a mutual recognition. Ricœur thus helps us to distinguish between two orders of gifts: those that aim at reciprocity and those that that aim at mutuality.

Alain Caillé (b. 1944), the main protagonist in the lively debates on Mauss' theory of the gift in French sociology, has drawn similar conclusions. Caillé founded the *Revue du M.A.U.S.S.* in 1981, and ever since contributors to that journal, instead of interpreting Mauss' ideas in utilitarian or normative terms, have engaged in the project of constructing an action-theoretical alternative to this dichotomy. In the course of his career, Caillé—professor emeritus at the University of Paris X and also the driving force behind the two *Convivialist Manifestos*—developed from a social theorist into a more practically minded, political figure who fights for a "third way" between an absolutization of either state or market. Convinced that gift theory is of great relevance to politics and society, he has contributed to public debates since the late 1990s: on demands for an introduction of a basic income, for a reduction of working hours, and for a revitalization of civil society, as well as on globalization and its problematic effects. Caillé has frequently argued in favor of alternative economies organized by civil society actors, as a way of combining non-capitalistic forms of trade and the ethics of giving.

Mauss' seemingly contradictory criteria for gift giving—voluntariness and spontaneity on the one hand, social obligation on the other—are discussed by Caillé in *Anthropologie du don* (2000a) and by Jacques Godbout and Caillé in *The World of the Gift* ([1992] 1998).[5] The gift is voluntary, according to Mauss, because it cannot be forced or claimed; and it is obligatory because violating the norm of reciprocity may entail social sanctions. A gift relationship always involves uncertainty, indeterminacy, and risk; at the same time, its very structural instability enables the building of trust. Since it is based on non-equivalence, spontaneity, and debt, neither a utilitarian-individualistic nor a normative-holistic approach can fully explain the gift relationship. Caillé (2000a) points out that as different the conceptions of Derrida and Bourdieu may be, they both insist that the gift relies on an absence of calculation and circulation; if this were not the case, we would not actually be dealing with a gift at all, but with an exchange. Caillé ascribes the theoretical misunderstandings often occurring in discourses on the gift to the fact that authors fail to clearly distinguish between utilitarian self-interest and another kind of "interest": that in others and their well-being. This latter form of interest corresponds with affection (*aimance*), play, and pleasure: occupations that are ends in themselves.

Voluntariness and spontaneity, then, are opposed to moral obligation (à la Kant), and "self-interest" is opposed to "interest in." It is between these four coordinates that Caillé locates the gift. If the gift relationship approximates the poles of self-interest, interest in, or obligation, it turns into an economic exchange, pure love, or deontology, respectively. But as long as it does not approach one of these extremes, the gift relationship constitutes a basic mode of social interaction in its own right. Gifts, reciprocity, and trust are of fundamental importance to cooperation and social order in general—but only because they are, paradoxically, at once obligatory and voluntary, self-serving and selfless. For Caillé, gifts are made without any expectations of reciprocation, but with the intent of establishing a social relationship; they are manifestations of a desire for attachment which is entirely autotelic. Other commentators have come to agree with his four-pole model. An example would be Marcel Hénaff (1942–2018) who likewise stressed that the Maussian ceremonial gift is neither economic nor altruistic in nature (Hénaff, 2010). Giving always implies the risk that the attempt to build trust may fail. And yet, gifts are indispensable for the establishment of communities and societies, both on the level of micro interactions between individuals or groups and on a larger, more structural scale.

Caillé's gift theory targets utilitarian economic approaches which simultaneously proceed in a reductionistic and an expansive manner: reductionistic because all actions are subjected to calculation and expediency; expansive because their analysis covers all areas of society (politics, family, art, civil society, and so on) instead of just the economy. Since the 1960s the reductive model of the *homo oeconomicus* has been applied to ever more societal fields, beginning perhaps with Gary Becker's work on a "new home economics" (1965). Caillé is highly critical of the dominant model of market economics with its focus on utilitarianism, self-interest, and rational choice. In neoliberalism, each and every human action is understood in terms of calculation, strategy, self-interest. Even the supposedly neutral social sciences are endorsing this one-sided view of "human nature"—a social fiction with very real consequences. As the French sociologists Michel Callon (1998) and Philippe Steiner (2019) have shown, economic theory not only describes economic realities but creates them as well: through education/socialization and by inscribing economic theory into the mechanisms and institutions of specific markets. People will then follow its provisions, and thus create the very reality that economists believe exists prior to and independent of their theory-making.

Caillé's anti-utilitarianism wants to counter all this. He calls on us to engage anew in sociological basic research in order to identify elements of giving on all levels of existence and prove that central aspects of human behavior cannot be explained by means of the utilitarian model. This is also the goal of the *Convivialist Manifestos*, which challenge their readers to partake in attempts at developing more just and sustainable forms of living together on earth. Caillé has variously pointed out that recognition theory, as first expounded by Hegel and substantially advanced by Axel Honneth ([1992] 2005) and others, is in principle compatible with gift theory. However, as long as recognition is first and foremost conceived of in terms of a struggle (as both Hegel and Honneth do), it cannot escape the primacy of self-interest. It is the grateful recipient of a gift who bestows recognition upon the giver, but that gratitude and recognition will hardly ensue if the receiver demanded what was given; that is, if it was given out of obligation or even involuntarily. Recognition presupposes a surplus of voluntariness and generosity; only then will the fundamental human desire "to be recognized and valued as givers" be satisfied (Caillé, 2006: 7).

In recent years, the idea that gifts involve an aspect of voluntariness and unconditionality, that they need not in fact be closely linked to reciprocity, has been taken up by cultural anthropologists—and no one tried harder to explicate non-agonistic gift giving from that perspective than David Graeber (1961–2020). In *Debt: The First 5,000 Years* (2011), Graeber argues that economic exchange is a rather new phenomenon; much older and more widespread is a form of economic activity along the lines of the Marxist motto: "From each according to his ability, to each according to his needs." Many premodern communities functioned that way, and even modern (capitalistic) societies, Graeber observes, build on that same foundation, namely, what he calls "communism." For him, familial relationships, friendships, spontaneous cooperation, collegiality, or friendly gestures and conversations are all examples of a communistic everyday morality which cannot be captured by utilitarian or normative social theories.[6] Wherever people do not keep accounts of the exchanges occurring between them, where they display trust, solidarity, dedication, and love, we are dealing with forms of giving. They act as if they thought they lived forever: you know that the other would do the same for you, but that situation may never occur. Reciprocity thus plays at best a minor role in such arrangements.

Exchanges can be stopped at any time; for instance, when you stop owing the other person. Debts are the result of a non-finished exchange between isolable individuals, but in communism there are no economic debts in this sense because no one is keeping track of who owes what to whom. One could also say that this "communism" constitutes a state of permanent mutual indebtedness which can never be dissolved since its exact circumstances are unclear (Godbout and Charbonneau, 1993). Graeber's idea does not rely on the liberal ideal of the autonomous individual but rather on a web of relations and mutual dependencies in which everyone gives or takes in proportion to their needs and abilities.

Above all, the gift is a one-way transfer—which may or may not elicit a reciprocation. Only exchanges warrant reciprocity; in gifts, it is not mandatory. Henceforth we should therefore distinguish non-agonistic gifts—based on *mutualité*, sharing, "communism," and weak reciprocity—from their agonistic counterparts. Agonistic gifts occur mostly in intercultural contexts. When groups (or individuals) are strangers to each other, the gift represents a test or challenge. Behind it is the question: are we friends or foes? Mauss' essay makes clear how common agonistic gifts are in many societies; and he explains that they usually serve the function of bringing about alliances. According to the anthropologist Philippe Descola, agonistic gifts are in fact a universal phenomenon, though of course there are differences as to how developed that tradition is in different parts of the world.

The fact that Mauss did not discuss *non*-agonistic gifts in his essay had the unfortunate effect that gift giving has been all but equated to its agonistic mode and as a result, is too closely linked to rivalry and competition. If we do not firmly disconnect gifts from exchange and reciprocity, we are bound to experience this conceptual confusion, or what Descola (2013) calls a "kinematic illusion." In this case, the gift's frequent consequence—a counter-gift and thus the closure of the cycle of reciprocity—gets mistaken for the gift itself. It is crucial that we realize that the movement of the gift is first and foremost uni-directional and asymmetrical. Just like a robbery, in which the asymmetry is negative, it is not intrinsically linked to reciprocity. Only exchanges are strictly symmetrical.

To sum up my reading of Mauss: on an everyday, non-agonistic level, people engage in giving relationships all the time: they help each other, listen to each other, give each other things as well as affection, recognition, and consolation. Then there are gifts that are less commonplace and sometimes agonistic in nature, as when somebody is given something extraordinary or when someone for-gives someone else. There exists, therefore, a propensity in humans to act in non-normative and non-utilitarian ways. Gifts entail aspects of surplus and unconditionality without which sociality would not be thinkable. At the very heart of the social, then, lie non-equivalences and asymmetries. Gifts, risks, and trust are fundamental components of cooperative relationships, not least in transcultural contexts. It is no coincidence that Mauss' *The Gift* is about intertribal relations, that is, relations between groups that each have their own system of values and norms.

3

Homo Donator: A Different Anthropology

Are humans egoistic by nature? Or, on the contrary, are they endowed with a disposition to give freely, unselfishly? What is cooperation based on? How do people come to agree in concrete interactions? These are questions that have occupied thinkers for years, and the answers they presented were very different, depending on their disciplinary background and the view of "human nature" prevalent in it. In what follows, I will defend the idea that there exists in human beings a tendency, with both biological and cultural roots, towards giving and sharing, a basic prosociality that is anthropologically prior to linguistic-reflective communication and explicit morality. Drawing on findings from the fields of evolutionary biology, developmental psychology and emotion research, neuroscience, and the pragmatist philosophies of John Dewey and George Herbert Mead, I will make that basic human propensity come to light. In doing so, I will try to avoid all naturalistic and culturalistic stereotypes and go beyond the traditional dualism of subject and object. In addition to Maussian gift theory, this pragmatist anthropology constitutes another major pillar on which I build my argument in this book.

A pragmatist model of action and emotion

Pragmatism is a school of philosophy that dominated American intellectual life from the 1890s to the outbreak of World War I and is commonly associated with the names of Charles Sanders Peirce, William James, Dewey, and Mead. In US history, this was a period of great upheaval, with processes of urbanization, industrialization, bureaucratization, and immigration shaking up the relative tranquility of 19th-century American society which was still largely agrarian in character. In politics, this was the time of progressivism and other reform movements, which would result in the introduction of welfare programs. Intellectual debates, too, were mainly concerned with adjusting the relationship of excessive self-interest—triggered by the new free market economy—and the common good.

Philosophical pragmatism assumes that truth does not spring from a single subject's intellectual confrontation of an object, but from a cooperative effort aimed at overcoming concrete social, political, or scientific problems. George Herbert Mead (1863–1931) and John Dewey (1859–1952) tried to escape the Cartesian dualism of knowing subject and to-be-known (and manipulated) object, and stressed the mostly preconscious nature of human behaviors. They understood that, more often than not, we act routinely instead of pursuing clear, preconceived intentions. Consequently, Mead and Dewey were highly critical of notions which suggested that subjects display an "instrumental rationality," thus reproducing the epistemological dichotomy of active subject and passive object (Joas, 1996).

According to pragmatism, our actions are embedded in situational contexts, in which there is no a priori separation between subject and object, mind and body, inside and outside. Instead, when we carry out actions, all these aspects form parts of one holistic experience, normally based on habits and without us consciously reflecting on our doing—Dewey ([1925] 2008) calls this "primary experience." Indeed, we routinely move through most of our days: we drowsily brew our coffees in the morning, apply a few well-practiced maneuvers to prepare breakfast, greet our colleagues with formulaic phrases, and check our emails as always. In all these situations, we are not acutely aware of any specific intentions. We are "in the zone."

Habits essentially ensure that we are functioning; they form a reservoir of behavioral patterns that we can resort to in all kinds of situations. Without habits, we would be incapable of orientation, of being-in-the-world (Heidegger). When a problematic situation arises though, that is, when our routines are disrupted by unexpected events, our habitual course of action is blocked and we suddenly become aware of the separation of subject and object as well as other aspects of the situation: intentions, means, resistances. For example, a colleague might one day tell us about his depression. The reflective process that now sets in—Dewey's "secondary experience"—is geared at continuing the course of action that has been interrupted. By thus breaking up routines, situated reflection and searching, problem-oriented action opens up new possibilities; in our example: concerning the relationship between us and our colleague.

It is hard to underestimate the role played by emotions in this process. Emotions, as Robert C. Solomon has argued (1988), constitute a sort of judgment, one that is not explicit, conscious, and deliberate, but bodily in nature: emotions combine judgment and perception in a directly felt manner. However, since they are usually directed at something external, emotions also signal a participation in the world (Nussbaum, 2001). We experience this whenever we are confronted with things that affect us. Oftentimes, our judgment is quick and direct—we feel either drawn to or repelled by something. In fact, all simple emotions fall into one of two categories: they are reactions to either liking or disliking something (Ben-Ze'ev, 2000: 94). In this way, an emotion, too, interrupts the previous course of action, or it highlights certain parts of the situation while pushing others into the background. Emotions alert us to a change within the situation we are in, either for the good or for the bad. Therefore, they are always judgmental and reflective—though primarily in a bodily anchored, not a cognitive-symbolic way. Like an extrinsic force, an emotion disrupts our natural interconnection with the world and the everyday routines we are engaged in.

Seen from a pragmatist perspective, then, emotions as bodily judgments make themselves felt, very directly and intensively, in problematic situations in which behavioral patterns and habits can no longer be continued. Both negative emotions (fear, anger, sadness) and positive ones (happiness, euphoria) can interrupt our flow of action in this way. They may appear when an action unexpectedly fails, or else when it goes especially well. As developmental psychology has shown, emotions are not subjective phenomena but common to us all—which, crucially, makes us capable of understanding others and emphasizing with them.

Embodied primary and secondary intersubjectivity in early childhood

Thirty years ago, the Chilean biologist Francisco Varela first called for an interaction-oriented approach in cognitive science (Varela, 1988; Varela et al, 1991). Ever since, this perspective has been developed further, and today neuroscientists and philosophers alike stress the importance of the body and its environment for cognitive processes (Noë, 2010). In a way, by using the findings of modern-day science (for example from perception research), these so-called "enactivists" continue the work of Dewey and Heidegger. The central insight is this: the living human brain cannot be examined in isolation but only in the context of the person's body, and thus within his/her environment, both natural and social; these are ties that the subject can never escape, try as it might (Fuchs, 2018).

In particular, this perspective has proved very productive in research on early childhood, revolutionizing our view of infants and their interactions with the world. Shaun Gallagher (2005), for instance, speaks of a social or embodied cognition in exactly this context. The once prevalent "idea of the asocial infant"—that is initially separated from its social environment and only starts interacting with it at a certain point—has by now entirely "lost its scientific credence" (Varga and Gallagher, 2011: 252).

In the first few months of their lives, infants go through a period of "primary intersubjectivity" during which their interactions are based exclusively on sensorimotor experiences: locking eyes with their parents, mimicking their facial expressions and gestures, and so on. Babies are very receptive to the nuances of their caregivers' expressions—for example to gaze directions, vocal variations, and levels of agitation—and they actively join this emotional communication. Even newborns are capable of differentiating between inanimate objects and human beings, and since they mimic facial expressions right from the beginning, we may assume that they are already endowed with some kind of body schema. It is further likely that in this kind of imitating behavior, mirror neurons play an important part: our brains display the same patterns when we watch others perform an activity as when we act ourselves. Thus, when an infant observes a facial expression, it does not need to cognitively understand that expression; the simulation takes place immediately, namely, while the infant's body is in a perceiving and imitating exchange with that of the caregiver. Our immediate, perception-based understanding of others, then, does not rely on an ability to infer the other person's hidden mental states (Gallagher and Hutto, 2008). Rather, there appears to be an inborn human capability for interaction, a comprehensive system attuned to the behavior of others.

Infants and caregivers engage in a constant process of giving and receiving (for example movements, looks, sounds), which both take pleasure in (Varga and Gallagher, 2011: 253). This primary intersubjectivity is complemented, though not supplanted, by a phase of secondary intersubjectivity that occurs when the child is about nine to 14 months old and first learns to understand the intentions of others. This understanding first arises in—and enables us to further immerse ourselves in—moments of "shared intentionality" (Tomasello, 1999). Such a shared focus of attention is given, for example, when the child learns to look at the object the adult's finger is pointing to, rather than the finger itself. And not only perceptions, but also affects can be shared in this way. As the psychoanalyst Daniel Stern (1985) has argued, intersubjectivity is the result of an intricate coordination of affects between caregiver and child. By modulating, albeit unconsciously, the intensity and rhythm of rapidly exchanged signals—say, laughing, cooing, babbling—a synchronicity develops, an experience of shared emotions. Such experiences are primarily about affects, about enjoying the newly created intersubjectivity, but they also enable the child to know itself. Conversely, if the adult does not mirror its emotions correctly (or not at all), confusion and a distorted self-image may ensue.

Emotions must not be misconstrued as inner, mental states. Instead, they constitute a space of interaffectivity: they evolve and move *between* individuals. If it were not for the presence of an other and their affective reactions to our own affects, self-awareness could not develop. This is how children learn about self-efficacy, that is, how their expressions affect others. In fact, already babies display self-regulatory faculties; for instance, when they make eye contact or withhold it, signaling a willingness or unwillingness to interact (Dornes, 1993). By means of these affective bodily practices, they regulate their own relationship to the caregiver in terms of closeness and distance, unity and differentiation (Downing, 2005).

One could also describe this as a process of giving and receiving (or else refusing to give and receive); the involvement in the affective logic of giving thus starts at a very early age. By repeating such interactions, a specific memory emerges, an implicit knowledge about the relationship, its rhythm and dynamics, and the affective connotations of past interactions with the caregiver—patterns that we are likely to unconsciously reproduce later in life. If successful, this synchronization goes largely unnoticed and serves the purpose of communitization: the contributions of both parties match each other, no dissonance develops, the two are affectively in sync. However, if the caregiver's responses to the child's interactive efforts and expressions are either too weak or too strong, the synchronization fails and the child is at risk of developing an affective disorder—depression or narcissism, respectively—later in life (Dornes, 1993).

The interactive social space of shared affects, meanings, and intentions, though itself pre-linguistic and pre-symbolic, is also where the foundation for our later acquisition of language is laid. But even as adults, we communicate our intentions and emotions not just linguistically, but also via our bodies, through voice, posture, facial expression, gestures, and movements. That adults, too, tend to synchronize their affects and behaviors is an insight that has been largely ignored by sociologists. An exception is Randall Collins whose book on interaction rituals (2004) focuses on exactly these processes, and whose study of violence (2008) is also based on a theory of interaction. In the latter book, Collins points out that situations of violence are surrounded by confrontational tension and fear. Violence only occurs though if both of these affects are transferred into emotional energy. Acts of violence run counter to our normal interaction rituals with their tendency towards synchronization; consequently, it is comparatively rare among humans, who generally find it hard to shape interactions in antagonistic ways:

> [H]umans have evolved ... particularly high sensitivities to the micro-interactional signals given off by other humans. ... We have evolved to be hyper-attuned to each other emotionally, and hence to be especially susceptible to the dynamics of interactional situations. ... Humans are hard-wired for interactional entrainment and solidarity; and this is what makes violence so difficult. (Collins, 2008: 26–7)

Prosocial primates?

If humans are "hard-wired for solidarity," what about their cousins in the animal kingdom? Increasingly, philosophers, social scientists, economists, and the general public are looking to ethology and evolutionary biology for answers, and not least regarding the question of how egoistic or altruistic humans are in comparison to animals, especially other great apes. While most scholars agree that *homo sapiens* is a highly social species, there is a fascinating debate taking place between those who see much continuity in that respect between humans and other primates and those who claim that empathy and prosociality are unique to us. The protagonists in that debate are the biologist Frans de Waal and the psychologist and anthropologist Michael Tomasello.

We turn first to de Waal. The Dutch primatologist, who has been a professor at Emory University since 1991, frequently emphasizes that apes, like humans, exhibit social tendencies, such as altruistic and empathic behavior, based on "emotional contagion" (2006). De Waal contends that primates do not just display emotional attachment; they are even able to comprehend another's situation by cognitively putting themselves in their place. For instance, although it yields them no apparent personal gain, chimpanzees have been observed to comfort the loser of a fight (de Waal and Suchak, 2010). For de Waal, empathy and reciprocity among apes are the foundation, in evolutionary terms, for human morality.

However, there are of course obvious differences in the behavior of humans and other hominids, especially as pertains their level of cognitive development. De Waal thus proposes a multi-level model of empathy at the center of which lies a perception-action mechanism: when a subject concentrates on the emotional state of another subject, corresponding neural representations are activated within its own brain, which are then translated into somatic and autonomic responses—pulse frequency, skin resistance, facial expressions, body posture—that resemble those of the perceived subject. This theory matches the hypothesis that so-called mirror neurons "allow individuals to understand and imitate the actions of others" (Preston and de Waal, 2002: 11). What occurs in such cases, then, is indeed an emotional contagion of sorts, which goes along with a synchronization of bodily phenomena. According to de Waal (2008), two further levels build on this basic capacity for empathy: sympathetic concern (as shown in comforting behavior) and the ability to see things from the other's perspective. For him, all these findings and theoretical deliberations suggest that humans are deeply marked by an evolutionary heritage, a heritage they share with other social animals. Human morality, even in its most sophisticated, uniquely human manifestations, is firmly rooted in this basic, evolved capacity for empathy—as is in fact all prosocial behavior.

Let us now consider what Michael Tomasello (1999, 2014) has to say on these issues. The American psychologist and long-time director of the Institute for Evolutionary Anthropology in Leipzig, generally focuses more on the differences between *homo sapiens* and its close evolutionary kin. How come, he wonders, that although our species shares 99 percent of its DNA with chimpanzees and bonobos, we are still so different? After all, modern humans, who entered the evolutionary picture roughly 300,000 years ago, are distinguished by a number of unique anatomical features, one of which—larger brains—results in cognitive capabilities that enable them to make and effectively use tools, and to cooperate to a degree unknown to other species. Another unique feature mentioned by Tomasello is the human capacity for symbolic communication and coordination, which in its most elaborate form manifests in such inventions as writing, money, or mathematical notations. Yet another is the human penchant for forming social practices, organizations, and formal institutions, and passing on what was learned to future generations. Human cognition, Tomasello insists, likewise does not develop in isolation but is dependent on the social environment, that is, on cooperation with others whose cultural knowledge we acquire and adapt in individual ways. We all are born into a world whose predefined characteristics (language, rules, institutions, and so on) we must adopt. And it is this process of socialization, and not the biological constitution of *homo sapiens* per se, that for Tomasello is the main precondition for the evolution of human self-awareness and specifically human cognitive achievements.

Like de Waal, Tomasello stresses the important role played by perspective-taking in empathic behavior—the ability, that is, to put oneself in another's shoes, to discern and interpret their intentions. But unlike de Waal, he regards this as a property that only humans have, whereas apes do not. As a result, only humans display "shared intentionality": that we are able to go for a walk with another person, for example, is no triviality; it requires a collective purpose (Tomasello, 1999). Indeed, the concept of shared intentionality goes a long way towards explaining our more pronounced sense of cooperation and norms like fairness and justice. While humans often act in this "we" mode, pursuing a goal together, other hominids largely remain stuck in an "I" mode. They seem incapable even of shared perceptions (that is, the knowledge that the other perceives the same object as me) and thus of joint attentional activities.

When we turn from empathy to altruism, insights from primatology and evolutional anthropology prove useful as well. For instance, it has been shown that apes never give unsolicited presents to each other (for example food) if it does not serve their own interest. What we do find in chimpanzees are forms of reciprocal altruism, in which both parties benefit from the interaction, but only humans appear inclined to help others even when they get nothing in return. Even human children, Tomasello claims, are "naturally concerned with each others' welfare" (2014: 190). Indeed, experiments have shown that one- and two-year-old children tend to behave in a much more altruistic and cooperative fashion than chimpanzees (which have about the same cognitive abilities): "infants as young as 14 months of age will help adults with all kinds of problems, from fetching out-of-reach objects to opening doors to stacking books with no concrete reward" (2014: 190). Tomasello infers that the motivation for altruistic behavior must be intrinsic, even though this almost unlimited willingness to cooperate shifts in the course of individual socialization: older children expect to be rewarded for their help or act strictly according to group norms. This orientation towards social norms, then, is uniquely human: apes know neither guilt nor shame, whereas humans are predisposed to conform, to internalize and enforce norms. One consequence of this predisposition is a frequent tension between ingroup and outgroup members, potentially resulting in aggression towards strangers (see also Bowles, 2006). This is why the history of mankind is shaped both by solidarity and by war.

Tomasello locates the origin of human prosociality in the dependence of group members on each other. The apparently inborn tendency towards cooperative behavior that little children display mirrors the earliest collective activities in human history: hunting and gathering. Cooperation was inevitable in these endeavors; and unlike nonhuman primates who usually compete for food, our ancestors shared it with other members of their group. Thus care came into existence. Or, as Tomasello puts it succinctly: "Interdependence breeds altruism" (2014: 192). But of course interdependence went far beyond foraging. In *Mothers and Others* (2009), the American anthropologist Sarah Blaffer Hrdy reveals how crucial cooperative rearing was for the evolution of empathy and prosociality. All apes have in common that their infants are raised almost exclusively by their mothers—except for human societies in which other caretakers (for example fathers, siblings, even non-relatives) support mothers in raising their offspring, which in humans is especially long. This is another reason why humans developed such exceptional cognitive skills and such intricate practices of sharing and caring. Adults had to learn to comprehend the emotions, needs, and intentions of infants, and (to some degree) vice versa—yet another instance of synchronization between humans. If this cooperation failed, infants were more likely to die. In evolutionary terms, empathy pays off.

Despite de Waal's and Tomasello's different interpretations on the singularity of the human capacity for empathy, they agree on one central point: human beings are "ultra-social animals" (Tomasello, 2014) and evolutionarily wired for cooperation. The dispute is really just due to different foci: while de Waal is more concerned with basal empathy and "emotional contagion," Tomasello addresses higher forms of social cognition, in particular shared intentionality. These more complex variants of empathy, it seems, are indeed unique to humans.

The will to cooperate

Now how can we correlate the issues discussed earlier—pre-reflective habits, unmediated emotional experiences, prosocial proclivities, altruism, empathy, affectively entangled subjectivities—to reflection, intelligence, or intended and controlled social change? After all, Dewey and Mead were not satisfied with showing how deeply we are affected by pre-symbolic and non-cognitive dimensions of behavior and action coordination. Rather, they were interested in how these competencies are connected to creativity and a potential transformation of society in radically democratic ways.

Dewey's political philosophy is based on the pragmatist idea that the pursuit of truth is a cooperative enterprise that serves the purpose of mastering practical problems of action, an idea he sees realized in the cooperation between scientists. Also, he is sometimes considered *the* philosopher of democracy (Bernstein, 2010: 70–88). In *The Public and Its Problems*, Dewey wrote:

> Regarded as an idea, democracy is not an alternative to other principles of associated life. It is the idea of community itself. It is an ideal in the only intelligible sense of an ideal: namely, the tendency and movement of some thing which exists carried to its final limit, viewed as completed, perfected. ([1927] 2008: 328)

Dewey is convinced that democratic values, far from being incompatible with "human nature," correspond to a basic human tendency towards cooperation. His belief in democracy rests upon his belief in human potential. And since "human nature" is indeterminate, so is the very constitution of democracy (Chanial, 2002).

Dewey avoided becoming subject to the reductionism of the so-called naturalistic fallacy: he never deduced an "ought" from an "is." The same is true of the latter-day proponents of philosophical pragmatism. Thus, Philip Kitcher's "pragmatic naturalism" (2012) stresses that altruism and moral norms are evolutionary mechanisms as well as normatively valuable human potentials, and we may add cooperation and democracy to these. Or, as Dewey and Tufts (1932) pointed out, moral concepts and processes arise naturally from the circumstances of human life. In other words: our inborn "ultra-sociality" (Tomasello, 2014) motivates certain behaviors more than others, for example empathic rather than aggressive behavior.

One can only speak of morality when an understanding of the future exists, when we are able to reflect on our own desires, when rationality (instead of instincts and emotions) guides our behavior. Only then can we live up to Kant's requirement that we act from duty even if it runs counter to our personal inclinations. It is not enough to have peaceful intentions and act accordingly; to behave morally, we must exert normative "self-determination," that is, scrutinize our intentions and actions, and sometimes defy them. Since it does not build on rule-governed behavior, the evolved human proclivity for altruism, while essential to the development of morality, is pre-ethical. "Generalized others" (Mead) or "impartial spectators" (Adam Smith) are needed to alert us to a lack of altruism. Only when we decide against yielding to an urge due to a social rule, we enter the sphere of morality (Kitcher, 2011, 2012).

We can conclude that "human nature" is social and that the roots of human ethics lie in this very sociality (which we partly share with other primates). What does *not* derive from this social nature is moral impartiality, that is, the ability to take into account the interests of others, judge our own actions from their perspective, and scrutinize whether or not these actions are based on generalizable rules (Singer, 2011). There is no evolutionarily formed impartiality in humans, but there is also no inherent tendency towards egoism or amorality in us, no Hobbesian wolf-like aggression.

To identify these anthropological possibilities and limits of morality is far from irrelevant from a pragmatist perspective because to describe and solve moral or political problems, we must first familiarize ourselves with the natural and social facts of the matter. Even though the "is"/"ought" dichotomy is ultimately inextricable, every vision of what ought to be must make use of empirical data on what is. The other main thrust in Dewey's naturalism rests on the reverse hypothesis, namely that every empirical description of facts involves normative assumptions and judgments. For Dewey, it is virtually impossible to describe the world in unbiased terms. Likewise, Hilary Putnam (1926–2016) suggested that all forms of experience are steeped in values and normativity, and that due to this entanglement of facts and values there can be no neutral notions of truth or rationality (2002).

As mentioned, to pragmatists science represents the paragon of cooperativity: it is a human mode of action that aims to overcome problematic situations collectively and is oriented towards social goals and values. Take for instance Dewey's own scientific work, which at all times bespeaks his democratic ideals. Instead of nature prescribing what is desirable (a position impossible to justify in post-metaphysical philosophical thinking), it is the scientist's own practices and value judgments that guide his or her research. Without an underlying ethical ideal, certain facts would not be uncovered in the first place. However, that same underlying ethical ideal makes scientific work forever vulnerable to (equally value-based) criticism. This is very much the case with this book as well, which is concerned with presenting an archaeology of the gift in a rather specific frame: that of our modern values of liberty, equality, and fraternity, that is, of radically democratic ideas.

Dewey directly derives *his* radically democratic ideas from an interpretation of scientific activity: only cooperative and transparent discourses, he is convinced, discourses that encompass the creativity, opinions, and objections of many, can bring about new insights, and thus scientific progress. Political philosophy has frequently adopted this conviction in discussions of democracy, arguing that such a collective pursuit of truth also results in the best political decisions and outcomes (see for example Putnam, 1992)—an argument that empirical data seems to confirm. Democracy, Dewey once wrote, "is more than a form of government; it is primarily a mode of associated living, of conjoint communicated experience" ([1916] 1997: 87). For him, it is apparent that we all can profit from cooperation—both individually and collectively, since these two levels are mutually dependent. In pragmatism, the epistemic ideal (democracy) therefore becomes an ethical one (individual and collective growth).

Individual self-realization is only thinkable for Dewey in the context of democratic participation; it relies on social interaction. As we will see, this argument can be extended to include interactions with nonhuman lifeforms—in fact, we have to extend it that way if we want to secure our survival on Earth (see Chapter 8). *Homo sapiens* can only exist in a "mode of associated living," and we should learn to embrace this mode and appreciate the contributions others make—as they will appreciate ours. Practices of reciprocal giving and receiving strengthen the individual's sense of community, a community that includes all life on Earth.

In Dewey, cooperation is not really distinguished from other forms of action. We find such a distinction in Jürgen Habermas' famous juxtaposition of instrumental or strategic action on the one hand and communicative action on the other (1984/1987), as well as in Hannah Arendt who insisted upon a genuinely political mode of action (1958). However, Dewey makes a distinction *within* what Habermas would call instrumental action: there are actions, Dewey holds, with "foreseen consequences" and "ideas ... of the measures ... required to bring the[m] into existence" ([1938] 2009: 207), and there are actions with merely "ends-in-view." In the latter mode, the objective of an action is not fixed but develops while carrying it out, in engagement with the means at your disposal (Hartmann, 2003). An example would be cooking spontaneously, with whatever is left in the pantry, as opposed to planning and fixing a meal according to a recipe. This distinction goes hane in hand with a normative valuation in Dewey. The "foreseen consequences" mode of action is associated with what he calls the "spectator theory of knowledge," which originates in ancient philosophy and rests upon a dualism of supposedly higher actions, especially philosophizing, and lower actions such as farming. Fixed ends, Dewey argues, have their roots in the Western tradition of searching for truth and certainty; once we "foresee" them, we are no longer open to new experiences and in fact vulnerable to instrumentalizing them for political purposes: the end justifies the means. By contrast, the "ends-in-view" mode of action provides openness and adaptability in view of changing conditions. Cooperations in that mode are potentially controllable by all parties involved; they may influence processes and contribute to the formulation of altered ends. This is an intrinsically democratic mode of cooperative action, and we will return to it in Chapter 7.

In a successful cooperation, actions attain not just meaning but also meaningfulness. As Dewey points out, the confrontation with others and their reactions to our behaviors teaches us self-reflection. Unlike Mead whose stress in this context is on conflictual situations (many of his examples hail from the field of boxing), Dewey focuses on joint activities in which, due to a consensus between the parties, a feeling of gratification ensues: the feeling to be a part of something bigger. For Dewey, experiencing a successful cooperation is not (just) of instrumental value; it is an end in itself which has a positive emotional and ethical effect on those involved. Whereas Habermas believes that the success or failure of interactions can be measured by the communicative outcome, for Dewey it is more about whether or not the cooperation works. Consequently, a misunderstanding is not the result of miscommunication but of unsynchronized actions—it is all about practice.

While we may be able to understand someone even though we may not want to cooperate with him, for Dewey communication is ultimately based on an accordance in action: our own willingness to participate in cooperative efforts, for example in democratic processes, is dependent upon our ability to trust in the willingness to cooperate of others (Hartmann, 2003). Trust and a readiness to support others are intrinsically linked to the concept of cooperation in Dewey. Without an advance of trust (in the form of a gift), many forms of cooperation are simply not possible—an insight that is strongly reminiscent of Mauss, even though Dewey never made this connection.

Trusting others is a risk because we cannot be certain if they will reciprocate, or perhaps even abuse our trust. But it is only by taking that risk that certain forms of cooperation become possible. The world-opening and -transforming power of trust was described by the psychologist William James (1842–1910), one of the founders of pragmatism, in his well-known essay "The Will to Believe." Here, James speaks of "faith" as a central "element of our active nature," which amounts to "the readiness to act in a cause the prosperous issue of which is not certified to us in advance" ([1896] 1979: 74). Faith—or trust, or the gift—has a motivating affective power that is directed towards uncertain things, actors, or actions. In fact, faith may only create that which one has faith in to begin with; its performative power anticipates the future and thus brings it into being. A case in point is love, which only exists when both parties are willing to trust in the love of the other, without any ironclad proofs. By enabling us to take a leap in the dark, faith/trust/the gift is therefore constitutive of the most valuable type of relationship.

In conclusion, let us return to Dewey's concept of "primary experience," which, we recall, describes a holistic experience that may only be broken up into its individual parts (perception, judgment, cognition, and so on) in a later reflective stage. In primary experiences, though we may not be aware of it, perceiving and judging go very much hand in hand. Honneth has examined this phenomenon with regard to research on infants. Take the observation by Daniel Stern (1977) that infant and caregiver engage in "a process of reciprocal regulation of affect and attention that comes about to a large extent with the help of gestural communication" (Honneth, 2001: 116–17). It could be said that infant and caregiver thus recognize each other, both as individuals and as human beings. Crucially, we do not need to "first acquire a cognition that permits us to perceive in our counterpart a small child in need of help before we can then apply the appropriate gestures of encouragement and of sympathy" (2001: 117). Instead, these "gestures" "express in abbreviated form the totality of the actions that are supposed to be accorded to the small child on the grounds of his situation" (2001: 117). In other words: perception, recognition, and care are performed simultaneously, in one holistic act, and this stimulates the infant to react. What Honneth wants to show is that, in terms of developmental psychology, identifying another person is not prior to recognizing that person. It is exactly the other way around: the infant learns to "read" the caregiver's expressions long before it is capable of cognitively comprehending its environment.

Conceptually, too, recognition is precedent to identification for Honneth, and what was learned by the infant survives into adulthood. Understanding another person does not mean having any abstract knowledge about their thoughts; it means sympathizing with them (Honneth, 2008: 48ff.). We can only understand the feelings of others when we realize that their emotional expressions are an "invitation to act" (2008: 50): they ask us for something, request that we do something. Only when I perceive these prompts can I really sympathize with the other person and recognize them. This form of existential recognition is precedent to more elaborate forms of recognizing someone (for something). Conceptual thought without sympathy results in objectification.

Primary experiences, then, are based on a form of recognition—or, as Dewey would say, valuation—which refers, beyond itself, to a potential cooperation between the two persons. We have thus found a theory which assumes that human actions are rooted in pre-reflective habits, and that reflection comes into play when we are facing problematic situations. This is linked to assumptions about affectivity: we never move in emotionally neutral spaces, and perception and action always go along with judgments, which we are forcefully alerted to by emotions. When it comes to actions, an affective logic of the gift constantly surrounds us. Each and every situation can be described as a constellation of giving and receiving—that is, giving and receiving attention, resources, affection, and so on. Gifts can be either anchored in habits and escape our reflective attention, or they can be quite evident. The latter is the case in particular when situations are problematic and demand solutions.

The tendency towards giving in humans is indicative of a willingness to cooperate that, with Dewey, we may call democratic. This tendency has its roots in both our phylogenetic and our ontogenetic heritage. We are wired for ultra-sociality and cooperation—*homo sapiens* is essentially a *homo donator*. Humans are ready to take on risks and bear the uncertainty that comes with giving. The gift precedes the establishment of a reliable interpersonal foundation; it represents a leap of faith which performatively calls into being possibilities for cooperation; it creates social order by simulating it. We even may go so far to say that every interaction involves an exploration of potential future cooperation. The history of mankind as well as our individual socialization has endowed us with a primordial tendency to actually recognize others (instead of just identifying them, as others) and open up to them in the mode of primary intersubjectivity, based on trust and cooperation.

PART II

Society's Gifts

4

Locating the Gift in Society

So far I have argued that there is a human propensity for giving that cannot be explained by way of either normative or utilitarian theories. Giving is different from exchanging things of equal value: gifts comprise aspects of surplus and unconditionality, which are constitutive for the emergence of sociality. Non-equivalences and asymmetries thus lie at the very heart of the social. Moreover, the alternatives of giving vs. receiving and recognizing vs. disregarding have neither the same value nor the same origin. In human behavior, a primacy of successful cooperation is manifest, a primal sociality based on cooperation, recognition, and giving. Humans display prosocial spontaneous impulses just as much as selfish ones. Within as well as between groups, gifts can bring about trust and cooperation.

It is now time to introduce a distinction that is linked to the one made earlier between agonistic and non-agonistic gifts: the distinction between ordinary and extraordinary gifts. As we will see, the latter variety plays a significant role in conflictual situations and intercultural encounters.

Ordinary vs. extraordinary gifts

Ordinary gifts are often not considered to be gifts at all. They form an implicit part of interactions, stay in the background, and are not labeled or framed as gifts by the involved parties. They rest upon practical skills and implicit knowledge (see Adloff et al, 2015), and it is only when our routines are no longer effective that what used to be implicit becomes explicated. Consider the many shared practices we engage in on a daily basis: we greet one another, practice turn-taking in our conversations, do each other little favors, ignore mishaps to make sure that the other is not embarrassed, help each other in countless different ways. While largely unconscious, these practices of appreciating the other, sharing attention with them, and synchronizing our utterances and body movements in fact amount to gifts.

However, even these implicit, ordinary gifts come with a risk because they, too, are marked by an aspect of unconditionality. Social niceties and other signals of attention are not actually exchanged; they are given. We cannot say hello to someone on the condition that they will say hello back; such reciprocation is only made a fixed condition in agreements and contractual exchanges. If we only smiled at others on the condition that they smile back, no one would ever smile. Our everyday life is characterized by uncertainty, and our ordinary gifts by unconditionality, even if we might not be aware of it.

The fact that in ordinary gifts only a short moment may pass between giving and reciprocating does not take away from their gift character; after all the risk involved is still the same. For Simmel, the eye contact between two people makes for an interaction par excellence: I look at someone and notice that I am being looked at as well. Giving and receiving here occur virtually at the same time, and ideally, both parties use the same normative register—that is, exchange good for good, or bad for bad. As we have seen, with gift-based reciprocity such normative and affective judgments are of central importance: giving and receiving always involves judgments; affective neutrality does not exist for subjects. Occasional gifts, such as presents, temporally stretch that process, so that its components (giving, receiving, reciprocating) become better discernable and a longer-term attachment, grounded in gratitude, may be formed (Simmel, [1908] 1950: 379–95).

In their ordinary manifestation, then, gifts can be implicit, and they invariably entail the giving of either a positive or a negative thing (from the point of view of the two people), as well as an aspect of risk and unconditionality which distinguishes them clearly from contractual exchanges. In a habituated and pre-reflective mode, cooperations or attachments may thus emerge. Only in problematic situations, that is, in moments when the flow of action is faltering, does reflection set in. Only then do we wonder whether we should give something (back)—and if so, whether that something should be good or bad. This is especially the case in actual crises of action and/or interaction (see Adloff et al, 2016). In situations of foreignness or interculturality, when suspicion and misunderstandings have turned into actual conflicts, actors can rebuild a joint basis of action by presenting the other with an extraordinary gift. As described by Mauss, extraordinary (agonistic) gifts are meant to initialize the (re-)creation of a shared world, and they involve some sort of test or challenge, as well as an underlying rivalry. They contain the questions: friend or foe? Peace or war? Extraordinary gifts are clearly marked as such, and the risk they entail is obvious to all parties—which is exactly what makes for their "greatness." The challenge to resume the "game" of cooperation is inherent in the thing given, which forms a third element in the interaction and draws the attention of both parties. At least for this moment of shared attention, the challenging gift creates a common world—notwithstanding the possibility that the recipient may eventually decline it.

By creating obligations, extraordinary gifts are supposed to restore trust, mutual intelligibility, and the possibility of cooperation. They are meant to build the very cooperative sociality they simulate: you advance trust without knowing if the other will acknowledge and ratify it. You challenge them by freely giving your generosity, and the other is just as free in their response. Such a gift, it could be said, transports the personhood and otherness of the giver. It foreshadows a joint world of cooperation which would be realized if the gift were received and reciprocated. The extraordinary gift thus transcends the existing order and amounts to an event. If it succeeds in ultimately establishing a shared practice of *ordinary* giving, it gets transferred into a state of peace (Ricœur) or of non-agonistic "communism" (Graeber, 2011). Extraordinary gifts are therefore meant to create the fundament of trust and cooperation that is already given in ordinary gifting.

Ordinary gifts occur in a mode of "play" to which both parties are already accustomed: you can rely on the other to know the rules of the game and comply with them, at least for the biggest part. If a person violates a rule, they can expect to be punished for it. But a singular rule violation does not call into question the validity of the game as such; it represents merely a breach of regulative norms. By contrast, a fundamental disruption of the game occurs when a person no longer follows its constitutive rules. The distinction between regulative and constitutive rules goes back to thinkers like Ludwig Wittgenstein, John Austin, John Rawls, or John Searle (see Rawls, 2012). The game of chess is frequently cited to illustrate this point: if a player deliberately moves the knight incorrectly to gain an edge over their opponent (provided the latter does not notice the maneuver), they are violating the regulative rules of chess; however, if someone moves their pieces totally at random throughout, they are likely to be unaware of the game's constitutive rules. If you don't know the constitutive rules of a certain practice—say, weather forecasting or baking—your course of action will make no sense to observers. In this case, no participation, and hence no cooperation, is possible: without any shared basis of meaning-making, your bewildered observer will withdraw, and the interaction collapses.

The essential importance of constitutive rules to joint practices and functioning cooperation was powerfully demonstrated by sociologist Harold Garfinkel (1917–2011) in *Studies in Ethnomethodology* (1967). Garfinkel argues that any cooperation—any successful social interaction really—is based on a coordinated (albeit implicit) reference of all participating parties to constitutive rules. These "basic rules" of the social (1967: 141) are more fundamental than norms (or regulative rules) which Garfinkel considers to be operating on a superficial level only. In fact, constitutive rules allow us to challenge and "play" with norms; they give us freedom. In his famous breaching experiments, Garfinkel managed to establish that everyday social interactions are indeed guided by such implicit basic rules. His student assistants would bring about interactional crises—for instance, by taking everything literally, requiring explanations for the most self-evident actions, behaving like strangers within their own families, or standing extremely close to others in elevators or on the subway. The constitutive rules or "expectational structures" (1967: 115) underlying these practices were thus worked out, and it was found that they reach deeper than mere norms.

According to Anne Warfield Rawls (b. 1950), a student of Garfinkel's, such practices based on constitutive rules gain in importance because we can no longer count on commonalities concerning culture, religion, language, and so on (2012). Actors must nowadays be able to participate in practices that require specific implicit knowledges and shared attention, practices contingent on an equality of all participants, which sometimes leads to situational solidarities. Such constitutive practices clash with top-down instructions and hierarchical institutional structures since they presuppose a moral and practical commitment to attention sharing and reciprocity. Rawls is convinced that the stability of our social orders relies ever more on such a commitment to egalitarian situational principles. She assumes an "Interaction Order Sui Generis" (1987) which ensures that face-to-face interactions are mostly characterized by mutual acceptance and consideration, and she describes this interaction order as a space of self-organization which is different from more institutionalized spaces (1990: 75ff.). It is not primarily a normative order, but it produces a commitment to ideals of reciprocity and equality of its own accord. This requires participants to be dedicated to the interaction and to focus on the subject at hand; else they will feel uneasy, or the interaction may collapse.

Rawls' early work is indebted to fellow sociologist Erving Goffman (1922–82) who in his book on *Asylums* (1961) had discussed "total institutions" and their systematic assaults on the selves of inmates, for example, by means of degradation and humiliation. Goffman showed how inmates managed to defend their selves against the inventions of the institution which tried to control their every move and action: they maintained some degree of leeway for self-expression, held on to their personal belongings, and established spaces of refuge. Moreover, even total institutions seem to be unable to totally redefine the egalitarian interaction order. For example, Goffman observed some "difficulty of sustaining a drama of difference between persons who could in many cases reverse roles and play on the other side" (1961: 112). Personnel and inmates, that is, had a hard time upholding the difference in status as structurally prescribed to their respective groups by the institution. Since there were no elaborate institutionalized procedures which would time and again establish that difference, the power of the everyday interaction order persisted, resulting in many instances of fraternization between inmates and personnel.

In a similar vein, Rawls conducted a highly interesting empirical study that demonstrates how it is possible to take part in collaborative practices even when there are no prior cultural commonalities between participants (Rawls and David, 2005). The long-term ethnographic field study involves a small convenience store in a multiethnic neighborhood of Detroit. Rawls found that, contrary to what one might expect in terms of cultural tensions, almost no altercations occurred between staff and customers. Their interactions were largely limited to the simple practice of selling and buying everyday items, and everyone engaged in "situated civility" (2005: 491). Conflicts arose only when this specific situational context was abandoned and racial/cultural narratives and stereotypes were mobilized, that is, when "othering" undermined the very basis of cooperation. But when the interaction succeeded, a "situated solidarity" set in (2005: 470), and potential differences were overcome by creating shared attention and mutual intelligibility. The trust thus produced by reciprocity is a prerequisite for all cooperation: if people trust each other, they are capable of mastering even complex situations and crises of communication. Accordingly, Rawls and David conclude:

> What a modern differentiated society in a context of globalization needs to maintain are situations in which diverse persons from diverse backgrounds, who do not share beliefs and values, can come together. ... [W]hat develops are shared background expectations that treat the practices that constitute situations as that which must be held in common and respected above all else. Trust becomes a matter of how one fulfills one's involvement obligations with regard to specific situated practices. (2005: 473–4)

Sequentiality is crucial for practices to succeed, which is to say that all utterances and actions must build on one another. The reaction of the other person tells you if they have understood, you can then in turn react to their reaction, and so forth. In this alternating reflective process, the two interactants may jointly clarify what they both mean. However, if one person is talking for too long, a space of meaning is formed that is too large to be confined in interaction in this way, and misunderstandings are likely to ensue.

As Rawls points out, things tend to go awry in intercultural situations when the concrete context of an interaction is abandoned, no "mutually intelligible grounds" in the form of shared "beliefs or ... concerns" are available (2005: 489), and participants begin confronting each other with group-specific narratives based on stereotypes. This is how the worst enemies of peaceful human coexistence—say, European racists or Islamist jihadists—operate, whose dangerous ideologies dehumanize whole groups of people (women, Jews, infidels, people of color, the disabled, and so on) in order for them to feel superior. Stereotypes are superimposed on actual interaction experiences, and what follows is a "forgetfulness of recognition" (Honneth, 2008: 52ff.), downright disrespect, or even reification. We may then still perceive the other's expressions, but "we lack ... the feeling of connection that would be necessary for us to be affected" by them (2008: 58).

While Rawls thus emphasizes the importance of trust and reciprocity in interactions, she fails to fully acknowledge how much the face-to-face interactions she describes are dependent on each interactant's willingness to actively participate in the situation and the social relation, that is, their willingness to give. For cooperative practices to succeed, actors need to freely and continually offer help and repairs. In *intra*cultural situations with shared knowledges, the constitutive rules of the "gift game" are taken for granted, and actors apply them automatically. Concrete norms may then develop which make the other's responses more predictable; for instance, the "norm of reciprocity" which ensures that we can expect our gift to be repaid (Gouldner, 1960: 177). When such norms are violated, such regulative rules are broken, there will likely be sanctions, but this does not threaten the "game" as a whole.

The extraordinary gift, on the other hand, which initiates a relationship, is created in a situation of crisis. It is meant to (re-)create a shared space of cooperation. When making such a gift, you take a risk, but at the same time you expect the other person to know the constitutive rules of the "gift game." A situational shared practice can then evolve based on the fact that both parties are committed to the rules. Constitutive rules are therefore not normative but normativizing; they facilitate a process of establishing norms which in turn makes shared practices possible. Expectations are then matched and adopted, mutual intelligibility develops, trust is advanced. This risky "game" is a condition for all cooperation in contexts of foreignness.[1] Practices of giving, I hold, are universally known in all cultures as a means of bridging foreignness, creating intersubjectivity, and thus building a basis for cooperation. This is true for extraordinary gifts in intercultural contexts as much as for ordinary gifts when some form of foreignness is involved (see Rawls and David, 2005). To put it bluntly: no gifts, no cooperation. I find confirmation for this argument in Unni Wikan's book *Resonance* (2012). The Norwegian anthropologist contends that there is a universal form of intercultural understanding "beyond the words." A former cultural relativist, Wikan was "converted" to this view, among other experiences she made during her fieldwork, when she accompanied a friend to a traditional Hindu healer in Bali (2012: 53ff.). At first, the friend, "a devoted Muslim" whose "family had long been afflicted with a series of misfortunes," was reluctant because she feared that the healer would "treat her as if she was a Hindu." Once Wikan convinces her to go, however, the man welcomes her very amicably and explains to her that her family's problems are due to the fact that their ancestors did not keep their oath to "place offerings in the Muslim holy place." Wikan is not happy about this turn of events, believing it to be an instance of interreligious misunderstanding. But her Muslim friend turns out to be delighted by the Hindu healer's statements and makes the decision to "take it upon herself to remedy the faults of the ancestors." She explains to Wikan: "He says *karma pala*, I say *taqdir*—it's all the same!" The anthropologist disagrees on theological grounds, but years later, when she is working on her book, she realizes that her friend went "beyond the words" of the healer, that she had recognized his intention to help her: "Resonance demands something of both parties to communication ... an effort at feeling-thought; a willingness to *engage* with another world, life, or idea. ... We can use this commonality—this 'shared space'...—to try to understand each other. Indeed we must, for we have nothing else" (2012: 57). To summarize the insights of the last few pages: we can assume a willingness to give as a basic anthropological principle (Godbout) that is effective even in transcultural situations. If there was just self-interested behavior on the one hand and behavior rooted in socialization and the internalization of norms on the other, we could only ascribe to the former the status of "natural" behavior. I argue though that our ability, willingness, and motivation to give to others is just as much present in spontaneous interactions.

Miso/meso/macro: where is the gift located?

Is the logic of the gift confined to personal relationships or to face-to-face interactions? The notion that the gift plays an important role only in that small realm but has no bearing on larger, structural phenomena is quite widespread. But of course it all depends on how you define these "micro" and "macro" levels in the first place. If you define social macro phenomena as a level *sui generis*, without acknowledging that they too can be broken down into micro situations, the aforementioned notion may apply. It no longer does, however, once we follow Theodore Schatzki (2015) that in fact "neither social structures ... nor individuals and their actions constitute distinct levels" (see also Latour, 2005). In a "flat ontology" of the social that does not make the mistake of "reduc[ing] everything social to the plane of individuals" (Schatzki, 2015), macro phenomena such as "capitalism" or "the state" are no longer located "above" micro situations, but instead are recognized to be made up of them. One could even say that we can only fruitfully analyze macro phenomena by de-constructing them that way.

In examining "where the gift is located," I assume such a flat ontology. A peculiarity of our contemporary interactions is that many of them no longer proceed face to face. Earlier examples of this phenomenon include letter writing, in which the time frame is considerably extended, or telephone conversations, which are limited to the auditory dimension. Likewise, our own ubiquitous computer-based conversations—messages, tweets, and so on—do not demand for the interactants to be physically co-present, and one obvious consequence of this is that you can no longer observe the other's non-verbal expressions. In our global communication networks, then, "embodied presence" has been replaced with temporal or "response presence" (Goffman, 1983); yet these "global microstructures" exist only in concrete situations (Knorr-Cetina, 2009). The difference between the macro and micro levels is gradual, quantitative. As Collins (1981) has pointed out, macro phenomena merely cover more space and a longer time span, and thus affect a larger number of people than micro phenomena.

The interaction order's logic of the gift is mainly dependent on the willingness of interactants to be fully immersed in a situation. By contrast, an institutionally more prestructured situation makes interactants appear as if remote-controlled: they follow fixed role scripts instead of reacting spontaneously to the requirements of the situation. This diminishes the egalitarian and cooperative potential of such interactions, which is due to the logic of the gift (here absent). Whereas personal relationships allow for considerateness and joint action coordination, unpersonal relations often do not since they are determined by membership in organizations. In this case, person A can hardly enter into a free dialog with person B because they are bound to their organization whose rules they follow—without usually disclosing anything personal. The organizational membership towers above everything, and interactants will not be considerate of each other, but of their organization's expectations. For instance, a policewoman is not allowed to engage in pleasantries with a traffic offender, and teachers are not supposed to become too personally involved with their students.

Organizations can enforce such desirable behaviors by means of gratifications or sanctions. While thus not normally applying between members of different organizations, the logic of the gift and of reciprocity does exists *within* organizations, even if only in the form of an exchange: in return for a salary, for example, you give away your freedom of action, including your freedom to engage in informal exchanges with people outside the organization. In effect, members of an organization are paid for their own reification and their contribution to a general desolidarization of interactional situations. At the same time, however, this unpersonal approach allows for a compliance with demands of equality and justice: those working in public bureaucracy are expected to treat everyone the same. Admittedly, the risk of corruption is bigger in gift-based exchanges. Which is exactly why many modern societies try to restrict them, arguing that the desolidarization is compensated for by the blessings of our modern division of labor: objectivity and justice for all. Reciprocity then primarily takes the form of secondary, indirect exchanges which frequently are very asymmetrical in character (Blau, 1964).

Organizations utilize a variety of means to induce their members to consent to their policies (Kühl, 2016), not all of which can be interpreted in utilitarian or normative terms. Whereas force only appears as an appropriate means in the realm of state authority—say, in the military—organization members are usually given incentives in the form of offers for identification with the organization, of bonding, collegiality, and so on. This is how the logic of the gift and reciprocity takes effect within organizations. Further incentives include the (size of the) salary and attractive working conditions. By all these means, organizations ensure that new members refrain from exactly predefining their tasks. There remains a space of indifference that the organization can freely command. Members give their organization carte blanche by thus selling their manpower and commitment in very generalized terms; they vow obedience to orders not yet known. This is not actually an exchange at all since the organization's expectations largely remain unspecified. The fact that people are still willing to agree to such deals speaks volumes. Organizations exploit their members' goodwill—or, in our terminology: their fundamental inclination to give. They could not survive without this, or without the informal, gift-based relations that develop between members. Without that solidarity within the organization, without their members' creativity in repairing formal procedures informally and their desire to be recognized as givers, no organization can manage (Hodson, 1991).

The argument that gift theory only applies to micro phenomena is untenable. Macro phenomena do *not* operate according to an autonomous logic, disconnected from processes of giving; after all, they are produced within concrete, local situations. And while the power of the gift is often contained by membership expectations of organizations, it can never be disposed of completely. In fact, organizations depend on practices of giving, as we have seen.

Many of today's social and ecological problems go back to the same principle: we produce negative externalities but cannot pay the affected party back because no networks of giving and reciprocating exist. As a result, distrust prevails, and a calculating, utilitarian logic reigns over us. Take, for instance, the stagnating international cooperation regarding climate change. It would certainly help if the spaces in which the various actors meet (states, companies, NGOs, and so on) were designed in a way that fosters real cooperation, if they were enabled to really interact and get into the mode of giving and reciprocating. This will not happen though, as long as organizations or states "remote-control" their representatives, as long as they compel them to play fixed roles: organizational logic then suppresses interpersonal logic (see Messner et al, 2013: 27ff.). Too much "culture" can also be detrimental to cooperation. If actors rely too much on predefined convictions, instead of engaging in real interactions with strangers, the logic of the gift will hardly take effect. Just like organizational demands, cultural ideas can undermine the potential for cooperation.

Motivations

Let us now turn to a theoretical issue that has somehow accompanied us since the beginning of this book, but has not really been addressed: what motivates actors in social situations to give, take, and reciprocate? So far we only know that utilitarian approaches identify self-interest and one's normative conformity as motives for gift giving, and that authors like Caillé stress the contradictoriness inherent in motives for giving.

First and foremost, we must distinguish between motivations and motives. Motivations refer to the elemental issue of what makes humans want to act and be in the world. This is the realm of social theory, psychology, and anthropology, and while some approaches, such as psychoanalysis or the utilitarian paradigm in the social sciences, have evolved explicit theories of human motivation, others work with mere assumptions. Instead of extensively discussing these, often conflicting, theories, I will resort to the convincing theoretical synthesis developed by American sociologist Jonathan H. Turner (1987, 2002). Turner posits five basic needs that drive human motivation, all of which must be satisfied otherwise we are exposed to "feelings of deprivation" and "diffuse anxiety" (1987: 23): humans strive for a) self-verification (the sense that others confirm their self-conception); b) profitable exchange payoffs; c) group inclusion; d) trust (the sense that they can trust others); and e) facticity in all transactions (the sense that others perceive reality in the same way) (2002: 137). I would argue that the last need, that for a "shared world" is prior to the other four, and in fact a condition for their fulfillment.

There are some interesting parallels between Turner's model of basic human motivations and Caillé's model of motivations for gift giving. Both assume that there are two basic needs focused on the individual and two basic needs that focus on an other, a group. One polarity that thus emerges is that between self-verification (Turner) or freedom and creativity (Caillé) *versus* group inclusion (Turner) or obligation and norms (Caillé). The second polarity is that between profit (Turner) or self-interest (Caillé) *versus* trust (Turner) or "interest in"/*aimance* (Caillé).

The latter pole involves an important difference, however, because whereas Turner's "trust" amounts to little more than a passive stance of expectation towards others, Caillé's *aimance* is more proactive. As our excursions into the fields of evolutionary biology, early-childhood research, and Deweyan pragmatism have shown, this active dimension of caring for another person is crucial when it comes to gift giving. Caillé defines the gift as a paradoxical amalgamation of all four motivations—as at the same time obligatory and voluntary, self-serving and selfless—and this implies that gift giving satisfies all four basic human needs. Furthermore, we have come to realize that the extraordinary gift manages to (re-)create facticity or a "shared world." Finally, we can conclude that each gifting interaction involves openness and spontaneity and is therefore a creative process.

So much for motivations. But what about the *motives* people pursue in concrete situations? Motives, too, build on the four basic needs, but are usually not identical to them. They can be more varied and differentiated, and they change along with a changing society. In sociology, the concept of motives is closely connected to that of actions. Classic action theory (Max Weber, Alfred Schütz, and so on) assumes that actors ascribe a subjective meaning to their actions, and it is this process that actually constitutes the action in the first place. In a strict sense, the actor is therefore the only one who knows about the meaning and motives of their actions. Schütz (1972) posited that it is the performance of behaviors the actor has previously imagined that gives their actions meaning. And it is true that actions can only come into being when people are able to imagine a meaning for them. Still, this answer to the problem of motives is unsatisfactory. After all, how do we know which imagined act is being performed by someone? You have to ask them. But the motives that people name may not actually be their real ones. As C. Wright Mills pointed out, what these named motives reveal, first and foremost, is the social constraints that the communicative situation is characterized by (1940: 907f.).

Of course most of our actions are not questioned like this anyway: we do not ask each other about our motives for routine procedures. Generally, we only have to explain our motives in problematic situations, namely, when there are diverging expectations or when a behavior is unintelligible to others. It is then up to the listener to decide whether or not our explanation seems plausible to them. However, there are situation-specific "vocabularies of motive" (Mills, 1940), and sufficient motives may vary, for instance, depending on who asks us. Consequently, descriptions of motives are not identical to motives themselves; they primarily fulfill a performative social function. We *attribute* motives to ourselves and to others. And these attributions are subject to situational as well as to historical changes. For example, in his article of 1940, Mills argues that Americans increasingly make use of a vocabulary of hedonism when describing their motives (1940: 913). Actions thus come about in social situations when actors attribute motives to one another. We infer typical motives from typical behaviors, and when asked for our own motives, we resort to a vocabulary that is appropriate to the situation we are in.

Now what does all this mean for gift theory? While we can safely say that gifts satisfy fundamental needs and motivations, on the level of social meaning-making things get more complicated: unless we are telepaths, we can merely attribute motives to others. When we apply this to Caillé's four-pole model of motivations for gift giving, an interesting scenario emerges: if person B is given something by person A, they are confronted with the question whether A's motive for giving was self-interest, *aimance*, obligation, or spontaneity. If either self-interest or obligation was apparently the sole motive, person B will not recognize the gift as a gift to begin with. On the other hand, they will consider it highly unlikely that either spontaneity or *aimance* was the sole motive for the gift—or in fact, that any *one* motive is at play. The answer to the question whether something is a gift or not cannot be found in the motives of the giver at all. That decision is made by the recipient according to their attribution of the giver's motive(s). And if they believe that the giver acted merely out of conventionality, duty, or even self-interest, they will not recognize the gift as such. Only acceptance and appreciation make the gift a gift. That gifts frequently include a mixture of very different motives is necessary: it is only due to this paradox and the risk it involves that they can create bonds and cooperation.

The gift as a medium of symbolic communication

Why is it that gifts are better at creating social cohesion than words? After all, humans, and only humans, have at their disposal very elaborate languages which they can use for coordinating cooperative endeavors. In sociology, there are two main notions with respect to the binding force of language, represented by Jürgen Habermas and Niklas Luhmann, respectively. For Habermas, a telos of mutual understanding is inherent in language. This means that via the exchange of arguments, we can come to a consensus about the objective world of things, the social world of norms, and even our subjective worlds—and on that basis, we enter bonds and commit to obligations (Habermas, 1984/1987, 1996). By contrast, Luhmann emphasized language's *dis*sensual potential. According to him, language produces a distance from the world and dissonance rather than consensus. Since it enables us to leave behind our everyday worlds and build abstract worlds that are not bound to the shared world of experience and action, language multiplies perspectives and, instead of binding us together, estranges us from each other. To this, Luhmann holds, modern society has reacted by developing symbolically generalized media of communication, such as money, truth, and power. The symbolic function of money, for instance, is to symbiotically connect to our needs so that we want more of it (Luhmann, [1997] 2012: 228). And communication media combine the world-creating dimension of language with the binding effect of the willingness to engage in specific behaviors. Language, on the other hand, is not thus designed to make us enter commitments to act; it has no or little binding force (see also Luhmann, [1984] 1995).

As of late, Habermas' position has moved in a similar direction. He now considers the binding force of language to be weaker than he used to. In a post-metaphysical world, he believes, it is perhaps strongest still in remnants of the archaic interconnection of myth and rite (Habermas, 2017). Earlier, metaphysical worldviews, while already aware of the world-creating function of language, preserved a close tie to rites, and this provided them with power over people. In the religious realm, the binding force of language has its roots in the sacred, which imposingly reveals itself to believers during ritual practices. Rites work much better in terms of group cohesion than narratives do. As language evolved, the close ties between perceptions of objective phenomena, expressions of subjective affects, and corresponding expectations as to the behavior of others were cut. As Habermas observes, "[i]n the single-word sentences of children—for example, the exclamation 'Fire!'—the three modes (communicating this occurrence, expressing fear at the sight of it and the call for help) still form a syndrome" (2017: 41). In more complex utterances, however, the propositional, expressive, and appellative components of meaning diverge, therefore making a binding effect less likely. For Habermas, in our rational and scientific modern world, the powerful binding force of language is thus forever lost. What is left are merely remnants of the sacred, for example, in "music and dance as media which involve ... an extralinguistic embodiment of meaning" (2017: 41).

We can now apply Habermas' model to Maussian gift theory. The gift, too, entails a ritual side known in every culture. It has a transcendent character since it transports an affective judgment as well as the foreignness and freedom of the giver. On the level of gestural communication, prior to grammatical language, it merges all three of the modes mentioned by Habermas: it transports the offer of a definition of the situation, it involves a strong aspect of self-expression, and it has an appellative and normative function. Objective, subjective, and social aspects are thus symbolically combined and endowed with a binding force. Like the symbolically generalized communication media, money, truth, and power, the gift can be considered a symbolical mechanism for increasing the probability that offers of communication are accepted. While rooted in symbolic gestural communication (Mead) and in rites (Durkheim), the gift's binding force still works in modern societies as well. And if the gift accompanies linguistic communication, such is my proposition, it can compensate for language's lack of binding force and the distances and proliferation of perspectives which result from that lack.

The gift provides a background mechanism that can accompany all communications in modern societies. Like other media of communication, it reduces the likelihood of offers of communication being turned down. The crucial difference between language and symbolically generalized communication media is that the latter are tied much closer to sanctions. Media formalize and sanction communication and challenge us to participate.

The use of money, for example, makes it more likely that an offer is accepted. This is what the American social theorist Talcott Parsons (1902–79) means when he speaks of money as a positive sanction (1968: 137): the asymmetry between money and goods motivates us to accept money as a general equivalent (Marx).

But the late Parsons made yet another important contribution to the debate. He posited that in modern societies there is a very general medium that stabilizes interactions: affects. Parsons considers affects the medium of the social system, that is, of society as a whole. For him, it is not so much shared values and norms that ensure social order. It is the communicative expression of affects that has a key function in constituting social bonds. A synchronization of joint action, he holds, is only possible since signs and symbols have the same emotional meaning for all interactants. In an interaction, you present your own affects, motives, and intentions to someone else, and synchronize them with theirs (Parsons, 1977).

Historically, affects as a communication medium evolved when certain bonds, especially those connected to status, had for the biggest part dissolved, when affectivity was no longer firmly bound to specific persons, collectives, or institutions (Parsons and Platt, 1973). One thinks of the medieval distribution of values and emotions along a fixed class hierarchy: peasants used to owe their lords esteem according to their higher social status. Only in (more or less) democratic societies, when people could (more or less) freely choose their own affiliations, affects assumed their socially integrating function. The freedom of association thus opened up new spaces for interactions, but it also created new uncertainties.[2]

For Parsons, then, it is no longer traditional cultural values that bring forth social order. Instead, it has to be created situationally, via the connection of affects to practices, objects, and subjects. However, as Harald Wenzel has argued (2005), Parsons never really defines what he means when he refers to affects. Are they emotions or moods; are they directed at an intentional object or diffuse? After all, not all affects are socially integrative: anger is not, and neither are depressive moods. For this reason Wenzel suggests, based on Garfinkel's earlier critique of Parsons, that we replace the concept of affect with that of trust. In Garfinkel's view, a consensus has to be reached actively, that is, while acting, and on the basis of constitutive rules and the trust that actors place in each other. And as I pointed out when discussing Garfinkel and Rawls, placing your trust in someone amounts to a gift. It signals a generalized willingness to cooperate that offers and invokes affects of attachment but is not identical with any specific emotion. A gift is an active offer of cooperation, whereas the concept of trust stresses the receptive, passive side of the action process. This is of particular importance in the paradigmatic case of an encounter between strangers who cannot yet rely on a shared social order but have to create it from scratch. As risky advances, gifts are a part of almost all interactions, and they are a necessary condition for all cooperation. The gift does not come with a normative foundation, and it cannot be forced or secured through self-interest either. As a background mechanism for cooperation, it is not institutionalized but works informally. Without freedom of association, its inherent equality will not take effect. Gifts make possible varied and flexible interactions, but without any guarantees or certainties.

5

The Gift between Socialism and Capitalism

Marcel Mauss was more than a scholar: he was a public intellectual involved in socialist party politics, activism, and political journalism. At the end of *The Gift* he mixes these two realms when he draws normative conclusions for the present from his analysis of premodern gifting practices. But this was a rare exception. Generally, he made a point of keeping science and politics apart—and this fact has caused major misunderstandings in the reception of his essay (Hart, 2014). For one thing, the socio-economic dimension of *The Gift* and its relevance for our own times has often been overlooked: a case in point is Marcel Hénaff (2010), a protagonist of modern gift theory, who downright denies the existence of this dimension in Mauss. For another, the presumption of a strict separation of science and politics has time and again encouraged readings of *The Gift* which claim that he strictly distinguishes between gift economies in "archaic societies" and our own modern market economy (see for example Gregory, 1982). And third, Mauss' political statements were repeatedly dismissed as half-baked, rash, and uncalled-for; even his closest colleague and friend Henri Hubert saw it this way (Fournier, 2006: 244). For example, in her 1990 foreword to *The Gift*, the anthropologist Mary Douglas opined that "[t]aking the theory straight from its context in full-blown gift economies to a modern political issue [is] really jumping the gun" (1990: xix). I could not disagree more.

Mauss, the socialist

In this section I will elaborate on Mauss' activism and his journalistic writings to establish which contemporary issues he had in mind while writing *The Gift*. Which social, political, and economic vision did he want to see realized? And what does this mean for *our* present? I will suggest that Mauss still has much value as a political and socio-economic thinker, that his version of socialism is now more relevant than ever. Crucially, he does not rely solely on either market or state, which, given the later excesses of both neoliberalism and state socialism, was far-sighted indeed. Combining the two will not do either. Instead, Mauss stresses the all-important aspect of self-organization, as realized, for example, in cooperatives. His objectives can be translated into the vision of a civil society-driven, radically democratic, and cooperative socialism, a "third way" that is not much concerned with the antagonism of private vs. state property but rather focuses on commons. Resources belonging to all do not have to be state property; they can be collective property within associations.

Mauss was politically most active in the period 1920–25. During these years, he wrote two thirds of his *Écrits politiques* (Mauss, 1997) and simultaneously worked on *The Gift*. But of course his fascination with socialist ideas had begun much earlier, namely, when he studied at the École pratique and first met Jean Jaurès, who was to have much influence on his thinking. Mauss was politicized in the midst of the Dreyfus affair, when his uncle Durkheim campaigned for a retrial of the wrongfully convicted Jewish army captain along with Émile Zola, Georges Clemenceau, and many others. Mauss supported the École socialiste, an organization dedicated to workers' education, and started contributing to the journal *Le Mouvement socialiste*, in which his first political text "L'action socialiste" was published in 1899. But his main focus was on the cooperative movement. In 1896, he joined a retail cooperative, and four years later he co-founded "La Boulangerie." He also wrote articles on the international cooperative movement for journals such as *Notes critiques* and *L'Humanité*. In 1905, he joined Jaurès' newly formed socialist party, the French Section of the Workers' International (SFIO) and took an active part in the party's debates.

Jaurès was assassinated in 1914, and it would take until 1920—that is, after the Great War had ended, in which he served as a "soldier interpreter" (Fournier, 2006: 174)—that Mauss would again take up his political activities. He now edited the writings of deceased friends and founded *L'Année sociologique*, thus reviving the legacy of Durkheim, who had died in 1917, in a collective working context. He also published articles in *La Vie socialiste* and *L'action coopérative*, mostly on bolshevism, exchange rates, and Germany's war reparations, and worked on his book on the nation. In other words, Mauss' 1920s were "inseparably intellectual and political" (2006: 189). Towards the end of that decade, he would begin to withdraw from political activism—despite some antifascist contributions in the 1930s and 1940s—and after World War II he would remain largely silent.

Let us now take a closer look at Mauss' political writings, starting with his essay of 1899. "L'action socialiste" illustrates that in the eyes of the then young socialist, the world is not constituted materially, let alone solely economically, but instead gets constructed socially: the social question is total for him since it touches on political, moral, and legal, as well as cultural issues. For instance, property rights and laws are not "material facts" but "mental facts" for Mauss, and socialism a "phenomenon of consciousness": a "new way of seeing, thinking, and acting" to be brought about by "conscious action in the interest of the collectivity." The agents he believes can achieve this change of consciousness—and perhaps even make it possible "to live the socialist life immediately," in capitalism—are trade unions and socialist cooperatives. Mauss felt that one could be a unionist without being a socialist, but never vice versa (cited in Fournier, 2006: 101–2; see Mauss, 1997: 72–82).

Like Jaurès, Mauss did not hope for a revolution; in fact, he frequently defended democracy and republicanism. The new society, he held, had to emerge within the old one and replace it nonviolently. Cooperatives to him are pioneers in this process since they experiment with "socialism here and now" (Fournier, 2006: 125). Mauss was a leading figure in the French cooperative movement. He wanted to find effective ways of abolishing wage labor, competition, and profit within a market economy, and, unusual for a French socialist at the time, the anglophile Mauss was inspired by developments in Britain, in particular the activities of Beatrice and Sidney Webb and their Fabian Society. Moreover, in his writings on the nation, he clearly self-identified as an internationalist: just as there are no self-sufficient persons, he thought, there can be no isolated societies. He acknowledged that here had always been economic interdependencies between nations and close contacts between societies who borrowed from each other economic, religious, or aesthetic technologies. Long-term peace can only be achieved, according to Mauss, if nations unite in federations and engage in fair international models of labor division. If Durkheim had stressed the solidarizing effect of the division of labor within societies, Mauss emphasized their pacifying effect on the international level.

Mauss' internationalism is most evident in the series of articles he wrote for the journal *Populaire* between December 1922 and December 1924 on the subject of the monetary crisis. As Fournier explains, "[s]uccessive administrations in France could not balance the country's budget and were even less successful in stabilizing the franc" (2006: 209), and the solution Mauss recommends in his articles is to devalue the currency. At the same time, he proposes to the Allies of World War I (including France) to grant Germany a moratorium on reparation payments and reduce these to a manageable amount (Fournier, 1997: 502)—not a popular opinion in France at the time, but one shared by the eminent British economist John Maynard Keynes (Mallard, 2011: 233–4; see also Cedrini and Marchionatti, 2017). Grégoire Mallard (2011) has suggested that Mauss here transfers the logic of the gift to the field of international relations. A moratorium would have represented a large (extraordinary) gift, with the potential effect of fixing French–German relations, at least to some degree. However, "no nation wanted to be the first to give, as a gift would be perceived as a sign of weakness" (2011: 236), and what followed instead was the Ruhr occupation, a renaissance of nationalism in Germany, and, eventually, a new war.

Starting in 1923, another series of articles by Mauss dealt with bolshevism: first with the problem of political violence, then with the question regarding to what extent bolshevism represents a socialist experiment. In short, Mauss believes that the bolshevists have failed, on moral grounds, due to their employment of violence. You cannot bring about a socialist society, he finds, by means of violence or laws, but only by gradually changing norms, mentalities, and habits. The "dictatorship of the proletariat" is to him nothing but a dictatorship of the Communist party, which he condemns for shattering all political, economic, and social intermediary institutions (1997: 522, 544). This does not mean that Mauss thought socialism could be victorious without massive conflicts, but he firmly opposed violence and tyranny. Concerning the second question he comes to the radical conclusion that bolshevism indeed does not represent a socialist experiment because it does not answer to the collective will (*volonté generale*). A minority of "naïve sociologists" ([1924] 1992: 199) cannot enforce a new political and societal system through violence. Socialism must be wanted by the people—and enthusiastically so.

Mauss is vehemently opposed to the idea of abolishing markets and instead proposes organizing them along socialist lines. Without free markets, without the interplay of supply and demand, there can be no economy, he believes, and in fact no society. A state-decreed collectivism does not correspond to the socialist vision. Only free association can simultaneously facilitate collectivism, individualism, and freedom. There are no purely capitalist or communist societies to Mauss; in reality, they are always a mixture of capitalist, statist, administrative, associationist, and individualist tendencies. Accordingly, a variety of organization forms must be recognized, and legal structures like inheritance law must be utilized as effective societal levers.

To recapitulate, Mauss aims for a cooperative socialism that asserts the principle of free association vis-à-vis state and market. His economic vision is strictly pluralist and experimental: it is necessary, he holds, to ascertain which forms of property and which control mechanisms (planned economy vs. market) ought to be implemented in what places. The logic of the gift, although it alone cannot build societies or economies, does take effect in multiple ways in this vision, both in its agonistic and non-agonistic versions. Non-agonistically it occurs *within* organizations, such as cooperatives or projects that rely on principles of sharing (Belk, 2009), while agonistically, it plays a role, for example, in international relations and other situations characterized by competition and distrust. Agonistic gifts are a challenge; they test the borders of communities and open them to others.

As a sociologist, Mauss was very aware that modern societies are complex structures based on a social division of labor, or what we would call functional differentiation today. This differentiation cannot be undone, but it can be controlled. Mauss' ideal is a society that has instruments of collective self-regulation at its disposal, which is reminiscent of Dewey's view of the public sphere as a space of societal self-reflection. Mauss' socialism addresses not just workers but all citizens—it has to, he argues, if it wants to succeed. Socialism to him is directed at social freedom because individual freedom can only be achieved in solidarity with others (see Honneth, 2017). Seen in this light, were the *homo oeconomicus* to triumph, this would indeed drastically curtail our freedoms. Mauss refuses to subscribe to the dichotomy of individualism, market, and utilitarianism on the one hand, and collectivism, state, and solidarity on the other. In voluntary cooperation, freedom and commitment go hand in hand. And in social experiments we may determine how to best realize the idea of social freedom under changing historical conditions.

Other than most 19th- and 20th-century socialist visions, Mauss' is still viable. This is the case since he a) does not abandon individual rights for the sake of a collective; b) addresses more than just revolutionary workers; and c) does not believe in an inevitable progression towards communism. It is because he avoids these three grave misjudgments of 19th-century socialist thought (Honneth, 2017) that Mauss' vision of socialism translates to the present so well. It is more kindred in spirit to early socialist, syndicalist, and libertarian-anarchist traditions than to "scientific Marxism." Mauss championed Proudhon's *mutualité* and economic experiments over (supposedly) fixed historical trajectories culminating in a dictatorship of the proletariat. This was not an unusual position for a French socialist at the time, whereas German social democracy was averse to anything that smacked of anarchism (Stowasser, 2006).

Mauss' socialist vision, then, focuses on civil society and self-organization, on empowerment, a solidary economy, and a democracy shaped by associations. He banks on reforms, not revolutions. By means of transformations in multiple societal niches, alternative economic and social forms emerge, which have to be defended and expanded so as to slowly but steadily erode capitalism. This is also what US sociologist Erik Olin Wright (1947–2019) had in mind when he spoke of "real utopias," that is, "real-world alternatives that can be constructed in the world as it is that also prefigure the world as it could be, and which help move us in that direction" (2010: 326; see also Chapter 9).

Beyond capitalism: solidarity economy and post-growth

Against the backdrop of Mauss' perspective, I will now consider some contemporary practices of an alternative economy and inquire how much non-capitalist potential is inherent in them and to what extent they intend to (re-)integrate the logic of the gift. It is difficult to keep track of the many varieties: some speak of a social or solidarity economy, others of a local economy; there are new concepts of bartering and complementary currencies; communes are being reinvented as eco-villages; give-away stores and communal urban gardening are still booming. All these phenomena are expressions of a tendency towards a social-moral reintegration of economy and civil society (Adloff and Kocka, 2016), of a general concern with creating a new relationship between individual and collective interests, between democracy, market, exchange, and gift. They all contribute to establishing a horizontal, self-organized economy in which human needs dictate economic practices—and not the other way around, as in neoliberal capitalism.

To illustrate that point, let us first have a closer look at the phenomenon of neo-cooperativism. Coooperatives are an invention of the 19th century; they emerged in the context of the early labor movement and came in social-democratic, Christian-conservative, liberal, as well as anarcho-syndicalist forms. While in England and France, the proto-socialist ideas of Robert Owen and Charles Fourier were taken up, in Germany conservative and liberal tendencies prevailed, so that by the 1980s and 1990s cooperatives had a very petty bourgeois image. Many of them now became corporations, and new cooperatives were hardly ever founded, partly due to strict specifications (Elsen and Walk, 2016). Currently, cooperatives are coming back in vogue, especially in the field of renewable energies. They are increasingly accepted as an effective alternative to ever more privatization and as a viable way of contributing to the much-needed social-ecological transformation.

Neo-cooperativism involves both producers' and consumers' cooperatives and is a global phenomenon. In many countries of the Global South cooperative movements are currently being revived, and they play an important part in transformational processes, for instance in Cuba (Walk, 2015). Under market conditions, cooperatives try to alter basic principles of capitalism and combine them with others. They are committed not to valorization, but to the satisfaction of the needs of their members, as well as to principles of democracy and solidarity. Profit maximization, individual property rights, and the division of capital and work are thus counterposed by nonprofit orientation, common property, mutual help, values, and voluntariness.[1]

In the West, the renaissance of the cooperative began in the countercultural milieus of the late 1960s and early 1970s (Curl, 2009: 204ff.; Reichardt, 2014: 319ff.). In our own time, interest in alternative economic practices has much increased since the 2008 financial crisis and in the wake of climate change. Internet-based endeavors—like Wikipedia, Linux, Open Access, or peer-to-peer networks—also need to be mentioned in this context. Currently, there are lively discussions about the common use of natural resources, such as rain forests or the world's oceans. But for these ideas to be taken seriously, it is necessary to first dismiss the old preconception that common goods will inevitably be exploited by selfish actors.

For the economist Jeremy Rifkin (2014), since the next years will see a further advance of the digital revolution, and therefore a drastic decrease of marginal costs, the future belongs to the commons: soon, he predicts, almost everything will be available for free online, and old-school capitalism will be pushed back into niches. Building on Rifkin, the socialist journalist Paul Mason speaks of a "project zero" (2015: 263ff.): emission-free energy supply, the production of machines, goods, and services with "zero marginal cost[s]" (Rifkin, 2014), and the by-and-large abolition of work in general are part of Mason's vision. Both agree that "[a]n economy based on information, with its tendency to zero-cost products and weak property rights, cannot be a capitalist economy" (Mason, 2015: 175).

Whether this enthusiastic vision of overcoming capitalism by means of technological innovation (or "productive forces") is realistic is anyone's guess. At the very least, however, practices of commoning can be considered a useful complement to the capitalist economy. In her book *Ecommony* (2016), Friederike Habermann names four main features of the commons: they can be used but not owned or sold; their users share with each other their knowledge and skills; these contributions to the commons are voluntary and not subject to the capitalist logic of exchange (they are gifts *par excellence*); and the access to resources is free. Wikipedia is a case in point: as a digital commons, it relies on voluntary, unpaid work; everyone can contribute to it (in compliance with certain rules); and it is accessible to all—a textbook example of sharing in the sense of non-agonistic gift giving. Wikipedia proves that gifts which are not geared towards reciprocation can facilitate a voluntary, decentral, discursive cooperation. Gifting practices and a sociotechnical system (the Wiki software) here intertwine in such a way as to create the most inspiring example of gift-based, global commons.

Services like Facebook or Google, by contrast, though they too are for all and for free, perform an indirect and uneven exchange by collecting user data and selling it to advertising clients (Big Data), a practice that has provoked privacy concerns and discussions about data protection and manipulated search results. The business model of both Google and Facebook rests upon the free provision of services, but these gifts are loaded with reciprocation. All who use their services are in fact giving back (that is, paying) in the form of their user data. This is not an explicit exchange nor a voluntary reciprocation: the gift is systematically entangled with the product, enabling immense profits. The classic concept of exploitation does not really do justice to such practices (Elder-Vass, 2016: 139f.). But there is definitely a major asymmetry in the control of data which encourages their misuse.

Critics like Jaron Lanier (2013) demand that users become direct exchange partners in the Internet economy. If companies like Google, Facebook, or

Amazon make money from the data their users disclose, then at least the latter ought to profit too: by means of micropayments. Also, these pure market spaces ought to be accompanied by state and civil society aspects. If a platform like Facebook primarily serves the free communication between peers, why should it assume the character of a commodity? Indeed one could ask if Facebook has not by now become a commons. If this were so, the company would have to content itself with a small monthly fee and cease its original business model, the sale of its users' data. At the very least, however, it should be possible to communicate across platforms so that those who are wary of Facebook's data policy could still reach their Facebook friends. These examples reveal that our current economy constitutes a complex system of competing principles of exchange, and that the digital economy in particular is characterized by hybrid composites of capitalist and gifting practices, with the latter normally being instrumentalized for profit-making purposes.

For some years now, debates on the future of capitalism have involved the question whether we ought to bid farewell to the idea of perpetual economic growth due to environmental and social reasons. In previous decades, science, politics, and large parts of the public agreed that modern societies were all about furthering growth, which was seen as guaranteeing social stability through what Ulrich Beck (1992) has termed the elevator effect: increasing prosperity made sure that the lower classes were loyal to democracy, immigrants were integrated in labor markets, and the welfare state curbed social inequalities. As plausible and effective as this system may have been during much of the 20th century, it is now evidently in crisis (see for example Nachtwey, 2018). The growth rates needed for its maintenance are a thing of the past, and the ecological consequences of growthism, as well as their potential social ramifications, are becoming ever more apparent. Given governments' inability to severely curtail the stupendous consumption of resources and the emissions released for the sake of capitalist economies, calls for a fundamental paradigm change are growing louder (see for example Jackson, 2009). More and more of us are beginning to realize that a transformation towards non-growth-based social orders will and has to occur—hopefully "by design, not disaster" (Victor, 2008). The issue of a post-growth society is at the center of our current crisis constellation, and even neoclassical economists seem to slowly acknowledge this. The stability of Western social orders is at stake because if we do not come up with a viable response soon, intensified competition, distribution battles, desolidarization, and further exclusions will ensue (Muraca, 2012; Blühdorn, 2017). What is needed are new institutions, new role models, new mentalities that go beyond the logic of growth.

The French term *décroissance* was coined by the French philosopher André Gorz in response to the Club of Rome's report "Limits to Growth" (Meadows et al, 1972). Gorz believed that it was absolutely critical to limit economic growth in order to preserve the Earth's ecological balance. These debates of the 1970s were all but forgotten until the early 2000s, when the concept of "development" first came under attack. Serge Latouche (2014) has argued for a "frugal abundance" as an alternative to the allegedly only way of economic development: growth, which relies on an ever-expanding use of resources and ever more consumption. Starting in France, and with early contributions from Spain and Italy, *décroissance* has become a fundamental critique of growthism and of capitalism in general. Practices and concepts of sharing, simplicity, commons, or care have been identified as paths to degrowth, and debates on the topic focus on a variety of issues (Kallis et al, 2015), such as CO_2 emissions and global warming, the GDP as an indicator of economic development, calls for a radical deceleration, for shorter working hours, or for a basic income, as well as critiques of our alienation from nature, of the division of labor in terms of gender, and of capitalism as such. What unites all of these tendencies is the search for an alternative economic system that is not dependent on growth, a system that enables us to break away from the ideals of a rationalized modernity and create a society that is autonomous in achieving its self-imposed goals and free to limit itself, instead of being heteronomously governed by economic laws (see Castoriadis, 1982). For Latouche, the protagonist of the French *décroissance* movement, this is a genuinely political task which requires us to initiate a cultural transformation of the productivist and consumerist mentalities of the West by developing a "concrete utopia" (Latouche, 2009: 31ff.).

In Germany, there exist two promising movements which aim at a transformation of the economy—in fact, a whole alternative milieu is currently emerging. I am referring to the degrowth network and the Economy for the Common Good organization (GWÖ). Whereas the latter has a rather practical orientation, the work of the degrowth network is of a more political and conceptual nature. Their website is hosted by the Konzeptwerk Neue Ökonomie in Leipzig which operates at the interface of science and politics and whose goal it is to build "[a]n economy by all and for all, ecologically sound and socially just."[2] The GWÖ, initiated by Austrian activist Christian Felber, pursues the vision of an ethical market economy that is mindful of human dignity, justice, solidarity, and socio-ecological sustainability.[3] Both movements are thus working towards a post-growth society—the degrowth network mainly by organizing conferences and summer schools, the GWÖ by establishing concrete alternative economic practices which democratize economic conditions on a local level. In the long term though, they too want to influence political parameters. The idea is to tax-support companies with a positive common good record, so as to incentivize more businesses to move in that direction.

Such social experiments in the spirit of conviviality are valuable contributions to a societal debate on controllable change ("by design").

They are "real-world laboratories" (Schneidewind et al, 2016: 10) in which members of the milieus likely to bring about the desired change can put to the test new values, subjective dispositions, and lifestyle practices. Specific examples abound, many of which may be found on the website of the GWÖ. In addition, I recommend having a look at the two Hamburg companies Quijote (coffee) and Premium (cola), both of which are commendably democratic and sustainable post-growth enterprises. An example of a classic cooperative still very much thriving is the Basque Mondragón Corporation, which was founded in 1956, manufactures industrial components (among many other ventures), and is currently Spain's seventh-largest company.

All these alternative economy projects serve non-economic purposes: generating social capital and trust, putting an end to alienated labor, fighting human commodification, creating local ties, overcoming hierarchies, fostering fairness, and behaving in ecologically sustainable ways. They combine elements of market capitalism, socialism, and civil society, thus showing that under global capitalist conditions there can still exist a variety of non-capitalist ideals and practices. The fact that both neoclassical economists and Marxists tend to not take seriously such projects is unfortunate. As the feminist geographers Katherine Gibson and Julie Graham argue, the "capitalocentric frame" in which we are accustomed to think obstructs our view at potential alternatives (Gibson-Graham, 2014: 149; see also Elder-Vass, 2016). This refusal to acknowledge that economy does not equal capitalism leads to a political disavowal and discouragement of existing non-capitalist initiatives, which we should instead integrate into our theories.

The prevalent capitalocentric perspective bespeaks a problematic understanding of the economy as an autonomous entity—either, in neoclassical economic theory, as guided by deliberations of individual utility and efficiency or, in sociology, as a self-referential societal system complying to a logic of profitability (Beckert, 2006). However, the economy is not synonymous with market processes or with capitalism; it also includes reproductive processes—namely, unpaid domestic and educational work—and relies on processes of reallocation and reciprocity. What is more, markets are not self-regulatory: they require governmental regulation and must be embedded in the normative framework of civil society. And finally, as is evident when we think of the previously mentioned cooperatives or of nonprofit organizations, not all economic enterprises are capitalist businesses. Such non- or weakly capitalistic practices may very well play a more important role in the future. After all, both the Global North and the Global South are currently confronted with a series of severe problems, most of which can be traced back to the fact that thus far labor, social security, redistribution, self-realization, and even democracy itself were intrinsically linked to, and dependent on, economic growth. Unfortunately, the post-2008 critiques of an anti-social financial capitalism still have not spawned concrete proposals for reform. Fostered by unabated political endorsements of the sector, you can still make more profits in finance than in any other economic area. Instead of being regulated, the financial economy is being pandered. Meanwhile, the distribution of income and especially of wealth is becoming ever more unequal, and the ever increasing use of non-renewable energies further accelerates global warming.

On our way to a post-growth society, the greatest challenge is to ensure that the underprivileged do not suffer. If the cake is shrinking, redistribution must be radical. Indeed, rather than socializing the economy, we should perhaps strive to abandon it altogether. To reduce people's dependency on companies and markets, however, we would need a functioning public sector that engages in new forms of cooperation both with businesses and civil-society or nonprofit organizations (Caillé and Les Convivialistes, 2016). We would have to preserve and newly create public property, subsidize cooperatives, and support regional complementary currencies. Consumer goods would have to be more durable, a life without cars would have to be made possible, and the dependency on money would have to be reduced by promoting non-monetary forms of exchange. Alternative indices and qualitative parameters for evaluating the economy would have to be introduced. Finally, we would need a radically different view of companies. In the Economy for the Common Good, for instance, they are required to be mindful of public welfare: collaborative enterprises that work towards generating common values which transcend the monetary, and which no longer externalize ecological and social costs.

In all this, the interplay of economy and civil society, their entanglements as well as their antagonisms, their mutual support and confinement is critical. Though governments are less and less trusted to successfully manage crises, most critics of hypercapitalism invest their hopes in them—while losing track of civil society as the most promising enabler of alternative forms of exchange (see Chapter 9).[4] There are currently a great many social movements and local initiatives around the globe which engage in experiments and transgress traditional limits. What is necessary now is to once again civilize capitalism (like the building of welfare states did in the 20th century) and come up with new, convivial forms of living together. The fact that the world seems to be developing in quite the opposite direction—with exploitation of human and natural resources higher than ever before and whole population groups being excluded and expelled (Sassen, 2014)—must not discourage our political hopes. One way forward will be via elections, protests, and lawsuits. In the meantime, we can already begin to build a convivial democracy and economy by participating in social experiments in societal niches and reviving the logic of the gift.

6

Commodities, Values, Money, Gifts

For some years now, the thought of the Hungarian economic historian and social scientist Karl Polanyi (1886–1964) has attracted renewed interest. Polanyi, who, just like Illich, was well acquainted with Erich Fromm, is perhaps best known for his unorthodox notion of markets as socially embedded, and he is regularly cited when it comes to their increasing separation from societal needs. In his famous book *The Great Transformation* ([1944] 2001), which is much indebted to Mauss' conception of premodern social forms, Polanyi points out that market economies rely upon demanding conditions of social dislocation and are historically a rare and very young phenomenon: before the 19th century, he asserts, economic activities were still firmly embedded in social life.

Polanyi is considered the founder of the substantivist school of economic anthropology. In his essay "The Economy as an Instituted Process" (1957), he criticizes economics for its too formal understanding of economic processes. Neoclassical economists proceed from the notion of the *homo oeconomicus*: they believe that all human beings think in terms of individualism and utilitarianism and ascribe all economic decisions to means–ends deliberations. Even though we know that in some historical societies there were no markets to speak of and some did entirely without money in our current sense, economists tend to treat these historical societies *as if* people had already made their decisions according to supply and demand. By contrast, Polanyi looks at the exact empirical conditions under which people then engaged in exchanges with others. He considers the economic activities of humans to be "embedded and enmeshed in institutions" (1957: 50) and points to three patterns of behavior that constituted the archaic and the premodern economy: householding, redistribution, and reciprocity. For him, reciprocity is a symmetrical form of exchange between equals, be it persons or groups. Redistribution presupposes a principle of hierarchy and centricity: goods were accumulated in a central space (for example, in the house of the leader) and then distributed among members of the group. Householding (Gr. *oikonomía*), that is, production solely for the individual household, is the oldest of the three patterns. Markets, Polanyi states, only played a minor part in economic life before the early modern era, and even as late as the 18th century they were primarily used in long-distance trading.

Polanyi's theories represent an important reference point for current work in economic anthropology and sociology (see for example Hann and Hart, 2011). It could be argued, however, that his historical juxtaposition of a reciprocity-based vs. a market-based economy is too absolute, in particular that he underestimated the prevalence of markets in premodern societies. Meanwhile, researchers in the field of moral economy, such as William James Booth (1994), have criticized Polanyi's dichotomy of embedded and autonomous markets as over-simplifying the matter. Even in modernity, they reason, markets are by no means completely dislocated from the social sphere. While it is true that modern economies are no longer as much subject to humanizing aspects as they used to be, even our current neoliberal economy is still to some extent embedded in culture and society (Fligstein and Dauter, 2007; Fourcade and Healy, 2007). Also, there have always been exchanges and self-interest, and even the monetary system, which is so often directly linked to the supposed historical rupture, can take on quite different cultural meanings. Anthropological studies suggest that any sharp distinction between gift and commodity, or in fact between premodernity and modernity, is bound to be empirically refuted.

Gifts, goods, and values

As the anthropologist James Carrier (1991, 1992) has highlighted, there are areas of transition and conflation between exchanging and gift giving. Goods can be more than impersonal and entirely exchangeable things; they often convey identities and attachments. Carrier thus proposes a continuum of commodities and gifts. For example, commodities can contain elements of gifts when objects attain a personal significance because they are connected to the "specific personal relationships in which they are transacted or in which they feature" (Carrier, 1991: 132). Such attachments can cause conflicts when one party disregards them and considers a transfer as merely an exchange, whereas the other party reads aspects of gift giving into it. An example would be a flea market or garage sale where used items are sold that "mean something" to the (previous) owners: these objects are steeped in biographical history, with lots of memories and sentimentalities attached to them—they are, paradoxically, "inalienable commodities" (Herrmann, 1997).

Jonathan Parry and Maurice Bloch have observed that in every society there are two "related but separate transactional orders: on the one hand transactions concerned with the reproduction of the long-term social or cosmic order; on the other, a 'sphere' of short-term transactions concerned with the area of individual competition" (Parry and Bloch, 1989: 24). But how exactly do these two transactional orders relate to another in our own modern, capitalist society? Parry and Bloch suspect, and I agree with this suspicion, that Western thought has for so long emphasized the categorical separation of the two orders that we have become all but unable to see the connections and interactions between them. We largely ignore the "long-term social or cosmic order" and fail to recognize that even capitalism builds on, and frequently exploits, the logic of the gift.

Examining the relationship between commodities and gifts may help us trace the lines that connect and separate different forms of value, and thus the social and economic spheres. As before him for Marx, the concept of the commodity is of vital importance for Polanyi (1968) who defines commodities as objects produced to be sold on markets. In capitalism, labor-power, land, and money—all key elements of the economy—are regarded as commodities as well. Polanyi argues that they are not since they do not fulfill the criterion of being produced for sale. Labor as a human activity, land as a synonym for nature, and money, which was invented to measure, not store value, and is government-controlled, are at best "fictitious commodities" (1968: 26). A society that is completely devoted to that fiction will destroy itself, Polanyi finds. The protective shield that societies need to survive will vanish once everything is treated as a commodity, as for sale. There are things, Polanyi holds, that must be saved from being instrumentalized and subjected to capitalistic valorization, because else they will not reproduce. This is especially true of nature, but also of humans: we did not "produce" our children so that they can profitably invest their human capital.

Marx called the process by which land and labor become commodities primitive accumulation. He related how in England, common land was enclosed and turned into private property, and how the expelled peasants became "free" wage laborers. To this day, Marxian economists think of this as the origin of capitalism: the worker lost his access to the commons, that is, his means of subsistence, and was forced to sell his labor-power to owners of capital, under purportedly fair and equal terms. In reality, the capitalists exploit the workers' dispossession by making them produce higher values than their labor-power is worth on the market (Harvey, 2014). Labor-power therefore produces more value than is necessary for its own upkeep, and the capitalists rake in that surplus value as profit. According to Marx, only labor creates (exchange) value, and the value of a commodity depends on how much labor (time) has gone into its production.[1]

Labor-power is a fictitious commodity since it cannot be sold completely. While it is temporarily transferred to the buyer, it remains tied to the body and skills of the worker and thus his property (Marx, [1867] 2019: 186–7). What the buyer acquires is not ownership of the commodity labor-power, but merely the right to use it. Labor can never be entirely separated from the rest of life. It cannot be stored and at best can be seen as an abstract commodity, and yet it is treated *as if* it belonged solely to the economic realm. As Marx was well aware, labor-power must be reproduced, a task that traditionally falls to women, whose household labor and child-rearing efforts are an indispensable factor in the capitalist economy. The commodification of labor relies on the existence of non-commodified spheres elsewhere. The domestic sphere still partly operates according to the logic of the gift, but it is in danger of becoming ever more colonized since commodity value is continuously derived from it.

Until quite recently, the private and public spheres were more or less divided among gender lines: commodities, labor, and public sphere were male; care, household, and private sphere female. But these divisions have become permeable, and the commodification of "social production" has advanced. For instance, an ever-increasing number of Western middle-class families are purchasing the labor-power of foreign care workers, au pairs, or underage babysitters, often via commercial providers. Converting all care work into wage work, however, is not really an option. Care is based on the logic of the gift which is incompatible with the capitalist logic of profit. Consequently, a future "care revolution" (for example, Neumann and Winker, 2020) cannot be capitalist in nature. While care work ought not to take place solely in the private sphere (where it tends to get devalued, as has traditionally been the case), it must not be subjected to the capitalist logic of exchange and profit either—because this would mean to allow capitalism to undermine the social foundations of human life. The more you treat fictitious commodities as real commodities, and not as gifts, the more our still non-commodified spaces of gift giving will be eroded. In a purely economic world, everyone indeed acts according to self-interest, and no one believes in the possibility of the gift any more (Callon, 2007); this is the dire scenario we are facing.

Following Mauss and Polanyi, we should emphasize how important gift giving really is for the economy. This is especially evident in our contemporary digital economy. eBay, for example—which has created the perfect market, bringing sellers and buyers together swiftly and easily—functions so well because of the feedback provided by users. "Without these gifts," writes Torben Elgaard Jensen, "it is almost certain that the level of trust and the volume of transactions would go down significantly" (2008: 187–8). Facebook's business model is another case in point: the platform's users contribute to it without either paying or getting paid, and the company profits by selling the data the users provide to advertising clients. Only if we realize how these gifting behaviors thus benefit capitalism can we protect the gift and the social sphere from being further co-opted and colonized by the logic of the market.

According to Marxist theory, capitalism obscures the fact that only human labor-power can create economic value. Even more so, it obscures the fact that value is also created by gift giving in the private sphere. David Graeber demands that:

> what is described in the Marxist literature as "reproductive labor," housework, child care, the making, shaping, education, nurturance, and maintenance of those who perform labor, should not be viewed as some secondary phenomenon, the mere reproduction of a workforce capable of producing marketable commodities, but rather, as the most elementary form of real value-producing labor, as the very core and essence of human creative life. (2013: 224)

While commodities belong to the world of equivalence and exchange, gifts emphatically do not. And social and cultural values differ from commodity values since "[t]hey cannot or should not be converted into money. Nor can they be precisely compared with one another" (2013: 224).

Value judgments and political processes play a big part in economic valorization. Values are politically constituted; they are normatively determined by societies. In fact, discussing what a society considers of value is what politics is mainly about. A good example are societies of hunters to whom the principle of sharing (that is, non-agonistic gift giving) is of utmost importance: "they share what they value, they share without receiving or even expecting returns, and they even—at times—value sharing itself" (Widlok, 2013: 12). In this sense, value does not derive from foregoing something for something else; it derives from foregoing that process of exchanging itself. Contrary to what Simmel believed (and many still do), as a societal factor value is *not* formed by comparing and exchanging objects. Simmel assumed that subjective values are objectified in the course of an exchange. However, as we have seen, value can be attached just as much to the disposition of labor-power, to care, or to objects symbolizing social relations. As Graeber stresses in his book on value (2001), it is ultimately not so much things that are valued, but actions and relations. If we value a gift, we value the relationship from which it has emerged. But if we value money, we value its ability to make others do something for us—usually, to hand something over. Money primarily creates (positive or negative) incentives; it is an instrument of strategic action. We can use it to influence, or even force others, and it is this persuasive potential that makes us value money so much.

Money can buy almost anything. At the same time, it decreases mutual obligations. By paying workers for giving their labor-power, the employer seemingly rids himself of his responsibility for them. This is possible because in our modern economy the amount of money that certain work is deemed to be worth is exactly defined. If obligations are more diffuse, as in gift relationships, you can never be sure whether or not you have settled your debt. For one thing, this means that you can never be even: you reciprocate a gift, but neither you nor the other really know who owns whom how much. This is true for non-agonistic gifts in particular, which involve a certain temporal fiction: "With all those things that we treat as eternal, that we assume will always be there—our mother's love, true friendship, sociality, humanity, belonging, the existence of the cosmos—no calculation is necessary, or even ultimately possible" (Graeber, 2011: 267). In these kinds of relationships, you are never even. You do not just quit them after "paying your debt," and you do not have to reciprocate every time you receive a gift either: when you live eternally, as it were, the right moment to give back may come later rather than sooner. Everybody is indebted to everybody, but in this constellation, this does not amount to a burden. Our debts tie us to each other without chaining us; there is no urge to settle them. Debt repayment, exchange, and reciprocity only exist as constraints where things are being merely distributed and bad faith prevails. In the mode of sharing, by contrast, you partake in things—for instance, in land, natural resources, or means of production. Whether or not a society allows or preempts such communing practices is a political question.

Interestingly, the logic of the gift can take effect even in the economy of debts. States reliably collect money through taxes and are regarded as trustworthy borrowers for this reason. While there are deadlines for redemption, their credits are usually rolled over (see Langenohl, 2018: 56). Their creditors thus habitually act as if states lived forever—the same mechanism we have seen with gifts. Sadly, when Greece went through its government-debt crisis in 2009, none of this was the case. Instead, it became very apparent that distrust results in the desire for debt relations to be terminable (see also Chapter 11).

The Canadian sociologist Jacques Godbout, who collaborated with Caillé on *The World of the Gift* (Godbout and Caillé, [1992] 1998), observed the same phenomenon in modern partner relationships: the partners' devotion is grounded in disinterested giving, but there is the expectation, albeit mostly unconscious, that our giving will move the other to give as well. This leads to a mutual positive indebtedness and an attachment based on the feeling that the other is giving more than we are (Godbout and Charbonneau, 1993; Godbout, 1994). The constellation changes as soon as money is involved and the two need to decide on who pays for what: a diffuse mutual indebtedness now turns into actual, countable debts, and the expectation is formed that these debts be settled. Therefore, diffuse debts enable voluntary attachments, whereas specific, countable debts allow for personal *de*tachment. Paradoxically, debts also produce unfreedom, namely, when they cannot be paid back. Once an equivalent exchange is not possible and permanent debts are accrued, formerly horizontal relationships become hierarchical. An exception to that rule are familial attachments which comply with the logic of the gift. How could we ever pay back our debts to our parents, let alone our ancestors? We do not have to. That is the whole point of gift relationships.

Let us have another look at the paradox we just encountered. In effect, gifts result in mutual obligations and thus, according to our modern sensibility, in feelings of constraint. It would follow that only market-based exchanges make us free because they allow us to settle our debts. In modern societies, exchanges rest on individual rights, which are meant to ensure that the personal interests and caprices of certain persons do not dominate. Nonetheless, our society is, perhaps more than ever, "the realm of private individuals pursuing their interests, and private interests are therefore seen as the natural basis for politics" (Menke, 2020). At the same time, morality or *Sittlichkeit* is being neutralized and individualism reigns supreme. Modern law enables us to want what we want without answering for it; for example, we can freely use, destroy, or sell our property.

The freedom that accompanies gift giving is different. If debts can never be settled anyway, they are not a burden but a symbol of attachment. And if the socially relevant resources and commodities belong to all, we cannot quantify who owes what to whom. You reciprocate if you can, even if it is just by means of your gratitude. This freedom of the gift can never be eliminated, whereas that is exactly what happens in exchanges as soon as debts are due. The communism of the gift consists in excluding the principle of exchange, equivalences, and quantifiable reciprocations, at least for the most part. The asymmetry and non-equivalency of the gift are the very foundation of social life—capitalism, on the other hand, is entirely focused on what can be compared and calculated. The gift thus creates what supposedly only labor-power can create: value.

In the history of capitalism the one-sided focus on labor-power has time and again led to the question of who deserves which income. Is it fair that people earn different amounts? The classic answer is yes: after all, those who earn more—say, managers—have completed a longer training and carry more responsibility than those who earn less—say, cleaners. Complicated economic models are mobilized to explain and legitimate these differences, but of course these issues are genuinely political in nature. We are dealing with a relict of the old feudal-system, in which the dignity and honor of people were determined by their status group membership. In law, we now have the concept of an equal dignity of all, but certain achievements are still valued higher than others (Habermas, 2010), and the more money someone has at their disposal, the higher their esteem. The Greek-French social philosopher Cornelius Castoriadis (1922–97) repeatedly stressed that such valuations are entirely arbitrary (see in particular Castoriadis, [1975] 1984, [1981] 2007) and demanded an egalitarian payment. He made clear that the question of value (of labor and of persons) is indeed a political one. It all comes down to what a society defines as adequate, fair, and valuable.

Castoriadis' own demand for an equality of income is not based on any theoretical economic argument, but likewise politically motivated (Castoriadis, 2010). He thereby points to the imaginary heart of capitalism: the belief that economic inequality is due to the different value of different lines of work and that social hierarchies are thus justified. It makes no sense, Castoriadis argues, to ascribe an economic result to one individual, to a group of people, or to an organization, once we realize that this result has come about through various synergies, cooperations, and societal advances. The generated surplus is a product of collective efforts.

Mauss and money

Who speaks of value and commodities must speak about money. Countless historians, economists, sociologists, and so on have thought about money, its merits as well as its alienating effects. Money, it is crucial to note, is not just a "thing," but an extremely powerful idea (Dodd, 2014). It is a medium of exchange which converts all qualitative differences between objects and activities into quantitative differences. To Simmel, money is an "absolute" medium since it can be transformed into every conceivable commodity, that is, it can buy virtually everything (Simmel, [1896] 1991, [1900] 2011). Of course, thanks to its ability to absorb uncertainty and remove doubt, money can also be used to influence others. In this way, it can become an end in itself, which very much appears to be the case in societies where money is all everyone wishes for. As Schopenhauer once wrote:

> [I]t is natural and even inevitable to love that which, like an unwearied Proteus, is always ready to turn itself into whatever object their wandering wishes or manifold desires may for the moment fix upon. ... Money alone is absolutely good, because it is not only a concrete satisfaction of one need in particular; it is an abstract satisfaction of all. (cited in Ganßmann, 2012: 133)

Alas, the pursuit of money creates distances between us and our things and activities. Everything can be subjected to the logic of quantification, and everything that has the same price has the same value. For Simmel, money is in fact the very incorporation of value. Its abstractness corresponds to an ideal of complete fungibility. At the same time, it is an expression of perfect freedom: with money, you can break free of traditional attachments, personal obligations, and material hardships.

In terms of history and theory, money—or as Marx had it, the "universal commodity" ([1867] 2019: 102)—is often derived from the concept of exchange: if two individuals with different things at their disposal enter an exchange, money simplifies matters by providing a standard of comparison and a medium. This "first exchange, then money" narrative is still rehearsed in most economy textbooks—even though many historical studies have shown by now that it is really only a myth (see for example Graeber, 2011; Dodd, 2014). An alternative theory of money's origins was submitted by the German economic historian Bernhard Laum ([1924] 2006) according to whom money initially had a political and religious function: subjects in the Ottoman Empire, in China, Africa, and elsewhere had to pay tribute to their rulers, and this usually took the form of sacrificing an exactly defined amount of goods or coins; a form of compensation that Laum traces back to Greek antiquity and its temple cult.

In this view, money was invented to pay debts owed to rulers or gods, which is reminiscent of Mauss and Hubert's argument that sacrifices were a means of trading with the gods ([1898] 1964). But Mauss also reflects on money in *The Gift*, namely, in a long footnote in which he discusses Malinowski's theory of money ([1925] 1990: 126ff.). Malinowski, Mauss asserts, understands money "in a restricted sense" ([1925] 1990: 127), that is, solely in modern terms: as a measure of value and means of exchange that is impersonal and frees us of obligations. Mauss observes that currencies used in earlier societies—"stones, shells, and precious metals"—served another function as well: "they have also a somewhat magic nature and are above all talismans—life-givers. ... [T]hey are still attached to persons or clans ... to the individuality of their former owners, and to contracts drawn up between legal entities. Their value is still subjective and personal." Like our own modern money, such ancient currencies had a quantifiable "purchasing power": "For such and such an American copper object, a payment of so many blankets is due. ... The idea of number is present" ([1925] 1990: 127).

According to Mauss, money has its origins in cultural and social processes and is ultimately a matter of faith: of value is that which has been determined to possess magical-spiritual force (*mana*) during affectively powerful collective processes (Mauss, 1914). This ancient form of money circulated between (members of) tribes; it was an expression of prestige and served the purposes of purchasing luxury goods and thereby gaining in authority. Only later, such objects would be further and further detached from specific persons and groups and ultimately be made into universal standards of measuring value.

Gift and money, then, are not mutually exclusive to Mauss but in fact intimately related in their historical origins. This insight allows us to look at our modern money with fresh eyes. If there once were personalized forms of it, money does not need to be cold, anonymous, and abstract, as Marx or Simmel claimed. Money can be personal and context-sensitive, which means that societal reforms could be tied to monetary reforms. As the sociologist Nigel Dodd notes, many of the practical attempts to "rehumanize" money go back to Mauss' hypothesis that money was once charged with social meanings. Mauss' work makes clear that even under the conditions of modernity, money is never as firmly decoupled from collective-affective processes as utilitarianist economics would have us believe (Dodd, 2014: 34).

Polanyi agrees that money need not be an anonymous, alienating, "absolute" medium. He distinguishes between special-purpose money, which prevailed in premodern times, and all-purpose money, which enables us moderns to buy almost everything. While different special-purpose monies could be used for different kinds of transfers, none of them was as universally appliable as our modern money (Polanyi, 1968: 175–203). In his well-known essay on "Principles of Exchange and Investment among the Tiv of Central Nigeria," the American anthropologist Paul Bohannan (1920–2007) took a similar view. Before the impact of Western economy made itself felt in Central Nigeria, the Tiv organized their exchanges in three separate and hierarchically ordered spheres, each of which had their own money (Bohannan, 1955). Thus, one kind of money was meant for the exchange of food, tools, and resources on the market; another for prestige objects, such as slaves, livestock, and brass rods; and the highest category of money was reserved for exchanging (non-enslaved) people, usually women or children. Though Bohannan's study has been criticized (see Hann and Hart, 2011: 59), it still teaches us that money does not have to be detrimental to social cohesion. However, both Polanyi and Bohannan assume that only premodern money was socially and culturally embedded like this, which implies an acceptance of the view that modern money is abstract and detached. It is exactly this dichotomy that we should question. There never was "pure" or "ideal" money, and even our modern forms of money are culturally and socially embedded. As Viviana A. Zelizer (2012) was able to show, money is always modified by social practices. For example, in everyday life, money may be used for compensation (for example, for housewives giving up professional occupations) or as a gift (Zelizer, 1996). We may therefore infer that money can serve non-monetary values and does not automatically transform all qualities into quantities (see also Guyer, 2004).

Whereas Zelizer shies away from drawing normative conclusions from her empirical findings, Keith Hart does not. The anthropologist directly builds on Mauss' and Polanyi's work and applies it to contemporary debates on societal reform. For Hart, the dichotomy of state vs. market money is misguided because in reality both are "two sides of the same coin":

> One side reminds us that states underwrite currencies and that money is originally a relation between persons in society, a token perhaps. The other reveals the coin as a thing, capable of entering into definite relations with other things, as a quantitative ratio independent of the persons engaged in any particular transaction. (Hart, 1986: 638)

But there is a third agent capable of creating money, one that is usually ignored or dismissed: civil society. The Internet has made it relatively easy for organizations to invent and use their own currencies, and thus counteract tendencies associated with money, such as alienation and depersonalization. In doing so, they rely on trust, a resource that, along with risk, we earlier on identified as closely tied to gift giving (see Chapter 3). Money, too, is fundamentally dependent on this background mechanism of the gift. Once people realize how the money they use is connected to all sorts of other currencies, it becomes clear how their local lifestyles are linked to those of others, far away. However, if these links (of payments) are obscured—allegedly because they are too complex for us to understand—the binding force of money, its "social life" (Dodd, 2014), gets lost. Money has the potential to make us understand that we are all part of one world—but only if we can discern that it does more than just connecting buyers and sellers temporarily, that there are communities behind it that recognize, trust, and use it. If we could trace money through all its transactions, the global division of labor—which we too are a part of, for better or worse—would be evident to everybody.

By way of a simple example, Hart (2005) demonstrates that things of the same monetary value may have very different cultural values:

> If you asked a British person how many toilet rolls a BMW is worth or how many oranges buy an Eton education, they would think you were crazy. Yet all these things have been bought with money for longer than we can remember. So the universal exchange introduced by modern money is compatible with cultural values denying that all goods are commensurate.

Monetary value, then, does *not* level everything. Commodities come with different affective values, and so does money itself. It is an expression of a collective faith; otherwise, it would never have evolved into a universal currency.

In modern society, money occupies a central position, almost like a god (von Hagen and Welker, 2014). It symbolically expresses a desire for freedom (from) and socio-economic power, but at the same time it contains aspects of exchange, affiliation, and interdependency, aspects of a positive freedom that we should strengthen by making money a symbol of social relations instead. By documenting our debts, money already serves as an instrument of "keep[ing] track" of our "proliferating connections with others," and thus as no less than "a means of collective memory" (Hart, 2005). Hart does not think that a national currency suffices to realize all of the needs for exchange that people living in the respective country (or group of countries, as with the Euro) might have. Instead, he makes the case for a pluralism of currencies with differing scopes and foci, as well as for "more informal means of regulation." This idea stands in a long tradition, but it never managed to gain much political acceptance: Robert Owen's equitable labor exchange comes to mind, Pierre-Joseph Proudhon's exchange banks, or, in the 20th century, Silvio Gesell's *Freigeld*, which gradually declines in value.

Since the 1980s and 1990s, alternative currencies have been booming, and in the wake of the latest financial crisis, interest in them has increased even further. While they all have specific goals, their very existence attests to the fact that money truly can be socially shaped. The time-honored concept of labor exchanges is also being revived, embodying a radical break with traditional ideas of value: every working hour is worth the same in this model, independent of the kind of work done, which prevents that labor gets over- or underpaid (cf. Castoriadis' demand for income equality). Currently, the idea of regarding human labor, that is, completed working hours, as an accounting unit is being utilized by so-called time banks. As Philipp Degens explains, these "social projects" are based on reciprocity and "primarily aim at integrating marginalised people" who thus experience some recognition as givers (2016: 28). Also, some senior cooperatives and other facilities for the elderly manage to implement the logic of the gift by detaching themselves from direct reciprocity and exchange: through care work people here earn entitlements to future benefits—without knowing whether or not they will one day have to redeem them.

Similar in principle to time banks, Local Exchange Trading Systems (LETS) represent another non-money-based complementary currency. According to supply and demand, goods and services are here being exchanged locally with the aid of a virtual accounting unit, which is meant to unfold a sense of community. Much more common nowadays than either LETS or time banks, however, are regional or local currencies. Increasingly used even in the formal economy, these alternative currencies are tied to the respective national currency and therefore secured. The rationale behind introducing them is usually to vitalize the local economy: equipped with negative interest rates, they typically circulate faster than regular money. All these alternative currencies are unsuited as stores of purchasing power, which corresponds to Gesell's idea that if money is hoarded, it is not available for circulation and therefore does not fulfill its basic function to serve as means of payment. Interest is an incentive for withholding and accumulating money, which is why in Gesell's *Freigeld* system, people have to pay fees for hoarding. After all, according to this vision, money is common property.

To differing degrees, gifts become a part of money circulation in these schemes. Advocates of currency pluralism and democratization emphasize the advantages of having different monies for different purposes (for example money as an accounting unit, means of payment, store of value). The Internet has brought forth currencies that combine a communizing effect with global interconnection, the prime example being the *Bitcoin*. However, the focus of such Internet-based alternative currencies is on their users' anonymity, and frequent increases in value entice users to hoard the virtual money, which makes them susceptible to speculative bubbles. What is more, *Bitcoins* are "mined," which means that there is a limited number of them; their inventors thus emulate the finiteness of gold as a resource in rather traditional ways. A real alternative is the Occupy movement's *Freicoin*, "a decentralized, distributed, peer-to-peer electronic currency designed to address the grievances of the working class and re-align financial interests of the wealthy elite with the stability and well-being of the economy as a whole" (http://freico.in/).

Ultimately, the gift is an implicit component of every kind of money, even of our abstract and impersonal modern variety. And as everyone knows by now, all risk and probability assessment by banks, companies, investors, and economists are subject to great uncertainty: the minute people lose their trust in a currency, it crashes. The economic sociologist Jens Beckert (2016) therefore claims that fictions are constitutive of the economy, with everyone acting as if certain anticipated results had already become reality, although the future is of course utterly unpredictable. This reminds us of gifts which, as we have seen, also simulate a future reality in order to make it happen. Similarly, we have to trust a currency; we have to trust that the willingness to exchange a piece of paper or a number on a screen for another value will prevail. This anticipated future depends on the acknowledgment and ratification of others, and the value of a currency on the amount of trust people place in it. It is this gift, performed by everybody, that explains the magical power of money. Consider the phenomenon of credits: the creditors *trust* for the credit to be paid back; they *give* a credit in that *faith*.

One main feature of our modern money system in particular makes clear how much money depends on gifts, trust, and faith. That feature is the capacity of banks—no matter if local or transnational—to create money from nothing. To be sure, banks do not print money, but they do create it by means of credits. This so-called book or deposit money only comes into being when a bank grants the sum in question to the debtor. In this case, banks give away something they do not have; they produce money, as it were, instead of just loaning it (Sahr, 2017: 74). In a way, they resemble a pastor who by blessing his parishioners merely passes something on: the blessing of God. What banks pass on to society at large is the belief in its own creditworthiness and in money in general. However, the profits from the production of capital flow right back to the banks and their owners—as if the pastor himself received the greatest blessing of them all. The purpose of our modern banks is to ensure that the yields from capital production are received by those who already own income from capital (2017: 67). The acquisition of profits works in an asymmetrical fashion: whoever has will be given more. Derrida (1992) states that you can only give time because time is nobody's property. That is exactly how banks proceed. It is amazing that politics and society still accept that the profits made on the basis of people's trust are thus being privatized, instead of benefitting the public good.

This is where political demands for a full-reserve banking system set in. Many economists are in favor of it, and in Switzerland there even was a legal initiative in 2018 in which 24 percent of the Swiss voted in favor of "money creation by the National Bank only." In a full-reserve system, you could only take out loans from existing savings deposits; there would be no more money-creating credits. Whether this would amount to a democratization of money creation is anyone's guess, but this example illustrates once more that debts are based on social relations. You believe in the trustworthiness of creditors and debtors, and this is a social phenomenon based on the gift. Unfortunately, the asymmetry of the present system makes it likely that these gift relationships will be instrumentalized for the sake of making private profit. Again: our societies are built on immense amounts of trusts, and it is sad that this resource is not used for the good of all.

The gift, then, has found its way into the monetary systems even of our modern societies—to different degrees and with different emphases. Therefore, we should not fall for the grand narrative of Horkheimer and Adorno ([1944] 1991), who held that the history of mankind, starting with the sacrificial rites of ancient times, is a history of instrumental rationality. For the two Frankfurt School theorists, sacrifices are a deliberate deception of the gods, so as to instrumentalize them for human purposes. The instrumentalization of others and practices of economic exchange are intimately linked in this view, and money here becomes just another means in the pursuit of self-interest. There is no room whatsoever in this gloomy vision for the non-equivalent and the gift.

Similar black-and-white portrayals of the world can be found in debates on alternative economies. In Germany, for example, proponents of commoning like Friederike Habermann or Silke Helfrich aim for a world of sharing in which money is obsolete. According to them, equivalent exchange is always accompanied by competition, antagonism, objectification, and alienation. And consequently, solidarity can only be enforced *against* the production and exchange of commodities. Only the communism of the commons is free from these capitalist pathologies in their view (Acksel et al, 2015). Needless to say that these authors idealize the principle of sharing and contrast too radically the non-agonistic gift on the one hand and the agonistic gift and exchanges on the other. This has little to do with Mauss' conclusion that gifts and money can mutually permeate each other, and he would not even have objected to an agonistic competition between individuals or groups. Moreover, gifts, too, may be quantified, without losing their gift character.

At the very least, a quantification of value does not automatically move gifts in the direction of rivalry and hierarchy (through indebtedness).

Nobody has the right to tell us what we and our practices are worth. But what follows from that is merely that we warrant different registers of value, and not that money necessarily has a corrosive effect and must be abolished. Some values you can exchange, others you can gift, and yet others—like our value as humans—should not ever be subjected to the logic of exchange. It is important to realize that gifts constitute values, and that all attempts at abstraction and quantification, while ignoring the asymmetry and non-equivalence of the gift, still depend on it. Once we recognize this qualitative and asymmetrical foundation of the social, we are better able to fend off the colonization of the gift.

PART III

Crossing the Borders

7

Science and Technology, Nature and Conviviality

We cannot understand our relations with each other and with nature—and thus the current ecological and social double crisis of capitalism—without considering the "progress" of science and technology. According to the founding father of sociology, Max Weber, Western modernity is designed for *world mastery*. Weber ([1905] 1930) saw this as closely related to religion, and he fruitfully compared Judaism and Protestantism to Eastern belief systems; in the latter he diagnosed a tendency towards *adjustment to the world* instead. For our context, his juxtaposition of the more ascetically oriented varieties of Protestantism (for example Calvinism, Puritanism, Pietism, Baptism, Methodism) with Chinese Confucianism is particularly instructive (Weber, [1920] 1963).

Since it lacked any tension between religion and mundane life, Weber contends, Confucianism historically knew only an ethics of the law, but no ethics of conviction. In ancient China, there was an established hierarchy of religious, magical, and worldly powers that demanded no "rational transformation of the world" (Weber, [1915] 1951: 240). While the Puritans were committed to a conduct of life they hoped their strict God would approve of, Confucians strove for self-improvement and harmony, cultivated literature and philosophy, and regarded this mortal world as the best one possible. Weber therefore distinguishes a rationalism of world mastery (Puritanism) from a rationalism of adjustment to the world (Confucianism) ([1915] 1951: 235). And he derives from this a stage model of rationalization describing to what degree magical thinking has been cast off in a certain society. How "disenchanted" is its world? And to what extent do people conceive of their relations with God and the world in a methodical and consistent way? For Weber, Confucianism is grounded in magic and does not devaluate the world, whereas among all religions, Protestantism displays the greatest potential for disenchantment. At the same time, through systematically distancing themselves from the world (by devoting themselves to a transcendent God), Protestants were best able to shape and master it. For Weber this is the hallmark of the Western way of approaching the world, even if in our secular times, the historical connection to Protestantism may be mostly obscured.

Let us have a closer look at the specific form of rationalization characteristic of the West. To rationalize first and foremost means to systematically relate ends and means—for example, to pursue truth by means of scientific experiments or to maximize efficiency and profit through the methods of economics. In Weber's writings, three versions of rationalization can be found: scientific-technological rationalization, which increases our empirical knowledge of the world and aims at predictability; metaphysical-ethical rationalization, which systematizes worldviews and ideas of meaningfulness; and a practical rationalism, which consists of applying certain guiding principles to our everyday conduct. That the West has been so successful at mastering the world is due to the fact that it is rational in all these senses. The sociologist Hartmut Rosa argues that modernity has resulted in a "permanent enlargement of the world scope" (2019: 756), which means that humans can now intervene in most aspects of our physical, social, and psychological environments. The world seems to us like a reservoir of resources that we can master, use, and thus instrumentalize: be it mineral deposits, animals and plants, other people, or our own emotions. The capitalistic logic of acceleration ("bigger, better, faster, more") is based on a utilitarian notion of human subjects as detached from the world, observing it and manipulating it as they see fit. In other words, the modern subject no longer feels embedded in the network of life with its manifold relations of giving and receiving.

Science and instrumentality

This diagnosis has accompanied modernity right from the start, as have critiques of its tendencies towards alienation, reification, and an exploitation of both humans and nature. As different as the theories may be—for example those of Rousseau, Marx, Weber, Adorno, Fromm, and Arendt—the core conviction is the same: modern life must be misguided because it falls short of achieving happiness and justice, the good life. Traditionally, the "birth" of the modern worldview is traced back to René Descartes (1596–1650) and his distinction between *res cogitans* and *res extensa*, soul (mind) and world. Souls were accorded to humans only, while all "matter," animate or not, was regarded as machine-like and thus describable by the methods of science.[1]

In the 1960s, the German-American social philosopher Herbert Marcuse (1898–1979) spoke of modernity's "technological a priori" and warned that "the transformation of nature involves that of man" ([1964] 2012: 154). Usually, modern science is seen (and sees itself) as value-free and not per se bound to any practical purposes or applications. It freed the conception of nature from all qualitative attributions (for example beautiful vs. ugly, sublime vs. low, good vs. evil) and made it quantifiable, resulting in a massive advancement of knowledge and in previously inconceivable technological innovations. Edmund Husserl (1859–1938) referred to modern natural science since Galileo as a "mere science of bodies," which "abstracts from everything subjective" and aims for a "mathematization of nature" ([1936] 1970: 6, 23). In the 17th century, Husserl states, a new striving for exactitude and logical stringency set in, a rationalism that disregarded both the senses and the contexts that knowledge was firmly embedded in before. While in Leonardo da Vinci's day, science was still grounded in humanism and linked to the local and temporal, from c. 1650 scientists were no longer willing to tolerate uncertainty, ambiguity, or a pluralism of opinions. Philosophical and scientific problems were now supposed to be "stated in terms independent of any historical situation, and solved by methods equally free of contextual references" (Toulmin, 1990: 36). This also meant that the gap between the everyday experiences of people and the scientific worldview got bigger. One could even say that for an ordinary observer, the scientific description of a phenomenon is somewhat irrelevant: the sun still *seems* to orbit around the Earth, although we know it to be otherwise.

Marcuse thought about the consequences this new mastery of nature had for humans. He stressed that the instrumentalization of humans by other humans can only be stopped if we change the very structure of science and adopt a different form of rationality: "Reason, as conceptual thought and behavior is necessarily mastery, domination. Logos is law, rule, order by virtue of knowledge" ([1964] 2012: 167). And if we keep objectifying and instrumentalizing nature, Marcuse cautions, our world could end up in a state of "total administration" (*passim*) that is harmful even to those who hope to profit from it. For the last 150 years or so, human mastery over nature was legitimized by pointing to the growing productivity of the economy, the parallel increase of technological innovations, and the global spread of consumerism.

Ever since the 19th century, the interdependence of science and technology has driven technological-economic rationalization, and that scientification of technology has become the greatest productive force: the main source of surplus value is no longer simple labor-power but scientific-technological progress (Habermas, 1971). Marcuse responds to this by demanding a new attitude towards nature and a new understanding of science. He wants us to no longer regard nature as an object to be controlled and instrumentalized by means of technology, but as a potential interactant of humans. A new model of interaction would attribute subjectivity to nature, and we would communicate with animals and plants rather than instrumentalizing them.

By contrast, Habermas, the leading exponent of the Frankfurt School's second generation, doubts that a new conception of nature would bring about a new understanding of technology as well. For him, there is no alternative to scientific and technological progress. He does think, however, that we ought to politically control the ever-increasing reach of technology and ensure that it serves the good life instead of being an end in itself. Habermas (2003) believes that not everything that is technologically possible should actually be done. For example, the cloning of humans could be prohibited without infringing upon the elemental structure of science and technology, their logic of world mastery. Communicative rationality, Habermas holds, constricts instrumental rationality without fundamentally calling it into question.

Naturalism, culturalism, and other worldviews

Critiques of modern science and technology go back to a long-standing ontological dualism of subject vs. object, culture vs. nature. One may wonder, though, if this dualism is really as stable as oftentimes assumed, and inquire since when it has dominated Western thinking and how other cultures relate to nature. Someone who has thought intensively about these questions is Philippe Descola (b. 1949), who until recently held the chair of "Anthropology of Nature" at the prestigious Collège de France. In his book *Beyond Nature and Culture* (2013), Descola reveals how deeply the West is indeed shaped by the dichotomy of materialism and mentalism: whereas one camp—natural scientists, but also many psychologists and philosophers of mind—attempt to show that everything, including human consciousness, can be ascribed to material processes, others tend to champion a semiotic idealism which states that we can only access the world via signs and language. In cultural studies and sociology, for example, constructivist approaches emphasize that we can only know nature by interpreting it in cultural terms.

But when did this powerful dualism of nature and culture develop? Descola identifies the roots of naturalism—the "notion of Nature as an autonomous ontological domain, a field of inquiry and scientific experimentation, an object to be exploited and improved" (2013: 69)—in the 17th century, and those of culturalism in the late 1800s. Around the turn of the century, "culture" was seen as something pluralistic and dynamic, subject to perpetual change, and for the first time an appreciation of the variety of cultural traditions emerged. The experience of culture's contingency was reinforced by a nascent globalized economy, by increasing intercultural contacts in the wake of colonialism, as well as by the first anthropological field studies (Adloff and Büttner, 2014). Henceforth, one could really only speak of cultures in the plural.

Also in the late 19th century and influenced by these developments, the differentiation between natural sciences and humanities was widely discussed, especially in Germany. Thus, the Neo-Kantian philosopher Wilhelm Windelband, in an 1894 speech on "History and the Natural Sciences" distinguished between a "nomothetic" and an "ideographic" approach to knowledge: the former is the method of the natural sciences, which try to derive general laws from individual phenomena; the latter is the method of the humanities in trying to explain one specific phenomenon as comprehensively as possible. Windelband therefore also speaks of "sciences of laws" and "sciences of events" (1894: 12). The problem is that this juxtaposition of a universalized nature, to be studied exclusively by natural scientists, and a multitude of culturally relative practices, conventions, and worldviews, to be studied by sociology, anthropology, and so on, is quite unique to our Western cosmology since c. 1900.

Descola (2013) requires us to acknowledge this and recognize that there is also a variety of views of nature and the nature–culture relationship. The non-Western ontologies are no less true for him than our own scientific dualism. All in all, he distinguishes four broad types of cosmologies, of which Western-style naturalism is only one. The second one, animism, can still be observed in the inhabitants of Amazonia and parts of Siberia, where nonhumans are believed to have subjectivity and intentionality as much as humans do an inversion of Western naturalism since animism knows just one "culture" (everything has a soul) but myriads of "natures." The third ontology is Australian totemism, which assumes a similarity of both mental states and physical constitution between humans and nonhumans. The fourth is what Descola calls analogism, which assumes a *dis*continuity of both mental and physical states. Analogism is prevalent in China, India, and West Africa—as it was in Europe up until the Renaissance.

By firmly separating humans and nonhumans, Western naturalism constitutes nature as a space for experimentation and a (supposedly) inexhaustible deposit of resources. Colonialism ensured that this view of nature was transported around the globe, so that even in non-industrialized societies, landscapes were massively altered: tropical forests were cleared to obtain wood, parts of the African savanna were turned from tranquil pasture to game reserve, and former hunting grounds became vast stock-breeding farms. To be sure, the interferences of humans with nature go back much further: the plant biodiversity of the Amazon rain forest is the result of millennia of human activities, and the Australian outback owes its appearance to the bushfires of the Aborigines. The difference is that such practices were not about "taming wild nature." They were seen as interactions between humans and all kinds of nonhumans: plants and animals, but also spirits and deities. For Descola, the nature–culture dichotomy is thus a purely historical and random affair and should not be mistaken for a universal formula. If scientists working in laboratories in India or China today use the same methods as researchers in the "West," this does not mean that they share the same naturalistic worldview. It is very much possible, Descola holds, to use Western scientific methods without embracing the Western cosmology.

Bruno Latour disagrees with Descola with respect to this last point. The French sociologist and philosopher of science (b. 1947) has examined, and fundamentally questioned, the nature–culture dichotomy in many publications over the last decades. Of particular importance for our context is his book *We Have Never Been Modern* (1993) in which Latour asserts that the strict separation of the natural and the social world, so frequently invoked in (self-) descriptions of modernity, has in fact always been restricted to Western scientific discourse. For him, the two worlds are rather intimately entangled, and our reality, Latour argues, is created by these very connections between humans and "things," natural as well as technological. Indeed we are witnessing a "proliferation" of nature–culture "hybrids" (1993: 1), that is, networks of actors, processes, or discourses in which humans, nonhuman lifeforms, objects, and technology mix—for example AIDS, energy policies, or the genetical engineering of animals. The problem is that "the moderns," other than "premoderns" beyond the West, do not realize that by changing the natural order, they will change the social order as well. "My hypothesis," Latour concludes in the first chapter, "is that we are going to have to slow down, reorient and regulate the proliferation of monsters. ... Will a different democracy become necessary? A democracy extended to things?" (1993: 12).[2]

For Descola, the modern nature–culture dualism remains crucial, and he accuses Latour of disguising this powerful mechanism of knowledge organization by focusing too much on hybrid forms. Be that as it may; what matters most to me here is Latour's demand that the West should acknowledge that it has created a world no longer well describable in terms of a nature–culture dichotomy. We should finally begin to think of ourselves and nature as parts of the same "collective" (1993: 4).

A new conception of nature, science, and technology?

Are Descola's and Latour's notions of Western "naturalism" correct? Is it true that humans have imagined nature as mechanical since the 17th century and have sharply divided the worlds of nature and culture since the end of the 19th century? I believe that this picture is incomplete because even in the West, the naturalist cosmology is not the only one. The phenomenological tradition in philosophy, for example, has always highlighted holistic experiences in which the separation between subject and object is partly overcome. When situations really take hold of us—say, at a concert or while mountain biking—we no longer distinguish between ourselves and "things." Instead of operating in a rational ends-and-means mode, we become absorbed in the situation and experience it as a whole. We know such "primary experiences" (Dewey) from various contexts, including encounters with nature. In our everyday lives, we do not view nature as merely a resource or as mechanical: we often feel a real connection to it. Such experiences have always been a part of modernity—and some modern art movements have capitalized on this (for example Romanticism)—but the scientific mainstream has tended to look down on them.

Us "moderns" really do live in two worlds at once, and the practical experiences we make, all the time, are not always compatible with our formal, scientific knowledge (Feenberg, 2010). The smoker knows that smoking harms him, but he enjoys it nonetheless. To be sure, our scientific knowledge changes our everyday experiences: knowing about photosynthesis alters our view of plants, astronomical knowledge our view of the stars, and so on. That which is not congruent with scientific knowledge, however, mostly lives in the shadows of modernity, and we are well-advised not to mention such "subjective," and "premodern" experiences in scientific discourse. But the world does not only consist of science. The "disenchantment" of our lives (Weber) is by no means as far advanced as Descola and Latour claim. In fact, fields in which holistic experiences play a major role are thriving: one thinks of alternative medicine or environmentalism, for example. Science itself—which has long known about the multiple interdependencies within ecological systems and supplies more and more evidence for our practical interconnectedness with other humans and nonhumans—could help us leave behind the naturalistic ontology. This will not lead to a regression into animism. We will not thank the pig that has ended up on our plate, but at least we could acknowledge our responsibility for its life and death. The broad appeal of vegetarianism, veganism, and the animal rights movement may be a first indication of Western naturalism's downfall.

The reductiveness of Descola's ontological model becomes even more apparent when we consider aesthetic experiences. Art history is full of examples that prove his claim of a nature–culture dichotomy wrong. One finds all kinds of crossovers, for instance in religious art (between sacred and profane subject-matter), in landscape painting (between wild nature and man-made countryside), or in still lifes (between natural substances and artifacts). Of course art just as often addresses tensions between nature and culture, as in portrayals of natural disasters as an existential threat to humans (see Böhme, 2017: 45ff.). The fact that we no longer adhere to a magical conception of nature but regard it in secular and rational terms can have positive effects on our relationship with it in the long run. Curiosity and freedom from fear sharpen the powers of observation and create spaces for aesthetic experiences beyond the nature–culture divide.

That scientific analysis does not necessarily disenchant nature and that science and culture can coalesce very productively is further suggested by the history of science. Perhaps the obvious example is Alexander von Humboldt (1769–1859), the German naturalist and polymath, whose *Cosmos: A Sketch of a Physical Description of the Universe* (1845–62) was conceived at the very historical moment when the professionalization of the sciences set in. Based on his travels in Latin America and Asia and bringing together what usually was kept apart—astronomy, geology, zoology, botany, archaeology, and history—Humboldt's five-volume treatise did not offer cold and detached observations of nature but rather expressions of excitement, astonishment, and awe. As an excerpt from Andrea Wulf's study *The Invention of Nature* (2015) makes clear, his understanding of nature was anything but mechanical:

> Unlike the scientists who had previously classified the natural world into tight taxonomic units along a strict hierarchy, filling endless tables with categories, Humboldt now produced a drawing. "Nature is a living whole," he … said, not "a dead aggregate." One single life had been poured over stones, plants, animals and humankind. It was this "universal profusion with which life is everywhere distributed" that most impressed Humboldt. … Life was everywhere and those "organic powers are incessantly at work," he wrote. (2015: 88)

For von Humboldt, this "universal profusion" was not divine in origin but came from the Earth itself. He drew no separating line between science, humanities, and arts, and conveyed the subjective within the objective. As Wulf insists, this interdisciplinary approach should serve as a blueprint for our own 21st century, especially in the fight against climate change (2015: 336). Thus far, von Humboldt's holistic approach was received with much reservation in the natural sciences, although there have been exceptions (see Lovelock's Gaia hypothesis which I discuss in Chapter 8). Instead, Humboldtian thinking was adopted in the humanities and arts. For example, Thoreau's *Walden* would be unthinkable without his *Cosmos* (Wulf, 2015: 249ff.).

We can now inquire what a new understanding (Marcuse) or an institutional regulation of technology (Habermas) could look like. Surely it cannot take the form of an absolute rejection of technology as merely "instrumental," of a reactionary call for going "back to the roots." Generally, critiques of technology warn of machines taking over, or at least lament the loss of human autonomy accompanying the proliferation of technological devices. I suggest that what we need instead is a conception of technology which recognizes a) that it is now mostly by means of technology that we encounter nature; and b) that the instrumental quality of technology does not have to lead to us dominating nature (Oberthür and Schulz, 2016).

All of our encounters with nature are mediated by technical devices (for example plows, cooking utensils, or airplanes), and technology is embedded in concrete socio-economic modes of production and culturally shaped practices. To be sure, our current technology is mostly capitalistically preformed, that is, designed for purposes like rationalization and growth. But there also exists what Ernst Bloch in *The Principle of Hope* called "alliance technology" ([1954] 1986), or what Ivan Illich in *Tools for Conviviality* named "convivial technology" (1973). A radical critic of modern technology, Illich deemed those societies convivial which impose reasonable limits of growth to all their "tools" (by which he means technologies as well as institutions). If a society fails to do so, he argues, the function of the tool in question tends to reverse into its opposite. In this view, science and technology are no longer only problem-solvers. They also produce problems, for example by transgressing limits and restricting human freedoms—to which our usual response is the employment of more technology. For instance, "[c]ars can monopolize traffic. They can shape a city into their image—practically ruling out locomotion on foot or by bicycle in Los Angeles" (1973: 55). Illich therefore believed that societal tools should be regulated, not by experts and specialized institutions, but by the general public, by the affected communities. Only such democratic control makes conviviality possible for Illich, and this requires a radical transformation of societal institutions according to criteria of conviviality. Under the conditions of utilitarianism and capitalism, convivial technology cannot thrive.

Andrea Vetter and Benjamin Best (2015) have specified Illich's rather general deliberations by introducing five criteria for a democratically controlled convivial technology: a) What kinds of interactions does a technology foster? Is its use free for all or mandatory, is it egalitarian or hierarchically structured? (relationship quality); b) Does the technology require certain knowledges? And if so, is that knowledge openly accessible or is it secret or patented? (accessibility); c) Can the technology be used flexibly? Is it extensible? Can it be used locally as opposed to only within transregional infrastructures? (adaptability); d) Which risks does the technology entail? Does it benefit the lives of humans and nonhumans? Is it recyclable? (bio interaction); and e) How sustainable is the technology? On which resources does it depend? Are these resources renewable? (resource intensity).

This list of criteria enables us to identify which technologies are convivial. Nuclear energy clearly is not, and neither are our current cars which exceed all emission standards and whose complex electrics no one knows how to fix any more. The Fairphone is more convivial than the iPhone. Cargo bikes are convivial, as is Open Design. Needless to say that such technologies run counter to the socio-economic framework of capitalism which relies on a constant search for new investment opportunities, gives exclusive production rights to individuals via patents, comprises practices of planned obsolescence, and continues to waste resources on a massive scale. Convivial science and technology can only emerge once mentalities and socio-economic conditions have radically changed. They require a post-growth society.

8

Gifts of Nature

In the year 2000, the Dutch atmospheric chemist Paul J. Crutzen and the American biologist Eugen F. Stoermer first proposed that we use the term "Anthropocene" for our current geochronological epoch, and thereby acknowledge the impact humans now have on fundamental biological, atmospheric, and geological processes on Earth. According to Crutzen (2002), we no longer live in the Holocene, which began some 12,000 years ago, but in a new era that was heralded by the beginnings of industrialization in the 18th century. The proposal was affirmed by an expert group at the International Geological Congress in 2016. We thus now know officially what we have always known: that humanity is disrupting the global ecosystem on a massive scale.

The Anthropocene denotes an ecological meta crisis made up of "such different phenomena as climate change, loss of biodiversity, air pollution, the hole in the atmospheric ozone layer, the proliferation of toxins and microparticles (e.g., microplastics), ocean acidification, changes in the watercycle, and so on" (Horn and Bergthaller, 2019: 20). No longer limited to merely local developments, the consequences of human lifestyles and technologies now assume a global, even a geological dimension. While major interferences with nature can be traced back to the Neolithic revolution in agriculture, only the advent of capitalism, private property, and modern technology brought about the ever-increasing human-made CO_2 emissions that are mainly responsible for climate change. Since the end of World War II, we have furthermore experienced a "great acceleration" regarding the pressure on the Earth system (Steffen et al, 2015).

Moreover, we are currently losing approximately a hundred species per day, and if this mass extinction continues, the Anthropocene will destroy half of all species on Earth. The American literary scholar Ashely Dawson (2016) sees this as analogous to capitalism and its destruction of the "commons of nature" (Bollier, 2002: 59ff.): plants, animals, clean air, clean water. When it comes to humans, due to the planetary scope of the Anthropocene it is often overlooked that not all of us suffer from its ramifications to the same degree—and not all of us are responsible for it: it is the Western (colonial) economy and the lifestyles associated with it that got the Earth into this trouble.¹

A new conception of matter and life

That all of nature is nowadays subjected to human influence is blatantly obvious. High time therefore that we bid farewell to the separation of nature and culture—which never applied in the first place. We must conceive of nature, but also of humans and the social, in new ways. To really understand agriculture, for instance, we need to reconstruct the interactions within a whole network of different actors: soils, micro-organisms, seeds, plants, livestock, farmers, tractors, and tools. The recognition that in the Anthropocene *everything* interdepends could lead to new forms of human-nonhuman cohabitation that do not threaten our very livelihoods.

This requires that we acknowledge the value of nonhuman life. In actor-network theory, which goes back to the science-and-technology research of Latour and Michel Callon, it has long been commonplace that even things possess agency since they cause certain effects: kettles boil water, guns shoot, speed bumps slow down cars. Of course all these things were invented and shaped by humans, but at the same time they shape us by enabling, if not enforcing, certain behaviors. Thus, hybrid networks of human and nonhuman actors are formed. As Latour writes:

> You are different with a gun in hand; the gun is different with you holding it. You are another subject because you hold the gun; the gun is another object because it has entered into a relationship with you. The gun is no longer the gun-in-the-armory or the gun-in-the-drawer or the gun-in-the-pocket, but the gun-in-your-hand, aimed at someone who is screaming. (1994: 33)

Without the interplay of actors and forces, then, no action would come about. It must be admitted, however, that Latour uses a rather weak conception of actions and actors in such examples: the effects he describes are caused without intention and consciousness. Also, no distinction is made whatsoever between human life, other forms of life, and matter. And yet, Latour's relational approach is useful because it stresses the agential potential of all subjects and objects. His is an influential voice in a proliferating transdisciplinary discourse that aims at overcoming the traditional nature-culture dichotomy by adopting positions that could be called monistic (as opposed to dualist). Versions of the metaphysical idea that all phenomena in the world hark back to a single substance or entity can be found, for example, in ancient philosophy, in Hinduism, in Spinoza, and in Deleuze.

All these approaches share the panentheistic belief in an impersonal creative life force and in active matter.

A major proponent of a new strand of monism, often referred to as new materialism, is the American physicist and feminist theorist Karen Barad. In *Meeting the Universe Halfway* (2007), Barad argues that in the wake of structuralism, we have come to overestimate the power of language and forgotten about matter. She posits that, instead of being constituted by language, matter has agency, and power, of its own: it is not passive but creative. Barad is particularly interested in the relations between things, in their networks and interdependencies, because it is from these that their agency arises. "[T]he object and the measuring agencies," she writes, "emerge from, rather than precede, the intra-action that produces them" (2007: 128). Thus, we should conceive of the world as always becoming, as a constant process of a "mutual constitution of entangled agencies" (which is how she defines her neologism "intra-action") (2007: 33).

Another famous new materialist is the Australian-Dutch philosopher Rosi Braidotti, whose posthumanist-monistic position is of a more normative nature and has proved quite controversial. Like Barad, Braidotti (2013) stresses the self-organizing power of living matter. She approvingly paraphrases Spinoza, according to whom matter, just like humans, is "driven by the desire for self-expression" (2013: 56). In this view, life is a pervasive power that connects matter with nonhuman and human beings. And this interconnectedness has, or should have, moral consequences: Braidotti makes the case for a "posthuman affirmative ethics" as a response to threats like climate change and species extinction, which in the end concern us all. Of course this is a far cry from the realities of global capitalism in which animals in particular are cruelly exploited: they serve as food resource and supplier of raw materials for the pharmaceutical and cosmetics industries, or they are used in scientific experiments. Braidotti sees nonhumans as our "companion species" (2013: 71), but without anthropomorphizing them—because if you speak indiscriminately, for example, of humans and animals being capable of empathy, you negate the uniqueness of both. Braidotti wants to think connectedness without denying species their identity; her vision is one of "unity in diversity." The collapse of the nature–culture divide, she holds, requires more than just a new way of looking at nonhuman lifeforms, it requires a "naturalization" of us humans who, just as much as other beings, are part of the milieu that is the planet Earth. This fundamental equality of all life demands that we renounce our rule over animals. We must realize that we too, are beings of nature, animals among other animals, and engage in alliances, in "joint projects and activities" with other species (2013: 190). This insight will change our view of humanity itself. A posthuman ethics does not imply to become indifferent about humans but to extend our ethical connections through a new understanding of community and relationality.

In other words: we should finally recognize nonhumans as givers whose gifts we very much depend upon.

Recent biological research points in similar directions. The German biologist Andreas Weber, for instance, is one of the most passionate proponents of a new science, ecology, and ethics of life. Weber wants us to perceive life in all its dimensions, to sense it, feel it, express it. The approach of traditional biology, he believes, is much too technical and thus reductionist; along with the other natural sciences, it has disenchanted nature by overlooking (or right out negating) its subjectivity and meaningfulness. Like Barad and Braidotti, Weber emphasizes that matter is creative, that "[s]ubjectivity, sentience, agency, expression, values and autonomy lie at the centre of the biosphere" (2013: 7). He rests this claim on a number of insights made in biology over the last decades, insights he thinks may revolutionize our conception of life. For instance, the American biologist Lynn Margulis (1998) discovered the importance of the principle of symbiosis (from Greek σύν *sýn*: living together) in all lifeforms, a field of research that is currently booming.[2] The concept of autopoiesis, which was introduced by Humberto Maturana and Francisco Varela (1980), refers to similar processes of self-organization. All living systems, according to the two Chilean biologists, are "autopoietic machines" (1980: 78): they create themselves and develop some degree of autonomy. The prime example is the cell which self-produces and self-organizes its components and structures. As Weber puts it, even the humblest organism "desires to survive unscathed, to grow, to develop, and to widen its life horizon" (2013: 62). Such degrees of autonomy are easily overlooked if one looks only for stimuli and responses.

Weber also mentions the field of biosemiotics which is concerned with processes of meaning-making within and between living organisms. An animal's metabolism, for example, is thus regarded as a semiotic process in which molecules act as signs and generate responses. Also, DNA is a sign system of sorts, which "has been able to branch into so many species only because all sorts of organisms could use its code, tinker with it and derive combinations that were meaningful and useful to them" (Weber, 2013: 39). Interactions between living beings—no matter if cells or, say, bird parents and their fledglings—could be said to always involve three aspects: the transfer of material substances, the exchange of meanings, and the entanglement of subjectivities. As the Swiss biologist Adolf Portmann noted as early as 1960, the instincts of animals are directed not just at self- and species preservation; they also display an urge towards self-expression. Living beings never just exist; they feel life, they want to be seen and heard, and they distinguish between good and bad, between what is and what should be.

If one treats nature like a thing, this whole dimension of meaning-making, sensation, expression, and experience is eliminated. Weber wants the natural sciences to pay more attention to relations between beings and the meanings conveyed in their interactions. Because only if we strive to understand these interactions, we can come to an adequate understanding of nature. Weber concludes that "interbeing" is geared at a "balance of individuality and the whole" and that the "economy of living nature" consists in a "cycle of the gift" (Weber, 2013: 37). The triad of giving, receiving, and reciprocating cycles around an approximate state of balance, and "stress" occurs when the ability of a system to respond is exceeded, when no more meanings and connections can be produced. At the moment of their death, "every individual offers itself as a gift to be feasted upon by others, in the same way it received the gift of sunlight to sustain its existence. There remains a largely unexplored connection between giving and taking in ecosystems in which "loss" is the precondition for generativity" (Weber, 2013: 39).

The biosemiotic perspective goes beyond the conventional conception of ecological balances which deals with the exchange of energy and substances only. The same is true of the new research area of multispecies studies (van Dooren et al, 2016) which ethnographically examines the lifeworlds of other species—be it livestock, frogs, fungi, or micro-organisms—and aims at reconstructing, in the form of thick descriptions in the first person, not just exchange processes but also the involved beings' interests and affects. What kinds of experiences do nonhumans make, what is of relevance to them? It goes without saying that we cannot ever know a tree's "feelings." And yet the charge of anthropocentrism routinely leveled against such approaches is not valid since the alternative would be to assume that other beings live in worlds devoid of meaning and meaningfulness. Certainly our empathy with them would increase if we seriously tried to immerse ourselves in their lifeworlds, broaden the limits of our experience, practice seeing the world from completely different perspectives. Aldo Leopold, a pioneer of environmental ethics, once famously wrote: we should "learn to think like a mountain" ([1949] 1989: 129). The feminist biologist and philosopher of science Donna Haraway challenges us to rethink our notion of kinship and display ethical behavior towards nonhuman species as well. "Right now," she stated in 2015, "the earth is full of refugees, human and not," and we ought to "join forces" with other species "to reconstitute refuges, to make possible partial and robust biological-cultural-political-technological recuperation and recomposition" (2015: 160).

How can we apply all these new approaches to nature? Do we need a new ontology to overcome the nature–culture dichotomy? Biosemiotics frequently invokes pragmatist philosophy, in particular the work of Charles Sanders Peirce (1839–1914) (see for example Wheeler, 2006). But John Dewey, whom we encountered earlier, can also help us get our bearings in this new terrain. Dewey's pragmatism assumes a continuity of nature and culture, a "biological continuity from the lower organisms to man" ([1917] 2008: 14)—even though the experiences made by these species of course involve different levels of complexity. If culture cannot be thought of without nature, nature cannot be conceived of without experience: wherever there is life, experiences are being made. For Dewey, experiences happen in interactions of a living organism with its physical and social environment: the organism influences the environment through its behavior and in turn is influenced by that environment, often through experiences of a hurtful nature: "experience," he writes, "means primarily ... ways of doing and suffering" ([1917] 2008: 26).

Dewey thus breaks with the subject–object dualism dominating the Western epistemological tradition, that is, with the assumption that human reason is positioned outside of the world of matter. For Dewey, there is no clear dividing line between a knowing subject and the world to be known. Since experience is always based on the interaction of an organism and its environment, there is neither a knowable world without living beings' concrete perspectives and their practical references to it, nor are there living beings independent of the specific conditions of their environment. Crucially, since the practical experiences resulting from such interactions do not rely on higher cognition, language, or signs, rudiments of "culture" and "meaning" can already be found on the level of pure being-in-the-world. Due to his vindication of the non-linguistic, affective, bodily aspects of human (and nonhuman) activities, Dewey can be considered an intellectual precursor of today's new materialists, biosemioticians, and so on. Instead of taking ontological boundaries as a starting point for theory building, a pragmatic perspective on life will radically scrutinize them all.

Gifts, values, conviviality

A new conception of nature and of experience would enable us to treat life on planet Earth differently. If we recognized (and felt) our interconnectedness with other beings, new worldviews and new practices could emerge (Gibson et al, 2015). In a first step, the sciences of nature and culture must enter into a real dialog, so that we can regard human interactions from an ecological and nonhuman life from an ethical perspective. Once we no longer consider nonhuman life to be free of meaning and value, we can ascribe to nature an ethical value of its own.

Beyond that, we must rethink the economy. It is time we left behind a view of the economy as an autonomous area within a society that is organized by supply and demand and independent of natural processes. The economy tends to ignore the fact that it fundamentally relies on countless gifts by nonhumans—without bees, there is no pollination of flowering plants, and thus without agriculture, there is no food to be sold. Nothing exists outside of nature. There is no "environment." We have to realize that the economy is already part of ecology and finally start acknowledging the "work" of nature, its gifts. Then, a new understanding of (value) production could ensue. So far, the economic surplus has rested upon the capitalistic utilization of values that are for free: the unpaid reproductive labor of humans, but also the "work" of bacteria, fungi, trees, farm animals, and so on.

The new form of living together that I envision could be called convivial. Human lives are not primarily based on autonomy, as the Enlightenment ideal of humanity implies, but on relationships and mutual dependencies. A new ecology would emphasize these connections between all beings and things and surely conclude that they are prior to singular entities. Association is primary—both in ontological and ethical terms (Boisvert, 2010). To hierarchically divide the world into culture and nature, humans, animals, and plants, or animate and inanimate entities makes little sense. Instead, we should proceed from the assumption of a "collective" (Descola) of human and nonhuman beings. Conviviality means that no one is alone, and no one can free themselves from the gifts of others.

This is not about treating the sick, the disabled, the elderly, children, or animals as objects of charity, which would make them into a separate class of being, different from "us." We all once were, and probably will be again one day, in need of help ourselves. Our relatively independent adult selves are the result of a great number of relationships, of being given what we needed. As the philosopher Alasdair MacIntyre puts it, all of us exist "within a network of relationships of giving and receiving in which ... what and how far we are able to give depends in part on what and how far we received" (1999: 99). In addition to the virtue of independence, there are for MacIntyre "virtues of acknowledged dependence" (1999: 9): you do not just give, you also receive, and part of receiving is showing gratitude. We should realize that this dependence on others cannot be shed, that we are all embedded in care.

This position is well compatible with debates in the field of environmental ethics where a recurring question is whether humans owe respect only to other humans or just as much, for instance, to animals, plants, and mountains? Thus, the philosopher Angelika Krebs inquires:

> Are we even allowed to kill and eat animals? Are we permitted to cut down forests, eradicate species, pollute rivers and oceans, destroy the integrity of landscapes—just because it is of use to us humans? Do not landscapes, oceans, rivers, plants, and animals possess their own dignity, their own moral value? And if they do, does this not necessitate a preservation of nature for nature's own sake? (1997: 7; my translation)

Put differently, do we not have to reconsider, and ultimately get rid of, the anthropocentrism of traditional ethics? After all, we already regard some animals—cats, dogs, horses—not as things but encounter them almost at eye level: we call them "you." They are more than objects of our observation; they are creatures we interact with, creatures with their own wills (Habermas, 1997). To some degree, then, we treat these animals as actors, and from this circumstance derive obligations towards them.

But what about animals unable to play the role of "second person," what about plants, what about landscapes? From a liberal individualist perspective, it is only possible to grant rights to those who are equipped with consciousness, who have interests, needs, and convictions and can express them by means of language. By contrast, the more radical strands of environmental ethics—for example Arne Naess' "deep ecology" or Aldo Leopold's "land ethic"—proceed from a holistic point of view. They emphasize the intrinsic value of ecosystems and contend that we are dependent not just on other humans but also on physical, biochemical, and biological systems which know no absolute boundaries. The philosopher Stephen Clark puts it like this:

> It's not as if "I" existed prior to my entering contractual or epistemological relationships with an external world: "I" have no existence at all outside of these relationships, which converge within myself. To respect "myself" means to respect nature and the tradition that is reflected in "my" unique character and "my" unique perspective towards the world. (1997: 160; my translation)

Everything exists solely in the mode of relation, of giving and receiving—including ourselves. And it would be foolish not to sustain that which we are a part of and utterly dependent on: our "kin."

In 2013, the *Revue du M.A.U.S.S.* published a 350-page special issue entitled "What Does Nature Offer? Ecology through Giving." The issue's editors—Caillé, Philippe Chanial, and Fabrice Flipo—begin their introduction by pointing out that traditional cultures conceived of their relationship with nonhuman nature in terms of gift giving: humans received something from animals, plants, mountains, stars, and so on, and gave something in return (Caillé et al, 2013: 1). In trying to rebuild these gift relationships, we must be careful not to retreat into premodern mindscapes or sound like new agists. Caillé et al argue that such a return to a familial relationship with nature presupposes that we once again ascribe subjectivity to it (2013: 2). As we have seen, there are currently strands in biology which do exactly that. It would be possible therefore to rely on the natural sciences in creating what Caillé et al call a "methodological animism" (2013: 19). This would mean to regard nonhumans as "quasi-subjects" (2013: 21), but without anthropocentrically attributing to them consciousness and intentionality (which it would be impossible to prove empirically). We could then recognize them as givers, as beings with an unconditional value of their own, instead of as a deployable form of capital. "Resources" do not have such an intrinsic value; they are merely instruments, a means to an end. It is not enough to just allocate an adequate monetary value to natural resources, as some economists suggest. The insight that nature has its own intrinsic value keeps any economic conception of its value within clear bounds.

I thus propose that we revive our alliance with nature. Just like gift relationships among humans, such an alliance with nonhumans would have an agonistic side. Our relationship with nature is never purely harmonious. Nature can refuse, take without giving, or give only bad things. And of course it is impossible for us to pay nature back in kind—there is no equivalent to the many gifts it bestows upon us. What we can do is to revive our alliance through an act of reciprocation, which consists in acknowledging the intrinsic value of nonhumans and recognizing nature as more than a passive stock of resources, as a partner. What I advocate is that we look at nature from a gifting perspective and extend the reach of our loyalties and sympathies.

There is an element of paradox to this view. From an ethical standpoint, it is absolutely imperative that we cease dominating nature and adopt an ecocentric perspective. But this idea is only seemingly altruistic since it corresponds to our own long-term self-interest of ensuring humanity's survival on planet Earth (Chanial, 2013). The general paradoxicality of the gift here expresses itself in the fact that it is in our interest not to act self-interestedly.

Us and Gaia: conflict or alliance?

Every time we refer to the physical world as "nature" (as I, too, have done so far in this book), this invokes the very dichotomy of "nature" and "culture" that we would be well-advised to leave behind. As our partner in a universal gift relationship, nature should bear a different name. Latour champions "Gaia"—one of the primordial deities in Greek mythology and Mother Earth personified. The "Gaia hypothesis" goes back to the early 1970s when the chemist James Lovelock and the biologist Lynn Margulis began to develop their theories of Earth as a self-regulating system. And while its name was no doubt one reason it became quite popular, it also attracted some utterly unscientific interpretations, much to Lovelock and Margulis' chagrin.

When we talk about *global* warming or *planetary* boundaries, we are addressing the Earth as a whole, a vast and complex formation. In view of the huge dimension of the problem we are facing, we tend to feel small and powerless, and perhaps it is thus only natural that we are inclined to ignore or deny the problem. Latour (2011) instead wants us to look closely at how the problem became so huge, which techniques and instruments have contributed to this. Since humans, like other creatures, are tied to their local environments, a "global view" (like that of Earth from outer space) does not come about easily, even for scientists. The notion of global warming, for instance, is based on countless local measurements and observations. Only by "recalibrating data points elicited from more and more stations" (2011: 7), that is, through integrative scientific modeling, such local perspectives can be transferred to a global level. For Latour, the task ahead is to "bring the whole Earth on stage" politically, to "do the same" that climatologists have done in science "in our efforts to assemble a political body able to claim its part of responsibility for the Earth's changing state" (2011: 8).

It is at this point in his 2011 London lecture that Latour introduces the concept of Gaia. Gaia, he holds, is very "different ... from Nature of olden days ... because it is highly and terribly *local*" (2011: 8). Also unlike impersonal Nature, Gaia is "extraordinarily sensitive to our action[s]" (2011: 8). This does not mean, however, that she is the nourishing "mother Earth" celebrated in "ecological New Age pamphlets"; on the contrary: she "follows goals which do not aim for our well-being in the least" (2011: 8). For Latour, the Gaia hypothesis is strictly a scientific affair, free from any esotericism, and Gaia herself is "just a set of contingent positive and negative cybernetic loops" (2011: 10; see also Donahue, 2010). Most emphatically, he counters the common misconception of Gaia as "a superorganism endowed with [some] sort of unified agency" (2011: 10). She is not a coherent whole, not a totality, but made up of the connections between multiple agents. And there is a "perfect symmetry" between her and us in this regard (2011: 10) since we do not amount to a unified agent either. There is no such thing as the collective will of humanity; both Gaia and humanity consist of a multitude of subcollectives.

Now, how should we encounter Gaia to initiate a positive gift cycle? As I have said, we must first overcome our old view of a "nature" that knows no agency, no meanings, aims, and values. Galilei's earth moved, but it had no agency. Gaia of the Anthropocene does. I am aware that such statements invite charges of anthropomorphism, but it ought to be clear that humans are not the only beings that shape their environments according to their needs: "the capacity of humans to rearrange everything around themselves is a *general property of living things*. On this Earth, no one is passive" (Latour, 2017: 99). In place of the materialist, anti-animist worldview we would build a "common world"; knowing that it "has to be slowly composed instead of being taken for granted and *imposed* on all" (Latour, 2010: 488). We should not expect a joint plan of action to arise from the competition between nation states. Latour reminds us that climate change represents a very serious threat, a threat that is not abstract and global, but takes concrete and local shapes (floods, storms, droughts) and thus concerns some populations more than others. "We understand nothing about the ecological questions," Latour insists in *Facing Gaia*, "if we don't agree to be divided over them" (2017: 245). Humanity as a unified agent is a dangerous fiction; in fact, populations are fighting over "the ecological questions." Some have to defend their very source of life—their part of Gaia—against others. Humanity is divided into those who still live in the Holocene and keep subduing the planet (us in the North/West) and those Latour calls "Earthbound" who have already arrived in the Anthropocene and strive for an alliance with Gaia. To the latter, it is crucial to figure out what exactly the source of life they depend on consists of, which territories they need to defend, and against whom. This has nothing to do with a nationalistic or racist defense of *Lebensraum*. The interdependencies in today's world reach beyond all national borders and beyond the nature–culture divide as the Holocene knew it:

> Nature was outside. How restful it was! But today, instead of finding enchantment in the clouds, it is our actions, in part ... that those clouds are transporting. Whether it is rainy or beautiful outside, from now on, we can no longer avoid telling ourselves that it is partly our fault! Instead of enjoying the spectacle of jet trails in the blue sky, we shudder to think that those planes are modifying the sky they are crossing, that they are dragging it in their wake the way we are dragging the atmosphere behind us every time we heat our homes, eat meat, or get ready to travel to the other side of the world. (Latour, 2017: 253–4)

The human populations most dependent on Gaia must create alliances with the components of her which are most relevant to them (for example rain forests, oceans, soils, or animals and plants in biodiversity hotspots)—to appease her and defend their basis of subsistence against the disruptive global forces of capitalism. And since nonhumans are not able to speak for themselves in the same way we are, humanity must take on the task of articulating the needs of their ecosystems. There is nothing astonishing about this: after all, we must represent and interpret things all the time: laws, companies, states, gods, the past or the future. Water and air also need spokespeople (Adloff and Busse, 2021; Latour, 2004). If we succeed in rearranging interests and collectives on planet Earth, the claims nation states lay to territories and their "resources" will soon seem odd—like it would appear anachronistic if a monarch today laid claim to absolute rule. In a world of conviviality between human and nonhuman beings, the old boundaries would be obsolete, and only our gift relationship with Gaia would matter. This would be nothing less than a radical break with fundamental patterns of Western rationalization as described by Max Weber (see Chapter 7). In the Anthropocene, modernity must come to an end.

9

Civil Society, Conviviality, Utopia

The venerable concept of the civil society was resurrected from oblivion in the 1990s and has enjoyed great popularity since. The term hails from classical European philosophy, namely, from Aristotle's use of the phrase *koinōnía politikḗ* (Lat. *societas civilis*) for the Athenian city state's citizenry. Its meaning perfectly illustrates what the polis in essence was: a community of citizens, united in their efforts of fostering the good—that is, virtuous and prosperous—life (*eudaimonia*). Our own understanding of civil society goes back to the separation of state and society in early modernity. The first genuinely modern theories of civil society were those of Hobbes, Locke, and Montesquieu, followed by Hegel and Scottish enlightenment thinkers like Adam Smith and Adam Ferguson.

Today, politicians and movements of all convictions invoke the term. Some associate "civil society" with radical political reform, with strengthening democratic self-rule and restraining the power of both governments and markets to infringe on individual liberties. Others use it to stress the idea that people should act on their own responsibility, for example, no longer rely on welfare benefits. Others yet mobilize the concept when deploring the undemocratic suppression of oppositional forces in countries like Russia or Turkey. All these uses of the term are politically motivated: the good form of societal organization that "civil society" is meant to designate is always contrasted to what is deemed its opposite, and what characterizes the latter, a "bad" form of society, differs according to political beliefs: the egoistical pursuit of self-interest in capitalist markets, authoritarianism, quietism, apathy, or dependence on the welfare state. Descriptions, judgments, and visions for the future apparently mix in the concept of civil society, as do scientificity and political ideals. It is this ambiguity that makes it somewhat fuzzy and quite fascinating at the same time.

One aspect of civil society that scholars disagree on is whether or not it should include the economy (Adloff and Kocka, 2016). Economic liberals and conservatives in the Lockean tradition are inclined to stress economic self-responsibility and argue in favor of a clear separation of state and society: the state, they believe, needs to keep its nose out of individual lives, private economic endeavors, and the societal sphere. In this view, civil society resembles an unpolitical shelter from the government's intrusion. By contrast, those inspired by republicanism and post-Marxism tend to draw the separating line between civil society and the economy. They emphasize civil society's genuinely political character, regard it as a mediator between the government and society, and sometimes aim for civic self-government. In this case, the intellectual forebears include Montesquieu, de Tocqueville, or Dewey (Adloff, 2005). Finally, current debates on civil society often focus on the question of social and political cohesion and on social capital (Putnam, 2000).

So how to neutrally define civil society? One strategy is to define it as a unique societal sphere of its own—made up of voluntary associations and not-for-profit organizations—as distinguished from the spheres of the family, the state, and the economy. Another definition is rather more normative and focuses on interactions. Authors like Robert Bellah ([1967] 1991), Edward Shils (1991), or Herfried Münkler (1998) have identified qualities like civility and community spirit as quintessential of "civic" behavior, which to them is not limited to any particular social sphere but can occur in politics and the economy as well. Historically, these scholars point out, civility goes back to the principle of religious liberty as established, for instance, in the Treaty of Westphalia or the US Constitution. The separation of church and state is a major feature of Western modernity of course: caesaropapism never gained much traction in Europe, and the need to tolerate religious pluralism prevailed. Most work on civil society, however, employs a combination of sphere- and interaction-centric definitions. For example, the historian Jürgen Kocka finds that civil society is characterized by a certain type of interaction to be found where state, economy, and the private sphere meet—an interaction type that recognizes plurality and is non-violent, geared at compromise, and at least partly guided by considerations of the public good (2003: 32). Moreover, civil society denotes a utopian project of complete democratic self-government for Kocka; in other words: it is never fully realized.

If we summarize these different approaches, an image of civil society emerges with these main features: it is a sphere of societal self-organization in which conflicts are resolved civilly so that integrative and solidary effects ensue, and it can actively influence political discourses and decisions but also has a utopian aspect in envisioning a self-governing citizenry. What this boils down to, in terms of concrete actions, is an engaged involvement in associations, a revolutionary option facilitated by Enlightenment thought and its political consequences (Tenbruck, 1989). Associations provide an opportunity to freely coalesce with others across traditional social affiliations: you choose the association you want to join, or even found one according to your own ideas. The dissolution of feudal society was in no small part due to the diffusion of the principle of free association.

Civil society concepts were first revived by political actors: by Eastern European dissidents and civil rights activists fighting against the totalitarian Communist regimes in the 1970s. In the West, it was the new social movements, concerned with radically democratic reforms, that first utilized the concept. And in the early 1990s, it boomed in the US where, in the wake of "Reagonomics" and the hyper-individualism of the previous decade, concerns regarding the social cohesion of American society grew bigger.

Gift and civil society

Civil society fundamentally rests upon the logic of the gift and the principle of reciprocity. When a number of persons found an association and join their resources (time, money, ideas) for a purpose other than making a profit, they do so by means of mutually stabilizing gifts. This form of solidarity based on a pattern of reciprocal giving and receiving is of the utmost importance for civic self-organization. Associations do not function hierarchically, and neither do they rely on market-style, money-mediated exchanges. The logic of civil society is rooted in voluntariness, obligation, spontaneity, and personal ties. As we have seen (see Chapter 4), gift relationships are usually of a personal nature, whereas organizations in the spheres of state and economy tend to disrupt the interdependency characteristic of the gift. The voluntary associations of civil society, however, manage to merge unpersonal societal relations with the logic of the gift: in the institutionalized sphere of civil society, *unpersonal gift relationships* are put to the test. This is the great achievement of associations, clubs, and societies since the 19th century. They elevate the principle of the gift to the same level as the principles of hierarchy (state) and exchange (economy)—but only as long as civil society manages to assert itself against the other two spheres (see Caillé, 2015: 279–305).

The principle of the gift, then, is realized within a functioning civil society, and it reinforces these principles: a) the individual (the singular and different); b) the common (though not the homogenous); and c) the mediating force of egalitarian reciprocity (Rosanvallon, 2013). These principles do not necessarily contradict each other; they can even mutually increase each other. There is no guarantee for this of course. But if one successfully balances these principles, a common world is created which does not negate differences, a community not based on close personal ties but on mutual dependencies. Civic political action is not compatible with the idea of homogenous collectives but rather with the concept of agonistic challenges in the form of gifts that test the willingness to cooperate.

That democracy relies on such forms of civic action is a conviction shared by the convivialists. Caillé and the other authors of the first *Convivialist*

Manifesto stand in a specific tradition of French political thought, that of Claude Lefort and Cornelius Castoriadis. Both disenchanted former Trotskyists, Lefort and Castoriadis collaborated in the libertarian socialist group *Socialisme ou Barbarie* which published an eponymous journal between 1949 and 1965 (Rödel, 1990). *Socialisme ou Barbarie* was highly critical of Stalinist totalitarianism and came to reject Marxist-Leninist theory in general. Instead, they championed the idea of an autonomous, self-generating civil society submitting to no power and self-regulating by means of democratic procedures. Castoriadis and Lefort agreed that a state-centered conception of politics that views civil society as a depoliticized sphere would not do. They believed that power needs to remain within civil society and must not be absorbed by quasi-independent institutions of the state. As Lefort wrote, in a democracy "the place of power becomes an empty place" (1988: 152). The place of power, which in the past was literally embodied by the monarch, must not be filled with new symbolic instances like "nation" or "class" because this would mean to give in to yet another antidemocratic, totalitarian fiction. To overcome all social and political antagonisms, as claimed by totalitarian societies, in effect means to eliminate democracy.

The *Convivialist Manifestos* also champion civic self-organization above all state-centrist models of politics. This resonates with recent debates on the difference between politics (*la politique*) and the political (*le politique*): for Lefort, Caillé, and others, the political cannot be reduced to the institutionalized space of politics (elections, government institutions, and so on) but has to be understood in much more wide and open ways (Marchart, 2007; Caillé, 2014). Of particular importance in this context is Castoriadis' concept of a social imaginary as influentially espoused in his book *The Imaginary Institution of Society* of 1975. Castoriadis contends that society is based on processes of institutionalization that are partly brought about by new cultural creations. Societal visions always include what he calls "the imaginary," that is, references to the future which reach beyond what is given and involve questions like: who are we as a community, what do we want, what are we missing? Societies constitute by providing answers to these questions: "by doing" and often implicitly. For Castoriadis, the greatest fiction our modern societies cling to is that they are ever so rational. In fact, goals like growth and mastery of the world are anything but rational, and they can become downright threatening when what has been institutionalized, for example, technology, takes on a life of its own.

To think about a different, a convivial society means to think about new forms of the social imaginary, to imagine and create a new *conception* of society. The neoliberal imaginary, which currently dominates our world, functions inversely to totalitarianism: where the latter eliminates civil rights and the political to achieve a total community, neoliberalism eliminates solidarities and social cohesion in favor of individual liberties and market decisions. Convivial alternatives will have to prevail over neoliberalism in a Gramscian war of position for cultural hegemony. What convivialism aims at—in political, affective, and symbolic terms—is to make a different organization of our life together thinkable again. Before engaging in specific policies, people must be enabled to imagine radical alternatives to the status quo.

My conviction is that conviviality is anthropologically inscribed in human interactions. It existed at all times and in all cultures, even though it was never fully realized. Now perhaps more than ever we need to ask ourselves how we want to live with each other (including with nonhumans). We need to focus on the political organization of our societies and on enhancing the quality of our social relationships—as an end in itself, free of self-interest (Lichterman and Eliasoph, 2014). "The only legitimate kind of politics," the first *Convivialist Manifesto* says, "is one that is inspired by principles of common humanity, common sociality, individuation, and managed conflict" (Les Convivialistes, 2014: 30). Accordingly, the "convivialist test" consists of normatively surveying social and political orders with respect to four questions:

a) Do they take principles of common humanity, of equality and human dignity into account, or do some groups externalize the negative consequences of their actions on others?
b) Is sociality considered the greatest wealth?

In addition to these two rather communitarian aspects, two more dissociating aspects are named:

c) Are the social orders in question mindful of the principle of individuation, i.e., of the fact that we are all different and want to be recognized and appreciated in our individuality?
d) Are conflicts allowed but controlled before they can escalate? (see Les Convivialistes, 2014: 30–1)

The second *Convivialist Manifesto* of 2020 introduces two further principles of convivialism:

e) The principle of a "common naturality," which entails that "[h]umans do not live outside a nature" but "are part of it and are interdependent with it";
f) The principle of controlling human hubris, self-indulgence, and the desire for omnipotence, which "is in fact a metaprinciple" that "permeates all the others and is intended to serve as a regulator and safeguard for them" (Convivialist International, 2020: 7–8).

Convivialism thus identifies six normative criteria for evaluating social and political orders and their stances towards nature, criteria that have evolved from a reflection and normativization of everyday practices of conviviality.

Convivial practices

When they talk about "common decency," the *Manifestos'* authors evoke the work of Jean-Claude Michéa. The political philosopher took up George Orwell's phrase in his book *The Realm of Lesser Evil* (2009: 88ff.) to argue that humans are not primarily rational egoists but display a "psychological and cultural disposition to generosity and fidelity" (2009: 94), a disposition politics and society can rely on when establishing their normative structures. Michéa explicitly refers to the gift paradigm of Caillé and other M.A.U.S.S. authors and requires that we "anchor socialist practice in basic human virtues, the forgetting, rejecting or despising of which is always the distinctive sign of ideologists and men of power" (2009: 94).

Much can be made of this positive view of "human nature." After all, the liberalism of Western modernity is based on a converse view of man: the war of all against all is only prevented by channeling private vices into the field of the economy and each submitting to the unpersonal mechanism of the law—so that issues of morality and value are in effect banned from the public sphere. Behind this is the utilitarian worldview, "this axiomatic of interest, forged in the specific conditions of seventeenth-century Europe" (2009: 91). Michéa finds that such a society robs itself of all normative structures and thus destroys the conditions in which civility and solidarity can thrive. He calls for a "reassert[ion] of the socialist primacy of virtue over justice" (2009: 107), and this includes taking seriously the working class in its insistence on decency, morals, and safety and conceiving of these qualities as potentially socialist and anti-economic virtues. Both totalitarianism and liberalism, Michéa notes, "drown the 'common people' in the icy waters of egoistic calculation" (2009: 113): "These rival ideologies both base themselves on the same negative view of man": liberalism takes people "as they are" and utilizes their weaknesses in its pursuit of competition and consumerism; while totalitarianism wants to create a "perfect world" but mistrusts its actual citizens and controls their every move (2009: 113). Again: such a negative view of humanity can become a self-fulfilling prophecy, and in fact we have lived in a context in which little else seems meaningful for some decades now.

Let me contrast this with the idea of the *homo donator*. We do not need to prompt people to change and finally become virtuous. Such practices are already ubiquitous, though we can and should still reinforce them. Conviviality is lived in all kinds of social constellations: in families and friendships of course, in which utilitarian calculation never superseded the logic of the gift in the first place, but also in hundreds of thousands of civil society associations and projects, in volunteer work, in cooperatives, in the solidarity economy, in fair trade and ethical consumerism, in NGOs, peer-to-peer networks, Wikipedia, the commons movement and many other social movements. Humans do care for others, they do support others spontaneously and empathically. Indeed, in our everyday acts of appreciation, assistance, and generosity we realize a "communism" of sorts (Graeber, 2011).

This insight is accepted by an ever-increasing number of social scientists. Conviviality research is done, for instance, on multicultural urban life, showing that people tend to handle diversity very respectfully, a finding that corresponds with the dispositions described by Caillé, Graeber, and Michéa (see for example Laurier and Philo, 2006; Wessendorf, 2014). Nowicka and Vertovec point out that "[c]onviviality is established in different routine practices of giving and taking, talking and sharing, exchanging news and goods and so on. ... These banal interactions across social and ethnic boundaries give a sense of togetherness" (2014: 346). The tensions and conflicts that arise all the time in such situations must be translated and negotiated. Unlike the cosmopolitanism of the 1990s and early 2000s, conviviality focuses not on elites but on everyday interactions, mostly in urban settings, in which residents develop practices of communal living by learning to cope with difference and conflicts. In this sense, conviviality represents a transcultural competence and a form of minimal consensus (Heil, 2015). It is no coincidence that contributions to this debate frequently invoke the term *convivencia*, which calls up the (more or less) peaceful coexistence of Jews, Muslims, and Christians in medieval Spain (2015: 318).

Conviviality: an analytical and normative model

Let us now properly tie together the concepts of civil society and conviviality. The convivial organization type per se, in which the principle of reciprocal giving and taking without payment is most important, is the voluntary association (Caillé, 2000b). The associative self-organization of civil society is crucial for both the theory and the practice of conviviality: gratuitous, free exchanges and self-organized assemblies form the basis of a convivial social order that rejects a version of prosperity and the good life defined only by material and quantitative-monetary factors. According to Caillé and other convivialists, we must not solely rely on institutions of the state, as traditional forms of socialism did, because true political change does not come about by means of parties and governments. Liberalism, too, with its one-sided focus on markets, tends to overlook the potential inherent in societal self-organization.

Convivial associations display an aspect of experimentalism (Dewey). The practices they engage in are characterized by self-organization, reflective figuration, and flexibility; this is how they differ from practices in more rigid settings such as organizational hierarchies and competitive market relations. Convivial practices do not correspond to the logic of functional differentiation with its highly specific action logics and selective objectives—profit-making in the economy, maintenance of power in politics, or the quest for truth in science (Beckert, 2006). Instead, they aim at creating social contexts for the good life, ways of living that are not based on exclusivity and cost-externalization but socially and ecologically generalizable (Brand and Wissen, 2017). A convivial conduct of life is not primarily guided by self-interest, it is averse to hierarchies and commodification, and it champions a solidarity grounded in gift relationships and recognition.

We can now distinguish between four dimensions of conviviality in a stage model of sorts:

- It requires minimal standards of civility, that is, nonviolence and tolerance of difference.
- It consists in forms of interaction in which people meet without mutual stereotypes, derogatory attribution, and objectification.
- It emphasizes equality, non-hierarchy, and democratic forms of self-organization.
- It eschews cost-externalization, that is, living at the expense of others.

It is the role of the social sciences to empirically determine different forms of conviviality and ascertain what their respective preconditions are. As to what currently obstructs conviviality, the *Convivialist Manifestos* first and foremost identify our proliferating utilitarian culture. While this indeed is an important factor, many others may be found once we begin to empirically and analytically inquire why the inclinations and abilities of people to act convivially constantly get impaired by all kinds of institutional orders. We should also ask ourselves whether civic practices of conviviality are not much too weak to present a real alternative to capitalism. As many commentators have objected, at present, far from being an actual threat to the status quo, conviviality remains a niche phenomenon.

Real utopias of conviviality

In his remarkable book *Envisioning Real Utopias* (2010), Erik Olin Wright described three possible paths into a post-capitalist society. The Marxist path historically favored a radical break with capitalism in the shape of revolutions. In the light of the tragic consequences of the revolutions of the 20th century, this approach has lost all emancipatory credibility: totalitarian terrorism claimed millions of victims and the statist economy of real socialism simply did not work, least of all for the "labor force." Social democracy's path of reform has lost credibility as well, since the interventions of governments and unions did not really succeed in changing the balance of power. For Wright, it is clear that both revolution and reform have exhausted their possibilities. But what could an alternative strategy of transformation look like? Wright proposes that we start taking civil society seriously and "build new forms of social empowerment in capitalist society's niches and margins" (2010: 303). In other words, he wants us to engage in alternative ways of living that are both attractive and viable, to build "real utopias" in the here and now that anticipate the future and make ever more societies actually move in this direction.

Even though this strategy is partly rooted in anarchism, Wright is wary about a radical distancing from the state. What if, he asks, the emancipatory alternatives developed in societal niches actually threatened capitalism? Then the state would intervene, and smash these alternatives to save capitalism. This is why we need to form intelligent alliances with state actors. Contrary to what Marxist theory too simplistically claims, the state must balance very different interests, of which capitalism is just one. In fact, the state could itself develop an interest in introducing an unconditional basic income (UBI) to reduce unemployment and social exclusion in the face of digitalization and automation. Wright argues that a UBI, though it may at first serve capitalist interests, could take on a dynamic that erodes capitalism in the long run:

> A tax-financed unconditional basic income provided by the state would ... enable workers to refuse capitalist employment and choose, instead, to engage in all sorts of non-capitalist economic activities. ... UBI would underwrite a flowering of the solidarity economy, noncommercial performing arts, community activism, and much more. Unconditional basic income thus expands the space for sustainable socialist—socially empowered—economic relations. (Wright, 2016)

Regardless of how plausible Wright's proposals may be in detail, they show that our quest for new forms of living together must involve responding to three basic questions: Is the envisioned alternative desirable in normative terms? If so, is it practical, self-sufficient, sustainable, and does it prevent non-intended effects? And finally: Is it feasible, are there realistic strategies to enforce and establish it? Which groups of actors could have an interest in this to happen? How can we win them over? What kinds of resistance must we expect? All taken together, these questions form a little manual for transformation.

A post-capitalist society must give much more room to self-organization than state-socialist societies ever did. That kind of socialism was undemocratic, and it rested on an economic system in which state officials controlled everything and everyone. Mauss' and Wright's socialism is different. It is a socialism of voluntary association and civic cooperation which demands a radical democratization that would subject even the state to the power of civil society. What is more, an adoption of collective property does not necessarily imply that economic activities can no longer be coordinated in markets. We should not conceive of socialism and markets or socialism and democracy as opposites, but combine their principles to create a "third way."

I have no blueprint for an alternative social order, and in fact we should be suspicious of all who claim that they do. But what I have in mind is a radical democratic, post-capitalist alternative based on Dewey's concept of experimentalism: association and cooperation will unleash a potential of creative solutions, and interactions will allow us to imagine new worlds. Orthodox Marxists and state socialists opposed the principle of experimentalism because they believed in universal laws of history, in fixed stages of societal development that they were even willing to enforce through violence. But only in social experiments can we figure out how to adequately combine liberty and equality, and learn how we want to live and shape our economic activities in the future (Honneth, 2017). Therefore, experimental spaces have to be created, expanded, and defended. In the resulting society, the state would be mainly responsible for regulatory tasks, for defining general rules and enforcing them, though never by violence. A productive correlation between the state, markets, and civil society.

PART IV

Worlds of Conviviality

10

Aesthetic Freedom, or The Gift of Art

In the early 1980s, the cultural scholar Lewis Hyde famously claimed that art is a gift. To be sure, it is also a commodity, but even more than in the realm of economics, art belongs in the realm of the gift: while it could exist without markets, it could never escape its gift character, insisted Hyde (1983). In the last few years, these reflections have been taken up again, and there is also an increasing number of exhibitions, plays, and performances that deal with the issue of giving and exchanging. Usually, these works do not reflect the gift on an abstract level but aim at generating and performing gift relationships by means of interaction and participation (Hentschel, 2018).

There are also artworks, however, which address the gift in its more theoretical dimensions. Thus, a pioneering exhibition, which would inspire many more, took place in Milan in 2001: "The Gift: Generous Offerings, Threatening Hospitality" (Maraniello et al, 2001). The American artist Ted Purves (1964–2017) wanted to demonstrate the myriad forms of giving that pervade our everyday lives, and performed the gifting of artworks to the public in many collaborative projects; his book *What We Want Is Free* appeared in 2005. The motto of the "Black Market of Knowledge" in Graz, Austria, organized by German curator and dramaturg Hannah Hurtzig in 2007, was "The Gift and Other Violations of the Principle of Exchange." And in 2017, the exhibition "Who Pays?" took place at Kunstmuseum Liechtenstein which brought together "artistic positions from the 1960s to the present" to "examine our notions of wealth and poverty, of give and take, and of participation from different angles, concepts that nowadays are mostly reduced to purely economic aspects" (2017). The curators in Vaduz prominently featured Joseph Beuys' adage "Art = Capital" which expresses his trademark "extended definition of art." To Beuys, the greatest capital of a society is its citizens' creativity, a point to which I will return shortly.

Theoretizations

Now, what does the gift have to do with art, with beauty and aesthetics anyway? Is Hyde correct in assuming that there can be no art without gifts? To answer these questions, we have to go a little deeper.

One proposition I am making in this book is that humans have a propensity for giving, and that gifts contain aspects of surplus, unconditionality, and creativity that are constitutive for social orders. At the root of the social are non-equivalences and asymmetries, which is incompatible with the exchange of equivalent values that characterizes economic exchanges. Gifts comprise irreducible aspects of freedom and transgression. It is in this sense that gift practices involve aesthetic qualities, though these are not restricted to the realm of art but closely tied to life itself. For Dewey ([1934] 2008), living in effect means making aesthetic experiences. And these are especially fulfilling when they achieve closure: "A piece of work is finished in a way that is satisfactory; a problem receives its solution; a game is played through. ... There is interest in completing an experience. The experience may be one that is harmful to the world and its consummation undesirable. But it has aesthetic quality" ([1934] 2008: 42, 46). Such experiences always rely on an alternation of active and passive elements, of acting and accepting. And they are always about dealing with tensions and resistance in an interaction with our environment: "That which distinguishes an experience as aesthetic is conversion of resistance and tensions, of excitations that in themselves are temptations to diversion, into a movement toward an inclusive and fulfilling close. Experiencing like breathing is a rhythm of in*takings* and out*givings*" ([1934] 2008: 62; emphasis added). For Dewey, art and experience go hand in hand. And making experiences is not an individual affair, nothing innerly. Experiences are made by engaging with the (animate or inanimate) external world, and *aesthetic* experiences tear down the shrouds of everyday life; they run counter to all routine. According to Dewey, works of art provide "the only media of complete and unhindered communication between man and man that can occur in a world full of gulfs and walls that can limit community of experience" ([1934] 2008: 110). And: "[W]hat is not immediate is not esthetic" ([1934] 2008: 123).

Dewey's view of art is in the tradition of Kant and Schiller who conceived of beauty as a mode of experience that can lead individuals to more freedom and autonomy, a mode of free reflection that breaks with routines of thought, is disinterested, and has invigorating effects. However, when we experience beauty, we are always aware that others are capable of feeling the same. And we feel connected to others when we experience something beautiful together. While we cannot verify aesthetic experiences and judgments, cannot persuade others of the beauty of a painting or a composition, for Kant there still is an aspect of obligation manifest in the aesthetic, a "subjective universal validity" ([1790] 2007: 46) based on the "free play of the cognitive faculties," that is, imagination and understanding ([1790] 2007: 49).

Whereas Kant believed that aesthetic judgments primarily reveal something about the relation of a subject to an object, Friedrich Schiller was more interested in the work of art itself. He inquired how an object must be constituted for us to find it beautiful. And his answer was that beauty amounts to "freedom in appearance" ([1793] 1971: 34), which is true for objects as much as for nature. If we think back to the debates introduced in Chapter 8—to arguments concerning the agency of matter (Barad) or the self-organization (Varela) and subjectivity of all lifeforms (Weber)—it is hard to deny that freedom and autonomy are manifest in nature as well. It would follow that aesthetic practices are those in which the uniqueness, idiosyncrasy, and intrinsic value of things, artifacts, or lifeforms expresses itself. With Schiller we could say that an aesthetic experience of the world is one in which "freedom appears," in which the spirit of liberty spreads all over culture and nature: Latour's "parliament of things" (1993: 142). "That is Schillerian idealism," writes Rüdiger Safranski:

> when things and humans come into their own and perform their whole potential, their whole vitality in the game of life; when spirit is manifest in all that lives, all the way down to mute and fossil nature. Beauty can be found there if you know how to find it, and you will find it everywhere if you have experienced it first in the power of your own self-realization. (2004: 361; my translation)

Experiencing this kind of beauty reconciles two seemingly conflicting aspects. It allows the individual to remain true to him-/herself, or find him-/herself in the first place, while at the same time connecting them to other beings, human and nonhuman. Aesthetic experiences are thus closely related to the logic of the gift: no gift giving without freedom; no gift relationship without recognizing the otherness or foreignness of those who give, be it an artist or nature. If you see only yourself in an artwork, you just subsume it in your own patterns of perception and cognition. You do not allow yourself to be touched, to be struck by the uniqueness of the other. Only when both sides remain free, when they both may preserve their autonomy, does the gift succeed as an aesthetic experience. Rosa (2019) describes this experience of responding to and touching each other as one of "resonance." Such resonance comes about in a successful cycle of giving, receiving, and reciprocating.

However, if you get overwhelmed by a giver, if a gift is forced upon you, the relationship turns hierarchical and asymmetric. Yet, some may still perceive this as an aesthetic experience, as the enthusiastic response to art in some far-right populist circles shows. The identitarian movement, for instance, which identifies with a blood-and-soil ideology, celebrates aesthetic experiences of shock and overpowerment (Ullrich, 2018). Once again, Heidegger and Ernst Jünger are being referenced in this context, once again they want to ignite bonfires, raise awareness of ethnic identity, and dissociate from everything "other." By means of aesthetically driven political actions, these ideologues want to coax the European peoples into embracing and fighting for their own heritage, to merge them into a "great community." But such an aesthetic of shock and overpowerment contradicts the inherent logic of beauty: no more connections between individual "freedoms in appearance" but collective self-aggrandizement through *Gleichschaltung*; aesthetic totalitarianism instead of an aesthetic of conviviality.

Art, just like the gift, is deeply entangled with the imaginary. For one thing, it is of course our imagination that gives birth to works of art; for another, we construct possibilities of living in art that cannot be realized elsewhere. Over the last years, the concept of the imaginary has been much discussed in the social sciences as well, due to the insight that individuals and groups do not solely comprehend the world through cognition and language, but that more than anything it is images, beliefs, moods, emotions, and narratives that inform human thought and action. Social practices would be unthinkable without the imagination, and in fact one should conceive of the imaginary not so much as an individual phenomenon but as a collectively shared dimension of meaning that enables humans to create novelty. As Castoriadis ([1975] 1987) taught us, the imaginary spawns more than new knowledge. Cognitive, evaluative, and affective factors go hand in hand when we imagine different worlds, for example positive or negative potential futures. We are constantly surrounded by an abundance of imagined, affectively connoted realities; we constantly make present what is absent or has not happened yet. To be more precise, we visualize these things, according to the Western tradition's primacy of the visual. Next to images, fictions are an important field for experimentation with what is not yet present (Fluck, 1988): stories, movies, and predictions give shape to the stream of images and moods and thus make it intelligible to others. The imaginary becomes acceptable when the world it creates is plausible, when it could be real (Esposito, 2017). Artistic as well as scientific and stochastic fictions, that is, reveal possible realities; like the gift, the imaginary operates in a mode of "as if." Something is seen in a new light, and we pretend that this new perspective, this other world is possible. The imaginary therefore transcends the boundaries of social standards.

For the philosopher Christoph Menke (2013: 13–14), the essence of art lies in its inherent power to form and re-form, its pre-subjective, active, purposeless force of innovation. For him, art is more than a standardized social practice, based on the artist's socialization and training; it is so immensely liberating precisely because it transcends the social. This power of art, I propose, is the same that gifts comprise. Gifts also have the power to constitute and at the same time transcend the social. They can create new reciprocities and social cycles and at the same time disrupt them. For Menke, "every work of art is an experiment because every work of art has to start from scratch—if it does not, but considers art secure, a given, it is not a work of art" (2013: 82; my translation). In an experiment you create arrangements and situations in which, depending on the receptivity and activity of those involved, something can happen. No artwork can be created without an act of surrender on the part of the artist: they have to immerse themselves in a strange environment and give up what is familiar. "This is the basic definition of aesthetic freedom," writes Menke: "as a freedom of play (of the shaping and reshaping faculties) it is a freedom from laws, a freedom from normativity" (2013: 155; my translation). Aesthetic freedom, that is, the freedom of the extraordinary, agonistic gift, underlies our standardized social practices. Art, aesthetics, and freedom are not areas separate from life but necessary conditions for our everyday performances of habitual actions. Art cannot exist without this form of aesthetic freedom, and nor can it exist outside of standardized practices.

Summarizing the insights of Schiller, Dewey, and Menke we could say that aesthetic experiences occur when play (and thus risk, freedom, and power) enters practice. Play is in turn constituted by the gift, which contains an aesthetic force of liberation from normality and habit in social practice. From when we are born (or even before) we possess the capability to open ourselves to the world; to take, receive, and reciprocate; to decline and withdraw, to connect or disengage. In these capabilities lies the condition of the possibility of rehearsing standardized social practices, but also of transcending these social boundaries. It is on these aesthetic foundations of the gift, I suggest, that art is built.

Take, for example, the performing arts: in a theater, a reciprocity between actors and the audience cannot be taken for granted. The actors present something to the audience, they give something without knowing for sure if their gift will be received and reciprocated through gratitude and applause. Consequently, a theater performance has an agonistic character: it amounts to a challenge and transcendence of norms, a game with unknown rules, a risk. If the actors could count on the norm of reciprocity, it would not be art—the performance would fail due to a lack of contingence and aesthetic surplus. And if the surplus or the aesthetic power moved too far from the audience's expectations, the cycle of giving, receiving, and reciprocating would not come about. An aesthetic experience in the sense of Dewey can only occur when the agonistic gift, with its power to transcend social boundaries, finds resonance, when the experience finds closure. Put differently: the disruption of symmetry generates symmetry. Asymmetry is a necessary requirement for sociality, and in art this is quite evident.

Reconciling art and life?

Over the last few years, artists have attempted to interact with their audiences more directly. They increasingly leave aside the traditional mediating institution of the museum and engage in performances meant to elicit immediate responses. As Ingrid Hentschel explains, a "deliberate destabilization of the boundaries between art and society, performance and life, is taking place, a process that is linked to the performative turn in art and has been referred to as deaestheticization" (2018: 122; my translation). This kind of art is still subject to art's principal as-if mode, even though it is less fictionalized than traditional art and chiefly aims at developing new social practices. The opposite of *l'art pour l'art*, this "artivism" operates on the crossroads of autonomous art and political action. And in fighting for the good life, it tends to draw on the logic of the gift. Frequently, the focus is on urban spaces dominated by neoliberal consumerism, which are now being reclaimed for public use and participation via creative resistance (Schmitz, 2015).

These tendencies are somewhat reminiscent of 1970s political performance art. But today's "artivists" are less dogmatic, more playful. They are concerned with living utopias in the here and now, with trying out new forms of the good life: *ars vivendi*. Related phenomena include DIY's collaborative version DIT (Do it together) or open source (Baier et al, 2016). Here, the boundaries between art and everyday life become fluid. Other art projects target those between human and nonhuman life; for example by attempting to present the world from the perspective of animals or plants. All these practices are social experiments that rely on collective creativity and aim for different ways of living, for a new conviviality beyond neoliberal financial capitalism. That this kind of activism makes use of artistic methods is not surprising; after all, art lends itself to creating different forms of perception and alternative spaces of as-if.

When it comes to an extended definition of art, we cannot disregard the now classic work of Joseph Beuys (1921–86). Beuys' concept of the "social sculpture" and his famous statement that everyone is an artist have often been misconstrued. He did not, of course, claim that all humans have got what it takes to become an artistic genius. However, he did want us all to take an active part in the shaping of society, to contribute our creativity to the public good (Hasecke, 2016). Beuys expressed this in an equation: "art = human being = creativity = freedom."[1] He envisioned a radically democratic society of free, self-organizing human beings resisting the blind forces of technological and economic change. Everyone is a co-creator of society, at least potentially.

French 1960s situationism likewise radicalized art for the purpose of political change. That movement and its artivist successors of today are particularly good examples when it comes to demonstrating the ambivalences inherent in such an endeavor. Because while linking art, politics, and everyday life can open up new creative spaces for conviviality, it can also lead to an aesthetic of overpowerment and an insistence on black-and-white categories.[2]

"Ne travaillez jamais" ("Never work") was a slogan written upon a Paris wall in 1953, perhaps by Guy Debord himself, founder and leader of the Situationist International. Making art against the system and the state's centralized power was the main motivation of the situationists. The Situationist International was a revolutionary movement intent on going beyond all its avant-gardist forerunners (Dada, Surrealism, Lettrism) in radically transforming everyday life itself. In terms of theory, situationism is close to Marxist thought, though rather to the heretics of *Socialisme ou Barbarie* and philosopher Henri Lefebvre than to orthodox Marxism. The situationists questioned hierarchies and classes and aimed to abolish capitalism and consumerism. Their big moment came in May 1968 when they played a major role in the revolutionary events in Paris.

To live life poetically, apart from the order of the social world, is the situationists' prime objective. In France, their ideas were adopted into popular culture, and their legacy can still be detected in art, advertising, literature, and so on. Their specific type of wordplay has become a permanent feature of French humor, even if those who engage in it might not always be aware of its roots. One of situationism's protagonists, Raoul Vaneigem, knew how much their vision owed to the paradigm of the gift. In his book *The Revolution of Everyday Life*, he wrote that "a truly new society can be founded only on the principle of the gift" ([1967] 2012: 16). "Everyday life embodies an energy," Vaneigem insisted, "which can move mountains and abolish distances" ([1967] 2012: 46). The distances he wants to abolish are those between us and other people, and in fact between us and ourselves. The path towards this goal, he suggests, leads via the creation of parallel micro societies which then experimentally develop alternatives to life in mainstream society.

Decades later, these ideas were taken up by the so-called Invisible Committee. Although anonymous (as its name suggests), everybody in France knows that Julien Coupat is a member of that group. Previously part of the Tarnac Nine—a gang of communards arrested on charges of sabotage and terrorism, but eventually acquitted—Coupat, along with his far-left co-authors in the Invisible Committee, is sometimes considered situationism's anarchist heir. In their view, the established societal order can only be overcome through new forms of social practice in which changed social conditions and changed selves go hand in hand. For the members of the Invisible Committee, there is no separation between inside and outside, between self and society, or culture and nature. In their militant and at the same time quite poetical texts, they advocate the shattering of Western dualisms and values. For instance, they consider the striving for individual self-realization to be closely related to alienation: "The more I want to be me, the more I feel an emptiness" (The Invisible Committee, 2010). All three of their pamphlets published so far counter this tendency with a theory of the interdependency of everything. After all, we are "[t]ied in every way to places, sufferings, ancestors, friends, loves, events, languages, memories, to all kinds of things that obviously *are not me*" (2010). Our cult of individuality relies on making invisible the myriad connections between us and others. But "[w]e can't rid ourselves of what binds us," and we should not want to. Because as it is, life in capitalism amounts to "pure boredom, passionless but well-ordered, empty, frozen space, where nothing moves apart from registered bodies, molecular automobiles, and ideal commodities" (2010).

The Invisible Committee envisions communities that experiment with new forms of sharing, unconditionality, and collective affectivity. In passages that sound like Latour in *Facing Gaia*, they stress that the left should let the Earth take center stage, the way the indigenous peoples of Latin American do in reaction to the neo-colonialist exploitation of their resources (The Invisible Committee, 2015). "There is no humanity, there are only earthlings and their enemies," that is, those who consciously destroy the earth system. For the Invisible Committee, the Western way of life and its consequences are "the real catastrophe" (2015). The alternative consists of making contact and acknowledging interdependency, "bring[ing] into immediate play parts of beings that discover themselves to be on the same level, that are felt as continuous" (The Invisible Committee, 2017). "This continuity between fragments is what is experienced as 'community.' An *assemblage* is produced. It's what we experience in every real encounter. Every encounter carves out a specific domain within us where elements of the world, the other, and oneself are mingled indistinctly" (The Invisible Committee, 2017). In the booklet I just quoted from, *Now* of 2017, the Committee appears more resigned than ever when it comes to the possibility of revolution or "the coming insurrection" (as was the title of their first pamphlet in 2010). Instead, they are now mainly concerned with a collective "deepening of perceptions":

> It makes no sense to share things if one doesn't begin by communizing the ability to see. Without that, living the communist way is like a wild dance in utter darkness; one crashes against the others, one gets hurt, one inflicts bruises on the body and the soul without meaning to and without even knowing exactly who to be angry with. Compounding everyone's capacity for seeing in every domain, composing new perceptions and endlessly refining them, resulting in an immediate increase of potential, must be the central object of any communist development. (The Invisible Committee, 2017)

Communism as an exercise in perception, as *aisthesis*, an aesthetic project.

The anarchism of the Invisible Committee not only eludes the political power struggle; they also want nothing to do with the economy. Instead of building an alternative economy, they declare, we should quit the logic of exchange altogether:

> Depending on the degree of proximity between beings, there is a commonality of goods, a sharing of certain things, exchange with an adjusted reciprocity, mercantile exchange, or a total absence of exchange. And every form of life has its language and its notions for expressing this multiplicity of regimes. Making the bastards pay is good warfare. When you love you don't count the cost. ... [E]xiting the economy is being able to ... push the hostile relations—and the sphere of money, accounting, measurement—as far away as possible. It's to banish to the margins of life that which is presently its norm, its core, its essential condition. (The Invisible Committee, 2017)

If this sounds to you like the usual—playfully subversive and ultimately harmless—deliberations of leftist intellectuals, think again. It is not for nothing that the Invisible Committee has been associated with violence in the past; for instance, in the aftermath of the riots during the 2017 G20 summit in Hamburg. Also, in their publications, passages can be found that defend the deeds of the German "black bloc" and other autonomist groups. The Committee holds that violence has the potential to create something divine and thus disrupt history. This inevitably reminded me of the "Critique of Violence" ([1921] 2007) by Walter Benjamin who believed that such violence can only be exerted by God: "divine violence." The Committee's writings are also reminiscent of George Sorel's mythology of violence. In his *Reflections on Violence* ([1908] 1999), which became a source of inspiration for far-left as well as far-right movements, Sorel claims that violent general strikes can unfold a mobilizing force. The Committee, too, speaks of violence as a mobilizing and community-strengthening experience; it is meant to fill activists with enthusiasm, create new collective values, and transgress existing boundaries of identity. Such a rhetoric which highlights the extra-ordinariness and liberatory potential of violence goes back to the early decades of the 20th century (Joas, 2003), when both communist and fascist movements regarded violence as a means of boosting solidarity among their members and increasing their dissociation from the enemy. The same could be said of the anti-colonial violence advocated by Frantz Fanon in the early 1960s. And in the case of 21st-century radical anarchism this enemy, embodying state violence, is usually the police.

What is most relevant about the Invisible Committee's writings in terms of our subject matter, however, is their apparent longing for an aesthetic freedom and power that is capable of bursting all the bonds of traditional orders, their pursuit of community and connection. Their pamphlet of 2017 is primarily a poetic intervention. By means of an aesthetic of intensity they want to trump the tedious political processes of democracy. Their flirt with violence is an expression of the same romantic desire for a freedom that transcends all norms, all order, that moved their parents' generation of leftist, bourgeois intellectuals 50 years ago. While the desire to be ungovernable and live in a mode of giving is beautifully performed in their writings, their fetishization of violence, insurrection, and states of exception makes the delicate poetry of the gift collapse into an aesthetic of overpowerment. The example of the Invisible Committee shows how close creativity, connectedness, and aesthetic freedom can be to violence. But their most radical gesture is seeing art and communism as exercises in perception.

11

Pluriversalism: Towards a European and Global Politics of Conviviality

Over its history, capitalism has appeared in many guises: as Manchesterism, as postwar welfare statism, as authoritarianism in some post-communist countries, and as our current globalized neoliberal financial capitalism. What all these historical varieties of capitalism have in common is that they were dependent on utilizing resources that are almost for free. This was possible through exploitation on a grand scale: of the colonies in the Global South, of the labor-power of women for the purpose of social reproduction, and of nature. Ostensibly, capitalism is based on economic exchanges between equals, but the liberal ideas of equal property rights and equal chances of participation in the economy obscure that the parties involved in most of these exchanges are in fact very unequally endowed with power.

We are currently experiencing a fundamental crisis of the Western world order: 500 years of European and 100 years of American dominance are coming to an end. Western colonialism is giving way to a growing influence of other powers, especially China. For many Europeans, the logical consequence of this development is that we must do our utmost to save our privileges and our wealth. But this will neither be possible, nor is it really desirable, for ecological reasons as well as reasons of social justice. We need a completely new societal vision, one that leaves behind economism and the externalization of social and ecological problems and aims for convivialism instead. So which ideas could we resort to in this endeavor? As we have seen with Mauss, it is possible to draw on old European practices of giving in order to create a solidarity economy. Beyond that, Western political thinkers seem curiously unimaginative—perhaps because, as the Canadian author and activist Naomi Klein writes:

> [i]n the West, there is little popular memory of any other kind of economic system. There are specific cultures and communities—most notably Indigenous communities—that have vigilantly kept alive

memories and models of other ways to live, not based on ownership of the land and endless extraction of profit. (2017: 220)

So if we want to counter "capitalism's matrix" (2017: 220), we have to look elsewhere and learn from the Global South. Just saying no to the banking system, to greed and hubris, to populism and nationalism is not enough. We need a yes: positive visions for our future life together on earth.

Colonialism and postcolonialism

Europe has been telling others how to solve their problems for 500 years, but now it hardly knows how to solve its own: the European Union has been in a crisis for over a decade, which has found its most conspicuous expression in Brexit. European obstinacy has a lot to do with its past as colonial ruler of the world, a role it still struggles to outgrow (Santos, 2017). Development policy, human rights policy, humanitarian aid: all these reputedly "universal" concepts are deeply Eurocentric, and we only now begin to question them. A new era of European learning—as opposed to teaching—must be grounded in horizontal relations with the Global South. Differences must be acknowledged and respected.

The "South" is both outside and inside of Europe. It comprises the former colonies, whose natural resources are now being extracted by transnational corporations based in the North and whose countries are coping with poverty, displacement, and ecological catastrophes. It also comprises Europe itself as a place of immigration: think of the descendants of Turkish "guest workers" in Germany, the big Maghrebi community in France, or the millions of Syrians and Afghans who escaped war and hardship quite recently. Finally, the "South" includes the countries of Southern Europe as peripheral places: during the European debt crisis of 2009–14, Portugal, Italy, Greece, and Spain were regarded as a political, economic, and cultural problem sphere unable to keep up with the savings principles of the North, as "PIGS."

There have been several attempts to counter such prejudices by declaring the Mediterranean a cultural sphere characterized by a high degree of civilization. Thus, Albert Camus ([1937] 2010) submitted that without "Mediterranean thinking" the project that is Europe is bound to fail. Camus believed the Mediterranean to be an area of close regional ties and a common culture of simplicity and moderation, and he contrasted this to the cold, instrumental rationality of the North with its inherent danger of self-destruction—a topos that pervades socio-ecological thought, from fears of a nuclear war to current concerns about global warming. Of late, the Mediterranean has been conceived of as a space that in many ways connects Europe, North Africa, and Western Asia and could thus in the future play a peacemaking role in the conflict-ridden Middle East (Leggewie, 2011).

This idea goes back to Hannah Arendt who proposed a Mediterranean federation in the 1940s, not least as a "reasonable solution of the Palestine question" ([1943] 2007: 197). But the fact remains that a glaring economic and cultural split divides Europe, and it is clear that this will not be fixed by a submission of the South to the principles of the North. Europe's South and its responses to the crisis of the EU must be taken more seriously. However, when Nicolas Sarkozy tried to establish a "Mediterranean Union" in 2007—an organization that would have included only countries, on all three continents, with direct access to the Mediterranean Sea—Chancellor Merkel vetoed the plan out of concern for the future of the EU.

But back to the actual, the "Global South." In Europe, we should get used to the fact that in regions of the world which were appropriated and exploited by our forebears, European and Indigenous traditions have merged into a hybrid knowledge that we would do good to adopt. But this would require overcoming deep-seated prejudices which also go back to colonialism and its underlying power relations between collectives. A minority of colonial masters unwilling to adapt to local circumstances made fundamental decisions about the lives of their subjects, decisions that were mainly based on their own political and economic interests (Osterhammel, 1997). The colonies were peripheral constructs permanently dependent on a distant center. Colonialism was shaped by racism and a sense of mission: the goal was to "civilize the savages" and convert them to the supposedly superior European religion, culture, and economy.

Colonialism proper came to an end in the aftermath of World War II, but colonialist racism and its structures of exploitation did not. While the former colonies are now formally sovereign nations, they are still far from independent, in particular economically. Policies of "development," as initiated by US President Truman in 1949, did little to change this (and were not designed for that purpose in the first place). Still, the countries of the South are bound in economic relations with the North from which they rarely profit. Despite all "foreign aid," the unfair relations of exchange continue to this day (McCarthy, 2009). In 1960, when decolonization was well under way, the per capita income in the richest countries of the world was 32 times higher than in the poorest county; in the year 2000, after four decades of foreign aid, that number had climbed to 134. Even more shockingly, if we add all financial resources flowing between poor and rich countries, it turns out that the "developing countries" actually contribute much more than they receive. "What this means," Jason Hickel (2017) concludes, "is that developing countries are net creditors to the rest of the world—the exact opposite of the usual narrative." Global justice and fair trade? Not yet.

The same is true of racism. Even though the pseudo-scientific race concept has been utterly discredited, racist discriminations still occur all the time. As the example of the so-called ethnopluralism championed by the alt-right shows, the post-biological neo-racism of today is compatible with formal concessions to liberty and equality. Racism and nationalism have been closely related since the 19th century. After all, both are all about distinguishing a "we" from a "they": "both invoked imagined collectivities with imagined similarities and differences ... and both identified certain 'others' as special threats to racial and national purity" (McCarthy, 2009: 8). Nationalist racisms—founded not on biology but on culture—play a major role in current debates on immigration, and just as with biological racism, they regard certain bodily differences as indications of supposed differences in "culture" and "mentality." It seems that the overall decrease of racism around the world has destabilized Western, White identities, and the simultaneous reinvigoration of far-right racist ideologies can be understood in terms of a defense of White privilege: culturally, politically, and economically (Mishra, 2017).

When groups or entire societies fail in their attempts at establishing prosperity and Western-style institutional orders, this is all too often ascribed to shortcomings concerning values, attitudes, or habits. Such culturalist forms of racism serve to legitimize a policy of capacity building, so that one can avoid compensation or tackling the real, structural issues. In effect, the argument that the poor and excluded can only help themselves legitimizes inequality. And this belief lies at the heart of all "development" efforts. The former colonies, Western politicians say, are ultimately responsible for their own achievements, and if they fail to climb up the ladder of development, it is their own fault—and not that of their former colonial rulers which continue to exploit them. The development concept, too, rests upon a we/they dichotomy, according to which the only way for "them" to "develop" is to become more like "us." The objective of development policies is to spread the Western ideals of prosperity and democracy. What the West should do instead, the philosopher and political theorist Thomas McCarthy thinks, is to concede its part in creating global inequality and finally make up for the damages: "Five centuries of imperialism and racism did not disappear without a trace in the fifty years since the postwar successes of decolonization and civil rights struggles" (2009: 17).

From universalism to pluriversalism

Of course Western modernity is not just the origin of inequality and exploitation. There is humanism, respect for human dignity, the idea of a universal morality, and the concept of human rights. If it were not for these European traditions, we would not be able to criticize unjust power relations to begin with. To advocate a normative relativism—which assumes that cultural traditions co-exist apart from another and should leave each other alone—means to throw the baby out with the bathwater. What such a relativism comes down to is the idea that a moral judgment is valid if it corresponds to the values of the judging person's society. The problematic underlying assumption here is that traditions are then the ultimate ethical standards, which would make solutions to intercultural conflicts of a moral nature impossible.

Western universalism, which harks back to the Enlightenment conception of human reason, conceives of the world as one. In the end, there is just one truth from this perspective, and one universal morality. Though within the universalist camp, there exist different opinions as to the degree to which normative issues are considered universalizable (Habermas, 1996), the consensus is that moral discourses serve the impartial regulation of conflicts and that questions of universal justice—and not, for instance, questions of how to live a good life within a specific community—are by far the most important. In recent decades, however, Western universalism has been attacked for being little more than a disguise for Western power politics. The West, the argument goes, has universalized its own cosmology and made it the norm all over the world, a cosmology that alleges a nature–culture divide and absolutizes individual freedom, autonomy, and rationality. Its critics further criticize that Western universalism is based on an ontology of separation: its reflections proceed from separate entities, not interdependencies. It is for this reason in particular that the concept of *pluri*versalism was introduced.

Pluriversalism takes seriously the fact that there are a variety of different cosmologies and moralities which correlate and argue with each other and are connected within power relations (Mignolo, 2011: 213ff.). Their interdependence cannot be detached from the global inequalities that are the legacy of colonialism and racism. To make the case for a pluriversalism means to embrace the decolonization of thought and action and to acknowledge that the West has gone too far in championing the autonomous individual. "Relational ontologies" like pluriversalism "eschew the divisions between nature and culture, individual and community, and between us and them" (Escobar, 2011: 139). This implies that we should take into account forms of nonhuman world-making as well. Because as Anna Lowenhaupt Tsing writes in *The Mushroom at the End of the World*:

> each organism changes everyone's world. Bacteria made our oxygen atmosphere, and plants help maintain it. Plants live on land because fungi made soil by digesting rocks. As these examples suggest, world-making projects can overlap, allowing room for more than one species. Humans, too, have always been involved in multispecies world-making. (2015: 22)

To prevent relativist interpretations, this pluralism of worlds and world-makings ought to be tied to a universalism. With respect to human coexistence, Caillé calls for as much plurality as is possible without jeopardizing social coherence; cultures must be equal but also have the right to differ radically from one another. Thus, pluriversalism amounts to a "relativistic kind of universalism" (Caillé, 2011a: 93; Les Convivialistes, 2014: 14). From a convivialist perspective, two demands follow from these arguments:

- On behalf of a common humanity and sociality we must globally fight self-indulgence, that is, extreme wealth at the cost of extreme poverty elsewhere.
- Instead of a cultural hegemony of the West, there should be a maximum of plurality and equality between the nations. Currently, the West tends to conceive of itself as solely a giver (of "development," money, technology, weapons, education, democracy, and so on). But mutual recognition requires alternating acts of giving and receiving.

In other words, we need what the Portuguese sociologist Boaventura de Sousa Santos (2014) has called "epistemic justice." Over the course of colonialism, the "Epistemologies of the South" were suppressed or even destroyed: local knowledges were pushed aside and existing political institutions removed. And yet there remain more approaches to knowing the world than the scientific-rationalist model the West would like to believe. But as long as we keep believing that no valid knowledge is being produced in the South, as long as we accept only the Western cosmology, existing solutions to our current global problems will be overlooked, ignored, or treated with contempt. In addition (and prior) to alternative forms of living together, we need an alternative understanding of alternatives because "there is no global social justice without global cognitive justice" (Santos, 2014: 124).

We could say, then, that a "sociology of absences is needed" (2014: 207) which would make the epistemologies of the South visible again. To solve the global problems, we cannot just rely on the experiences of the North. Recognizing alternative, non-scientific knowledges will not devalue scientific knowledge. It will demonstrate its limits though and reveal that it is just one form of knowledge among others. Scientific knowledge will one day enable us to travel to the moon, but indigenous knowledge allows us to protect biodiversity in Amazonia (see Santos, 2014: 206). Thus, every knowledge is limited. However, the North refuses to acknowledge what it does not know and what others do; it is convinced that its own hegemonial epistemology is the only (valid) one. A pluriversal dialog, Santos believes, would spawn important new insights. Cultural translations are required, and a cultivation of what already exists in germinal form: a "sociology of emergences" (*passim*) which identifies promising solutions and elaborates them.

In this way, important blends of indigenous and Western thought have emerged in recent years. Article 71 of the constitution of Ecuador, adopted in 2008, was the first piece of legislation to award rights to nature:

> Nature, or Pacha Mama, where life is reproduced and occurs, has the right to integral respect for its existence and for the maintenance and regeneration of its life cycles, structure, functions and evolutionary processes. All persons, communities, peoples and nations can call upon public authorities to enforce the rights of nature. ... The State shall give incentives to natural persons and legal entities and to communities to protect nature and to promote respect for all the elements comprising an ecosystem. (cited in Perra, 2020: 344–5)

The "rights of nature" concept is a hybrid phenomenon: it combines the Western conception of (human) rights with an indigenous conception of nature (Acosta, 2010). It is closely tied to the concept of *buen vivir*, which has been popularized in recent years by the Ecuadorian economist Alberto Acosta, who also chaired the country's Constitutional Assembly in 2007–08. In sketching a new social and ecological vision of the "good life," *buen vivir* draws on Andean indigenous knowledges that emphasize communitarianism, and it opposes conventional (Northern, capitalist) models which assume a linear progression of "development" and aim solely at economic growth. The break with anthropocentrism here clears the way for a recognition of the intrinsic values of nature and the interdependency of all living beings (Acosta, 2015a).

Other examples of cosmologies that contain much potential when it comes to solving issues of social and ecological justice are Ecoswaraj (India) and Ubuntu (Southern and East Africa). Also referred to as Radical Ecological Democracy, Ecoswaraj (or ecological "self-rule") is a South Indian movement which is made up of various poor and lower-caste communities and is concerned with ecological sustainability, social well-being and justice, direct democracy, economic democracy, as well as knowledge commons (Kothari, 2016). Ubuntu had its heyday in post-apartheid South Africa, but the concept is known under different names in all Bantu countries (and beyond). Based on a relational ontology according to which all humans are closely connected, the main insight behind Ubuntu is that "a person's humanity is dependent on the appreciation, preservation and affirmation of other persons' humanity" (Eze, 2008: 387). Similar to European conviviality, the concept is communitarian in that it stresses the individual's duties towards the community: respect, care, forgiveness.

Beyond "development"

What is common to all these concepts is their alternative understanding, or rather, their rejection of the notion of development. Attached to that term and its varieties (modernization, sustainable development, and so on) is the promise of progress. It divides the world into a sphere of "developed" societies and one that is "undeveloped," "underdeveloped," or at best "developing": European and North American societies are the role models that other nations are supposed to emulate. Over time, the emphases and objectives of development policies have changed: creating markets, establishing a functioning health and education system, and so on. However, economic growth has continuously been considered to be the prime criterion for assessing a society's prospects for development. Just as constant is the view that "developed countries" are giving something to "developing countries," namely, "development." "Giving development" goes along with all kinds of disparagements and tensions (Karagiannis, 2004: 105ff.), and development relations are characterized by a fundamental inequality between those who give and those who receive. A reversal of these roles is unthinkable because one of the parties is thought to have nothing of value to give. This results in self-ascriptions as modern and progressive on the one hand and, fatally, deficient or backward on the other. To be sure, over the last years development policy has moved in the direction of an economic exchange between North and South, but in fact only one side benefits from such inequal transactions.

In response to this fundamental imbalance of the international constellation of giving and receiving, the concept of development has of late been challenged. In Latin America in particular, the neoliberalist spirit of the development paradigm was much criticized by leftist governments which countered it by making fighting poverty a top priority. But, as Acosta objects, "their policies are nevertheless informed by the development concept: just like colonialism, they espouse a development policy dedicated to the exploitation of resources and farmland for exports—what has been called 21st-century extractivism" (2015b: 192; my translation). The Western conception of development and modernity first came under attack by so-called dependency theory in the 1950s through to the 1970s. Marxist theorists like Paul A. Baran (1957) or André Gunder Frank (1967) pointed out that underdevelopment was not a historical phase, to be followed by development, but the consequence of the exploitation of the South by colonialism and capitalism. But even though this heterodox perspective criticized basic tenets of the Western model of development, it clung to the same old idea that development can best be achieved through economic growth, that is, through industrialization and an efficient utilization of natural resources.

As a result of the debates on the limits to growth (Meadows et al, 1972) and the necessity of ecological sustainability, since the 1990s the focus has been on "sustainable development," meant to reconcile ecology and economy. In particular, the 1992 UN conference in Rio, also known as "Earth Summit," represents a watershed of sorts since it yielded a declaration and an agenda in which the right to sustainable development was incorporated for the first time (Adloff and Neckel, 2019). This is also when the talk of a green economy, of green growth, and a green new deal started. The idea is that increasing technological efficiency will result in a decoupling of economic growth and the use of resources. However, there is no indication whatsoever that this solution, which amounts to little more than a trade-off between economic growth on the one hand and a preservation of natural resources on the other, really works (Jackson, 2009).

By contrast, concepts like *buen vivir* and degrowth offer real alternatives to the development paradigm itself. Consequently, they were summarized under the heading of "post-development," a term that goes back to authors like Wolfgang Sachs, Gustavo Esteba, and Arturo Escobar whose work deconstructed the development concept, and especially its inherent notion of linear progress, decades ago (Demaria and Kothari, 2017). Post-development discourses and practices are concerned with the establishment of a plurality of models which differ radically from Western growthism: relational, non-anthropocentric ontologies that reject the nature–culture dichotomy; local practices of a solidarity economy; as well as community-centered ideas of the good life (Escobar, 2011; Acosta and Cajas-Guijarro, 2020). Post-development is opposed to both capitalist and socialist concepts of development (Gudynas, 2013) and thus represents a fundamental critique of modernity as it is similarly voiced in the Global North by proponents of eco-feminism, deep ecology, Gaia theory, and post-growth approaches.

To take the relationships between countries of the North and South to a new, convivial level and overcome the linear concept of development, horizontal, equitable relationships are needed. But how can such relationships be established in a world of post-colonial power asymmetries? How can the ideal of a common humanity be realized when a part of humanity was denied the status of being human for centuries? Acknowledging cultural diversity and formally recognizing the dignity of all is not enough. We need to dissolve the power mechanisms that continue to produce such discriminations. But that can only be achieved by way of political reconciliation and material compensation.

The political theorist Ina Kerner (2015) suggests that extraordinary gifts could initiate a process of forgiveness and the creation of a community of equals. Of course it is not the job of the degraded and exploited to forgive those who have caused them so much suffering; the obligation is entirely that of the Global North. Already Frantz Fanon (1925–61), the Caribbean psychiatrist and anti-colonial cultural critic, thought that reparations were essential. Kerner sees them as prerequisite for "a twofold new beginning: economically for the post-colonies and politically for their relation with the North" (2015: 235; my translation). Compensations would materially confirm that an injustice has occurred and that the North owes something to the South. This may well be the only way to build a world in which both sides are on equal terms. It would be up to the South to decide whether or not to accept the offer of economic and moral compensation. After all, it is always the receiving party that decides if a gift relationship among equals comes about, in which both are then givers as well as receivers. Only thus can the convivialist principle of a common humanity be realized.

For Europe, this would mean to move away from the logic of a so-called *Realpolitik*. It would be unwise for Europe to assume the role of the world's policeman, once played by the US, even in its own periphery. But what could an effective international fight against Islamic terrorism look like which ultimately results in more conviviality and not less? This is a difficult question to answer of course, but a sensible first step would be to reassess and revise the traditional Western strategy concerning the Middle East—and concede that it has been based on colonialism, oppression, arbitrary favoritisms and demarcations, an expropriation of mineral resources and interference with their extraction and distribution, armament orders, and a permanent struggle for spheres of influence. The Middle East's experience with modernity has been one of exploitation and despotism. This we need to acknowledge if we want to face the question why "so many people feel offended and humiliated by the West and why terrorism has at its command a seemingly inexhaustible reservoir of people" (Ulrich, 2015; my translation). The (post-) migrant reality of many youths in France, Belgium, or Germany is anything but convivial, and for lack of ideological alternatives some of them come to join the global jihad.

A new, convivial policy towards countries of the Middle East would have to begin by conceiving of their history as a failed project in colonialism, marked by violations of the West's own declared ideals on a massive scale. A new chapter of Western foreign policy can only be written once the former colonial masters and imperial powers very publicly plead guilty—to their colonialism, their racism, their self-interested behavior, their acts of caprice. Reparations, though no doubt hard to imagine for many today, would guarantee justice for all under conditions of decolonization.

These reflections on the Global North–South relationship may be transferred to the circumstances within Europe as well. After the financial crisis, the so-called European troika, made up of the International Money Fund, the European Central Bank, and the European commission, imposed radical reforms and austerity measures on Greece in return for desperately needed aid. Privatizations and cuts to salaries, retirement and health care benefits were brutally enforced. Regardless of the question whether these cuts made economic sense, such policies can only be interpreted in terms of debt bondage and outright humiliation. The convivial way of making up for this, thus bringing about a new beginning, would be a policy of granting Greece more debt relief (Leggewie, 2015).

The US would also do well to be guided by the gift-related concept of compensation as regards the injustices of the past. The violent removal of indigenous tribes—some speak of a genocide—as well as 200 years of slavery and racial segregation have given rise to passionate debates. As the American author Ta-Nehisi Coates argued forcefully in 2014, only reparations would be capable of initiating a much-needed process of reconciliation in the US.

Quo vadis, Europe?

In conclusion, I want to briefly reflect on Europe's inner and outer state. Its current crisis has put the question of what a convivial Europe could look like firmly on the agenda, and much of what I said in previous chapters about economism and growthism can be transferred to this issue. But beyond that, the crisis of Europe has raised the question of what "Europe" actually means to us. Should Europe as a project be carried forward, even intensified, or should nation states be given back part of the sovereignty they have lost? The latter solution is favored not just by right-wing populists but also by some leftist politicians—for instance, Jean-Luc Mélenchon in France or Sahra Wagenknecht in Germany. To me this is the wrong way forward. As the philosopher Étienne Balibar said in an interview in 2018, "the leftists who want to revive the nation as a bulwark against neoliberalism are mistaken. ... We need a united Europe, but not as it is now" (my translation). This different Europe would have to be post-national and feature a strong parliamentarian counterweight to the executive arms and bureaucracy of the EU. It would have to take seriously again the idea of social justice, prevent further cuts to the welfare state, and stop the deregulation of financial capitalism. It would have to pursue paths towards a solidarity economy that is free of any growth imperatives. This appears to be the only way to exit the fatal race for competitiveness between economic regions. We could then ask what Europe may learn from the South, perhaps starting with the South of Europe, and begin leaving behind a world of asymmetries and exploitation.

For a while, Europe was justified in considering itself the center of the world. But that time is now over: Europe has become provincialized (Chakrabarty, 2000). Instead of aspiring to a new powerful role in world politics, we would be well-advised to expand European humanism, in order to save it. We should strive for true equality—between people, between nations, between humans and nonhumans. Because beyond the objective of maintaining our prosperity, there is really just one *raison d'être* for a unified

Europe (see Offe, 2016: 87ff.): preserving peace among the nations, curbing aggressive nationalisms, and furthering social inclusion—all things that Europe has (more or less) successfully achieved during the last 75 years. In contradistinction to the US, a united Europe could play a role in foreign policy that relies on soft, not hard power. Its capacity for self-criticism and willingness to condemn injustices represent a specific potential that we should not waste. Their own bloody history—from the wars of religion to colonialism, two World Wars and the Holocaust—has taught Europeans to favor post-national positions. This disposition we should build on in creating a vision of a post-colonial and post-capitalist Europe, a society of conviviality.

Unfortunately, there are not many progressive civil society actors that operate in all of Europe. Most organizations are either local/regional, national, or global in orientation and have little influence on a continental level; we should thus be prepared that the project of rebuilding the European project will demand realism and a willingness to compromise. For the most part, leftist positions are much concerned with *global* justice. And they should be—we owe this to the normative principle of a common humanity, or rather, to our responsibility for all life on earth. However, since humans as social creatures always strive for community and collective identity, a convivial Europe has to grant a right to rootedness as much as to rootlessness. Of course, that rootedness can no longer express itself in an aggressive exclusion of others or at their expense in other ways.

Let us return once again to Marcel Mauss. In the course of his work on the subject of the nation, Mauss came to the sociological insight that collective identity is no fixed matter ([1920] 1969). Rather, group identities depend upon exchanges with other groups, and it makes a great difference if these groups antagonize or compete with each other, or if they cooperate. Nations, too, *were made*—whether from below, that is, by national movements, or, which was much more often the case, from above, that is, by means of governmental decrees relating to education, conscription, linguistic homogenization, and so on. A "social division of labor" (Durkheim, [1893] 1964), consisting of cooperative relations that go beyond the frame of the nation state and are not based on economic self-interest, may well take on international dimensions. Mauss believed that under conditions of equality, socialism would first emerge within nations and then spread through cooperation between nations. Mutual dependencies that are not solely grounded in power asymmetries and competition are thus capable of opening up boundaries of identity; they pacify social relations. For Mauss, the idea of the nation is synonymous with such mutual economic and social dependencies, which are controlled democratically.

Mauss' thoughts on nations, it becomes clear, are closely related to his ideas about the gift. In fact, one could conceive of Europe as a network of reciprocal gift relationships. Such post-national, convivial connections need not be insubstantial, as some communitarians are likely to object. Entering connections without espousing ideas of essential identities would create *new* identities beyond nationalisms and ethnocentrism. This is what Mauss wrote enthusiastically on a form of solidarity born from mutual dependencies:

> An intentional, organic solidarity between the nations, a division of labor between them according to soil conditions, climate, and population, will ultimately create a peaceful atmosphere in which they may enjoy life to the fullest. This will have the same effects on collective individualities as it did on the people within nations: freedom, singularity, and greatness. ([1920] 1969: 633; my translation)

Whether this new Europe will take the shape of a republic made up of cities and regions, as the German political scientist Ulrike Guérot (2019) recently proposed, is anyone's guess. What is clear is that Germany's political and economic dominance has paralyzed all reform efforts and keeps driving apart the countries of the European Union: the "black zero" policy of former German Finance Minister Wolfgang Schäuble, who insisted on balanced budgets in member states, has effectively divided the EU into a Northern and a Southern half. The German government will not bring about the new Europe, and neither will the neo-nationalist governments of certain EU member states, anti-European populists, the technocrats of the European Commission, the ECB, or the European Council (Offe, 2016: 16).

What has to be done, what I have been calling for in this book, is of a utopian nature and highly unpopular in large parts of the EU. Which is why civil society groups and social movements must first influence values and attitudes by building networks that span all of Europe—in the end, building "real utopias" locally will not be enough. This counter-hegemonial work has only just begun. I believe that it should focus on a convivial Europe which could act as an intermediary, since a cosmopolitanism is neither achievable anytime soon nor normatively desirable from a pluriversalist perspective. Europe could then become an important experiment in conviviality within the larger context of a great transformation towards an ecological and decolonial post-capitalism—a pioneer on the path that takes us beyond neoliberalism, individualism, and utilitarianism.

Conclusion

The English translation of the first *Convivialist Manifesto* came out in 2014, and the German edition of this book in 2018. As I write this chapter in early 2022, we continue to face many of the same social and political problems. Other developments, however, are new and were not really foreseeable then. Currently, we are experiencing an unprecedented polarization of certain tendencies.

To begin with, Donald Trump's election as US President brought with it a deterioration of American democratic culture and a disruption of erstwhile continuities in foreign policy around the globe; one thinks of his readiness to engage in economic warfare, his relativization of human rights, and the withdrawal of the US from multilateral accords like the Paris Climate Agreement. Bruno Latour (2018) has argued that Trump's presidency marked the first genuinely "climatic regime": his determination to carry on fossil policies and flatly ignore climate change was tantamount to forsaking the shared, confined sphere of planet Earth, the "safe operating space for humanity" (Rockström et al, 2009). Then again, the boundless use of resources is nothing new, but rather a continuity of Western hubris and capitalist accumulation, which has been exploiting the free availability and inexpensiveness of nature for centuries. In juxtaposition to Trump and what he stands for, another, by now iconic, figure has emerged: Greta Thunberg, the initiator of the global Fridays for Future protests, who has made the public aware of climate change like no other individual has been able to. Whereas Trump's planet knows no boundaries, Thunberg's planet trembles under the weight of humanity.

Such polarizations have become ubiquitous. In Germany, while there had been a welcoming atmosphere and much solidarity with refugees in the summer of 2015, the mood soon changed. The profiteer was the "Alternative for Germany" (AfD), a new party with nationalist and racist positions which entered all of the country's regional parliaments as well as the Bundestag, and thus made Germany move to the right. Now, during the ongoing COVID-19 pandemic, more and more people are joining forces via social networks to rebel against the government's measures and spread outlandish theories and misinformation. Already, this movement is being used by right-wing extremist groups to undermine democracy and the rule of law.

When it comes to climate policy, despite the publicity Fridays for Future generated, we can now observe a yellow-vest effect of sorts. Ever since the *gilets jaunes* protested en masse against President Macron's plans to increase fuel taxes, European politicians are afraid that every additional expenditure for climate protection will result in more votes for right-wing populist parties. This elucidates our current political dilemma: as long as we expect the lower and middle classes to shoulder most of the additional costs required to create an ecologically more "sustainable" society, these classes will not be persuaded and may even move to the right. We will only achieve a majority in favor of a socio-ecological transformation if the lower and middle classes were to materially profit from it—that is, by means of redistributions of wealth. As I have stressed at various points in this book: the social and the ecological question are intimately connected.

Thus far, there are no signs of a move away from the neoliberal variety of redistribution: bottom-up—not in Germany, nor anywhere else in the world. Social inequalities, especially as regards the distribution of wealth, keep on rising rapidly, even as demands for capital and higher estate taxes are getting louder (Piketty, 2020). As do critiques of capitalist growthism: when the first manifesto came out, its post-growth reasoning sounded exotic, if not absurd, to many; by now, the degrowth movement has in fact become quite influential in Europe.

In summary, we can state that the search for new forms of solidarity, for a fundamental transformation of our ways of living together, and thus for an expansion of principles of the gift and of conviviality, is being conducted on very different levels of society. The goal is to limit ourselves ecologically and at the same time dissolve the boundaries of democracy. Democracy has recently come under attack in many places, with claims for political participation being denied and oppositional voices being suppressed in countries like Hungary, Russia, Turkey, India, and Brazil. Civil society spaces that are dependent on the freedom of opinion and assembly are increasingly under pressure (see Forum Menschenrechte et al, 2016).

The three regulating principles of the second half of the 20th century—liberal democracy, market-based capitalism, a pluralistic and individualist culture—have become somewhat unstable of late. In this period of transition, very different paths could be pursued. Right-wing populism, illiberal nation states, and notions of homogenous collectives are opposed to movements that fight for more democracy, want to overcome the logic of growth, and aim at reconciling individualistic and communitarian principles. But these movements will only be effective if they manage to bring home to the general public what benefits a convivial life could have. That is why this book as well as the two *Convivialist Manifestos* strive to find an inclusive language in providing a theoretical basis for transformative approaches and political movements. It goes without saying that this is but an attempt, and that the inclusive language of the *homo donator* has to be reinvented and expanded time and again—after all, self-reflexivity is at the heart of the convivial experimentalism presented here.

Since spring 2020, the COVID-19 crisis has highlighted problems that were always virulent, like the fragility of financial capitalism, massive digital and educational asymmetries, gender inequalities (for example regarding care work), or global disparities with respect to the distribution of vaccines. These old problems have recently come to light more clearly than ever; and they are joined by the consequences of our current crisis management: recessions, newly indebted countries, rising unemployment, and so on.

For a few weeks during the 2020 lockdown, fantasies of omnipotence and the controllability of nature had to be thrust aside. It became clear that existing certainties can be shattered in no time whatsoever, and that there is simply no basis for an everlasting business as usual. False certainties were replaced by an awareness of contingency. This makes the new more easily imaginable—but at the same time this loss of supposed security produces fear. The question is whether our societies can endure this fear, or even better, turn it into something productive.

Many of us are beginning to realize that the COVID-19 pandemic was just the beginning. In comparison with the effects of climate change, handling COVID-19 will likely prove very easy. In fact, the COVID-19 crisis has illustrated that we are dealing with very different levels of temporality in the Anthropocene. That the virus probably originated in animals and was transmitted via zoonoses, and that the loss of biodiversity, which has been going on for millennia, facilitates pandemics: these are connections that more and more people know about. Even though COVID-19 conquered the world within just a few weeks, it was prepared by over 100 years of globalization and ecocide, and fueled by over 40 years of neoliberal privatizations and health care cuts. This goes to show that the current crisis was long in the making, and the overlapping temporalities make it likely that we will soon experience the next crisis.

After all, the climate crisis also causes sudden shocks and catastrophes: heavy rains lead to massive floods, droughts to a scarcity of water and food, people are fleeing from extreme heat, and so on (Wallace-Wells, 2019). These shocks have been in the making for decades, if not centuries. In the Anthropocene, preventive action to curb climate change and the establishment of resilient social infrastructures go hand in hand.

We used to believe that the history of human societies plays out against the backdrop of a relatively stable nature. This belief has now become untenable. Earth system science, philosophy, and the social sciences have long been critical of the separation of nature and culture in modernity. With the COVID-19 crisis, the insight that this separation has become obsolete has gained currency. There is just one shared nature, and we humans don't exist outside of it.

Modernity is fundamentally marked by excess and fantasies of human omnipotence—and COVID-19 has had the impertinence to reveal to us the limits of this historical path. Various movements from the North and South thus call on governments, the economy, and science to forsake the hubris of a desire for world mastery, and so does convivialism (Caillé, 2011b). Self-limitation and a convivial coexistence of humans and nonhumans must appear like a valuable alternative path. We have to create new connotations of meaningfulness, which do not negate but affirm contingency and interdependence.

COVID-19 has demonstrated how interdependent our world is, how we all, humans and nonhumans alike, are dependent on each other—even if not symmetrically. From this feeling of interdependence solidarity could arise, as was the theory of Émile Durkheim in the late 1800s. Whereas he had the nation state in mind, today these dependencies are manifest on a global level. And yet, this does not lead us to a new narrative of progress. Thus, the coming years will bring us new conflicts, and old ones will intensify. One key question we are going to face is how humanity will deal with the new contingencies and the associated fears. Will fears, exclusions, inequalities, and conflicts over resources of all kinds increase? Will anxieties of the future still be countered by means of individualism and privatism? Or will we manage to invalidate these fears through more solidarity and convivial solutions?

Announcing a convivial world for tomorrow might seem both desperately ambitious and excessively timid—compared to what yesterday's secular religions such as socialism, communism, or liberal modernization promised us (see Adloff and Caillé, 2022). All of them held out the prospect of a better and brighter tomorrow. We would end all forms of domination or exploitation of man by man. Or, at the very least, everyone would see their material living conditions assured, their health protected, their education sufficiently guaranteed, and would become fully respected citizens. These great hopes have been fading away over the last few decades. Today, for a whole range of reasons, it is rather despair and a dreary future that looms on the horizon. We no longer look to the future full of hope; on the contrary, the horizon of the future has closed. Claiming that tomorrow's world could be more convivial, less violent, less unjust, more secure, more symbiotic or ecological seems almost foolish.

It is obvious that a convivial society has no chance of coming into existence if a global shift in public opinion is not triggered, a sort of axiological great transformation. A huge amount of energy would be needed for that. In addition, the rise in influence of the universal religions or quasi-secular religions has taken a long time, sometimes centuries; but now we live in times of absolute urgency. The climate crisis in particular demands that we act fast. Our time is running out. But perhaps we could even utilize the fact that our age is one of continuous acceleration: ideas circulate and passions are unleashed at a speed unimaginable only a few years ago. Often for the worse—but why should it not be for the better?

The most urgent thing now is to show as many people as possible what they would gain from a shift to a post-neoliberal and post-growth convivial future. It would be a world in which, at least in the richest countries, living better means less material wealth, with less money for the wealthy or upper middle classes (Neuhäußer, 2018), and one that stops exploiting humans and nonhuman beings. Therefore, it is necessary to collect accounts of an alternative future world, one that is attractive to a Russian worker, a Spanish peasant, a farmer in Senegal, an inhabitant of a *favela* in Rio or a slum in Bombay, an Egyptian employee, an Iraqi doctor, a Chinese student, but also one that a French company director would be happy to live in. Whether the future will be more convivial in this sense is decided by our actions in the present, which in turn are guided by the ideas we have about the future. Thus, my bold bet is that convivial ideas about the future can help decide which future becomes the present.

Notes

Chapter 2
1. For biographical information about Mauss I am drawing on Fournier (2006) and Moebius (2006).
2. The anthropologist Marshall Sahlins later came up with a convincing interpretation of these rituals, regarding pacification by means of gift exchanges as an alternative model to a Hobbesian "war of all against all" and the subjugation to the will of a sovereign. By reducing distrust and establishing social bonds, alliances, and solidarities, gifts prevent conflicts between competing clans. Sahlins (1972) therefore considers gift-based reciprocity to be an "in-between" kind of relation, a means of establishing cooperation between two parties that do not share certain cultural values (see also Chapter 4).
3. As later research has shown, extreme potlatch practices—as described, for instance, by Franz Boas—were to a large extent a consequence of European colonialism (Godelier, 1999).
4. See Randall Collins' concept of "emotional energy" (2004).
5. It was Godbout (2000) who first introduced the concept of the *homo donator* as a radical alternative to the *homo oeconomicus*. On a psychological level, he asserts, as much as there is a natural urge towards greed, there is a "temptation to give."
6. See Max Weber who wrote in *Economy and Society* that family households amount to "a communist economy … on a small scale" ([1921] 2019: 222).

Chapter 4
1. Extraordinary gifts can take the form of forgiveness (see Ricœur, 2006)—or, on the part of the liable party, an apology or offer of compensation. In an intercultural context, these two options are based on the assumption that all parties know the constitutive rules of "repair" rituals.
2. Parsons and Platt observed that in the 1960s and 1970s, emotionally more intense relationships had developed between infants and their caregivers than in earlier decades. This attachment endows the child with more self-confidence, and therefore the ability, later in life, to deal with diffuse or unstructured situations more effectively (see Parsons and Platt, 1973). As the findings of Stern illustrate (see Chapter 3), mutual expressions of affect in early childhood generally result in a high action competence. By contrast, affectively rigid familial forms of interaction are more suitable to affectively rigid social systems.

Chapter 5
1. The decidedly subversive nature of the cooperative movement has never been discussed in any detail in sociology, and the concept of the cooperative has long vanished from the discipline's radar. This is not least due to the fact that Max Weber was solely focused on

the attainment and retention of power, while he dismissed attempts at democratization as futile or even ridiculous (see Rothschild, 2016).
2   www.konzeptwerk-neue-oekonomie.org/english
3   www.ecogood.org; see also Felber, 2015.
4   See, for example, Colin Hay and Anthony Pane's book *Civic Capitalism* (2015) which entirely focuses on the state without even so much as a side glance at civil society actors.

Chapter 6

1   For Marx, economic value has always relied on the value of labor—even in early societies unfamiliar with practices of commodity exchange. It has been objected that the value of labor as a commodity is unique to capitalism and that Marx's argument is ahistorical and quasi-metaphysical (see for example Castoriadis, 2010).

Chapter 7

1   It appears that science increasingly conceives of humans as part of the *res extensa* as well—at least this is what recent statements by materialist brain researchers suggest that a "self," endowed with a free will, is scientifically impossible.
2   The cultural historian Hartmut Böhme (2017) states that we are living in a "post-nature" era in which nature is seen solely in terms of its availability for human-technological intervention. For more on the Anthropocene, see Chapter 8.

Chapter 8

1   Alternative terms—such as Chthulucene, Capitalocene, or Technocene—have been proposed to express this disparity (Haraway, 2015).
2   For example, forests would not exist without the symbiosis between tree roots and fungi.

Chapter 10

1   See https://beuys2021.de/en/art-human-krefeld-ii
2   In what follows, I am drawing on Adloff and Rotkopf, 2017.

References

Acksel, B., Euler, J., Gauditz, L., Helfrich, S., Kratzwald, B., Meretz, S. et al (2015) "Commoning: Zur Konstruktion einer konvivialen Gesellschaft." In *Konvivialismus: Eine Debatte*, edited by F. Adloff and V. Heins. Bielefeld: transcript, pp 133–45.

Acosta, A. (2010) "Toward the Universal Declaration of Rights of Nature: Thoughts for Action." *Revista AFESE* 54: 11–30. Available at: https://web.archive.org/web/20190909155204/https://therightsofnature.org/wp-content/uploads/pdfs/Toward-the-Universal-Declaration-of-Rights-of-Nature-Alberto-Acosta.pdf [Accessed 28 May 2022].

Acosta, A. (2015a) "Buen Vivir: A Proposal with Global Potential." In *The Good Life beyond Growth: New Perspectives*, edited by H. Rosa and C. Henning. London: Routledge, pp 29–38.

Acosta, A. (2015b) "Vom guten Leben: Der Ausweg aus der Entwicklungsideologie." In *Mehr geht nicht! Der Postwachstums-Reader*, edited by Blätter für deutsche und internationale Politik. Berlin: Edition Blätter, pp 191–7.

Acosta, A. and Cajas-Guijarro, J. (2020) "Ghosts, Pluriverse and Hopes: From 'Development' to Post-Development." In *The Routledge Handbook to Global Political Economy*, edited by E. Vivares. London: Routledge, pp 292–307.

Adloff, F. (2005) *Zivilgesellschaft: Theorie und politische Praxis*. Frankfurt: Campus.

Adloff, F. (2014) "'Wrong Life *Can* Be Lived Rightly': Convivialism: Background to a Debate." In *Convivialist Manifesto: A Declaration of Interdependence*, translated by M. Clarke. Duisburg: Centre for Global Cooperation Research. Available at: www.gcr21.org [Accessed 28 May 2022].

Adloff, F. (2016) *Gifts of Cooperation, Mauss and Pragmatism*. London: Routledge.

Adloff, F. and Busse, T. (2021) "Gegen das Massensterben: Warum die Natur Rechte braucht." *Blätter für deutsche und internationale Politik* 66(11): 43–52.

Adloff, F. and Büttner, S.M. (2014) "Kultur versus Sozialstruktur: Einführung." In *Kultursoziologie: Klassische Texte—Aktuelle Debatten*, edited by F. Adloff, S.M. Büttner, and R. Schützeichel. Frankfurt: Campus, pp 23–34.

Adloff, F. and Caillé, A. (eds) (2022) *Convivial Futures: Views from a Post-Growth Tomorrow*. Bielefeld: transcript.

Adloff, F. and Heins, V. (eds) (2014a) *Konvivialismus: Eine Debatte*. Bielefeld: transcript.

Adloff, F. and Heins, V. (2014b) "Was könnte Konvivialismus sein?" In *Konvivialismus: Eine Debatte*, edited by F. Adloff and V. Heins. Bielefeld: transcript, pp 9–20.

Adloff, F. and Kocka, J. (eds) (2016) *Kapitalismus und Zivilgesellschaft*. Special issue of *Forschungsjournal Soziale Bewegungen* 29.

Adloff, F. and Neckel, S. (2019) "Futures of Sustainability as Modernization, Transformation, and Control: A Conceptual Framework." *Sustainability Science* 14: 1–11.

Adloff, F. and Rotkopf, M. (2017) "Unregierbar sein: Poetische Kraft oder die unmögliche Rezeption des Unsichtbaren Komitees in Deutschland." *Mittelweg 36: Zeitschrift des Hamburger Instituts für Sozialforschung* 26: 75–90.

Adloff, F. and Sigmund, S. (2005) "Die *Gift Economy* moderner Gesellschaften—Zur Soziologie der Philanthropie." In *Vom Geben und Nehmen: Zur Soziologie der Reziprozität*, edited by F. Adloff and S. Mau. Frankfurt: Campus, pp 211–35.

Adloff, F., Gerund, K., and Kaldewey, D. (eds) (2015) *Revealing Tacit Knowledge: Embodiment and Explication*. Bielefeld: transcript.

Adloff, F., Antony, A., and Sebald, G. (eds) (2016) *Handlungs- und Interaktionskrisen: Theoretische und empirische mikrosoziologische Perspektiven*. Special issue of *Österreichische Zeitschrift für Soziologie* 14.

Altieri, M.A. and Bravo, E. (2009) "The Ecological and Social Tragedy of Crop-Based Biofuel Production in the Americas." In *Agrofuels in the Americas*, edited by R. Jonasse. Oakland: Food First Books, pp 15–24.

Arendt, H. ([1943] 2007) "Can the Jewish-Arab Question Be Solved? [II]." In *The Jewish Writings* by Arendt, edited by J. Kohn and R. Feldman. New York: Schocken Books, pp 196–8.

Arendt, H. (1951) *The Origins of Totalitarianism*. New York: Harcourt, Brace, & Co.

Arendt, H. (1958) *The Human Condition*. Chicago: University of Chicago Press.

Axelrod, R. (1984) *The Evolution of Cooperation*. New York: Basic Books.

Baier, A., Hansing, T., Müller, C., and Werner, K. (eds) (2016) *Die Welt reparieren: Open Source und Selbermachen als postkapitalistische Praxis*. Bielefeld: transcript.

Balibar, E. (2018) "Jetzt regiert Hegel." Interview with Pepe Egger and Leander F. Badura. *Der Freitag* 28 March 2018. Available at: www.freitag.de [Accessed 28 May 2022].

Barad, K. (2007) *Meeting the Universe Halfway: Quantum Physics and the Entanglement of Matter and Meaning*. Durham, NC: Duke University Press.

Baran, P.A. (1957) *The Political Economy of Growth*. New York: Monthly Review Press.

Beck, U. (1992) *Risk Society: Towards a New Modernity*, translated by M. Ritter. London: Sage.

Becker, G. (1965) "A Theory of Allocation of Time." *Economic Journal* 75: 493–517.

Beckert, J. (2006) "The Moral Embeddedness of Markets." In *Ethics and the Market: Insights from Social Economics*, edited by J. Clary, W. Dolfsma, and D.M. Figart. London: Routledge, pp 11–25.

Beckert, J. (2016) *Imagined Futures: Fictional Expectations and Capitalist Dynamics*. Cambridge, MA: Harvard University Press.

Belk, R. (2009) "Sharing." *Journal of Consumer Research* 36: 715–34.

Bellah, R.N. ([1967] 1991) "Civil Religion in America." In *Beyond Belief: Essays on Religion in a Post-Traditionalist World* by R.N. Bellah. Berkeley: University of California Press, pp 168–89.

Bellah, R.N., Madsen, R., Sullivan, W.M., Swidler, A., and Tipton, S.M. (1985) *Habits of the Heart: Individualism and Commitment in American Life*. Berkeley: University of California Press.

Benjamin, W. ([1921] 2007) "Critique of Violence." In *On Violence: A Reader*, edited by B.B. Lawrence and A. Karim. Durham, NC: Duke University Press, pp 268–85.

Ben-Ze'ev, A. (2000) *The Subtlety of Emotions*. Cambridge, MA: MIT Press.

Berking, H. ([1996] 1999) *Sociology of Giving*, translated by P. Camiller. London: Sage.

Bernstein, R.J. (2010) *The Pragmatic Turn*. Cambridge: Polity.

Blau, P. (1964) *Exchange and Power in Social Life*. New York: Wiley.

Bloch, E. ([1954] 1986) *The Principle of Hope*, translated by N. Plaice, S. Plaice, and P. Knight. Vols 1, 2 and 3. Cambridge, MA: MIT Press.

Blühdorn, I. (2017) "Post-Capitalism, Post-Growth, Post-Consumerism: Eco-Political Hopes beyond Sustainability." *Global Discourse* 7: 42–61.

Bohannan, P. (1955) "Some Principles of Exchange and Investment among the Tiv of Central Nigeria." *American Anthropologist* 57: 60–70.

Böhme, H. (2017) *Aussichten der Natur*. Berlin: Matthes & Seitz.

Boisvert, R.D. (2010) "Convivialism: A Philosophical Manifesto." *The Pluralist* 5: 57–68.

Bollier, D. (2002) *Silent Theft: The Private Plunder of Our Common Wealth*. New York: Routledge.

Booth, W.J. (1994) "On the Idea of the Moral Economy." *American Political Science Review* 88: 653–67.

Bourdieu, P. ([1980] 1990) *The Logic of Practice*, translated by R. Nice. Stanford: Stanford University Press.

Bourdieu, P. (1986) "The Forms of Capital." In *Handbook of Theory and Research for the Sociology of Education*, edited by J.G. Richardson. New York: Greenwood Press, pp 241–58.

Bowles, S. (2006) "Group Competition, Reproductive Leveling, and the Evolution of Human Altruism." *Science* 314: 1569–72.

Braidotti, R. (2013) *The Posthuman*. Cambridge: Polity.

Brand, U. and Wissen, M. (2017) *The Limits to Capitalist Nature: Theorizing and Overcoming the Imperial Mode of Living*. London: Rowman & Littlefield.

Brillat-Savarin, J.A. ([1825] 2009) *The Physiology of Taste: Or, Meditations on Transcendental Gastronomy*, translated by M.F.K. Fisher. New York: Knopf.

Caillé, A. (2000a) *Anthropologie du don: le tiers paradigme*. Paris: Desclée de Brouwer.

Caillé, A. (2000b) "Gift and Association." In *Gifts and Interests*, edited by A. Vandevelde. Leuven: Peeters, pp 47–55.

Caillé, A. (2006) "Anti-Utilitarianism, Economics and the Gift-Paradigm." *Revue du MAUSS*. Available at: www.revuedumauss.com.fr/media/ACstake.pdf [Accessed 28 May 2022].

Caillé, A. (2011a) *Pour un manifeste du convivialisme*. Lormont: Le Bord de l'Eau.

Caillé, A. (2011b) "En guise de prologue: Vers le convivialisme." In *De la convivialité: Dialogues sur la société conviviale à venir*, edited by A. Caillé, M. Humbert, S. Latouche, and P. Viveret. Paris: Éditions La Découverte, pp 15–24.

Caillé, A. (2014) *Anti-utilitarisme et paradigme du don. Pour quoi?* Lormont: Le Bord de l'Eau.

Caillé, A. (2015) *La sociologie malgré tout: Autres fragments d'une sociologie générale*. Paris: Presse universitaire Paris Ouest.

Caillé, A. (2020) *The Gift Paradigm: A Short Introduction to the Anti-Utilitarian Movement in the Social Sciences*, translated by G. Connell and F. Gauthier. Chicago: Prickly Paradigm Press.

Caillé, A. and Les Convivialistes (2016) *Éléments d'une politique convivialiste*. Lormont: Le Bord de L'Eau.

Caillé, A., Humbert, M., Latouche, S., and Viveret, P. (eds) (2011) *De la convivialité: Dialogues sur la société conviviale à venir*. Paris: Éditions La Découverte.

Caillé, A., Chanial, P., and Flipo, F. (2013) "Que donne la nature? L'ecologie par le don." *Revue du MAUSS* 42: 5–23.

Callon, M. (1998) *The Laws of the Markets*. Oxford: Blackwell.

Callon, M. (2007) "An Essay on the Growing Contribution of Economic Markets to the Proliferation of the Social." *Theory, Culture & Society* 24: 139–63.

Camus, A. ([1937] 2010) "The New Mediterranean Culture." In *Albert Camus's "The New Mediterranean Culture": A Text and Its Contexts*, edited by N. Foxlee. Oxford: Peter Lang, pp 37–50.

Caputo, J.D. and Scanlon, M.J. (eds) (1999) *God, the Gift, and Postmodernism*. Bloomington: Indiana University Press.

Carrier, J. (1991) "Gifts, Commodities, and Social Relations: A Maussian View of Exchange." *Sociological Forum* 6: 119–36.

Carrier, J. (1992) "The Gift in Theory and Practice in Melanesia: A Note on the Centrality of Gift Exchange." *Ethnology* 31: 185–93.

Castoriadis, C. ([1975] 1984) "Value, Equality, Justice, Politics: From Marx to Aristotle, from Aristotle to Ourselves." In *Crossroads in the Labyrinth*, translated by K. Soper and M.H. Ryle. Cambridge, MA: MIT Press, pp 260–339.

Castoriadis, C. ([1975] 1987) *The Imaginary Institution of Society*, translated by K. Blamey. Cambridge: Polity.

Castoriadis, C. ([1981] 2007) "The 'Rationality' of Capitalism." In *Figures of the Thinkable*, translated by H. Arnold. Stanford: Stanford University Press, pp 47–70.

Castoriadis, C. (1982) "From Ecology to Autonomy." *Thesis Eleven* 3: 7–22.

Castoriadis, C. (2010) *A Society Adrift: Interviews and Debates, 1974–97*, translated by H. Arnold. New York: Fordham University Press.

Cedrini, M.A. and Marchionatti, R. (2017) "On the Theoretical and Practical Relevance of the Concept of Gift to the Development of a Non-Imperialist Economics." *Review of Radical Political Economics* 49: 633–49.

Chakrabarty, D. (2000) *Provincializing Europe: Postcolonial Thought and Historical Difference*. Princeton: Princeton University Press.

Chanial, P. (2002) "La démocratie est-elle naturelle? Sur l'humanisme démocratique de C. Cooley et J. Dewey." *Revue du MAUSS* 19: 80–96.

Chanial, P. (2013) "Does Nature Give Once and for All? The Ethics of Earth Seen from the Gift." *Revue du MAUSS* 42: 83–96.

Clark, S.R.L. (1997) "Gaia und die Formen des Lebens." *Naturethik: Grundtexte der gegenwärtigen tier- und ökoethischen Diskussion*, edited by A. Krebs. Frankfurt: Suhrkamp, pp 144–64.

Coates, T-N. (2014) "The Case for Reparations." *The Atlantic* June 2014. Available at: www.theatlantic.com/magazine/archive/2014/06/the-case-for-reparations/361631 [Accessed 28 May 2022].

Coleman, J.S. (1988) "Social Capital as the Creation of Human Capital." *American Journal of Sociology* 94: S95–110.

Collins, R. (1981) "Micro-Translation as a Theory-Building Strategy." In *Advances in Social Theory and Methodology: Toward an Integration of Micro- and Macro-Sociologies*, edited by K. Knorr-Cetina and A.V. Cicourel. Boston: Routledge & Kegan Paul, pp 81–108.

Collins, R. (2004) *Interaction Ritual Chains*. Princeton: Princeton University Press.

Collins, R. (2008) *Violence: A Micro-Sociological Theory*. Princeton: Princeton University Press.

Convivialist International (2020) "The Second Convivialist Manifesto: Towards a Post-Neoliberal World." *Civic Sociology* 1: 1–24.

Crutzen, P. (2002) "The Geology of Mankind." *Nature* 415: 23.

Curl, J. (2009). *For All the People: Uncovering the Hidden History of Cooperation, Cooperative Movements, and Communalism in America*. Oakland: PM Press.

Dahrendorf, R. (1968) *Essays in the Theory of Society*. London: Routledge & Kegan Paul.

Därmann, I. (2009) "Wie man wird, was man gibt: Marcel Mauss und die Erkenntlichkeit der Gabe." *Journal Phänomenologie* 31: 20–31.

Dawson, A. (2016) *Extinction: A Radical History*. New York: OR Books.

Degens, P. (2016) "Between 'Market' and 'Reciprocity': How Businesses Use Local Currencies." *Money's Future and Future Monies*, edited by A.T. Paul. Special issue of *Behemoth—A Journal on Civilisation* 9: 22–36.

Demaria, F. and Kothari, A. (2017) "The Post-Development Dictionary Agenda: Paths to the Pluriverse." *Third World Quarterly* 38: 2588–99.

Derrida, J. (1992) *Given Time: I. Counterfeit Money*, translated by P. Kamuf. Chicago: Chicago University Press.

Descola, P. (2013) *Beyond Nature and Culture*. Chicago: Chicago University Press.

Dewey, J. ([1916] 1997) *Democracy and Education: An Introduction to the Philosophy of Education*. New York: Free Press.

Dewey, J. ([1917] 2008) "The Need for a Recovery of Philosophy." In *John Dewey: The Middle Works, 1899–24*, vol 10, edited by J.A. Boydston. Carbondale: Southern Illinois University Press, pp 3–48.

Dewey, J. ([1925] 2008) *Experience and Nature* = *John Dewey: The Later Works, 1925–53*, vol 1, edited by J.A. Boydston. Carbondale: Southern Illinois University Press.

Dewey, J. ([1927] 2008) *The Public and Its Problems*. In *John Dewey: The Later Works, 1925–53*, vol 2, edited by J.A. Boydston. Carbondale: Southern Illinois University Press, pp 235–372.

Dewey, J. ([1934] 2008) *Art as Experience* = *John Dewey: The Later Works, 1925–53*, vol 10, edited by J.A. Boydston. Carbondale: Southern Illinois University Press.

Dewey, J. ([1938] 2009) *Theory of Valuation*. In *John Dewey: The Later Works, 1925–53*, vol 13, edited by J.A. Boydston. Carbondale: Southern Illinois University Press, pp 189–251.

Dewey, J. and Tufts, J.H. (1932) *Ethics*. New York: Holt.

Dodd, N. (2014) *The Social Life of Money*. Princeton: Princeton University Press.

Donahue, T.J. (2010) "Anthropocentrism and the Argument from Gaia Theory." *Ethics & Environment* 15: 51–77.

Dornes, M. (1993) *Der kompetente Säugling: Die präverbale Entwicklung des Menschen*. Frankfurt: Fischer.

Douglas, M. (1990) "Foreword: No Free Gifts." In *The Gift: The Form and Reason for Exchange in Archaic Societies* by M. Mauss. London: Norton, pp vi–xviii.

Downing, G. (2005) "Emotion, Body, and Parent-Infant Interaction." In *Emotional Development: Recent Research Advances*, edited by J. Nadel and D. Muir. Oxford: Oxford University Press, pp 429–49.

Durkheim, É. ([1893] 1964) *The Division of Labor in Society*, translated by G. Simpson. New York: Free Press.

Durkheim, É. ([1897] 1965) *Suicide: A Study in Sociology*, translated by J.A. Spaulding and G. Simpson. New York: Free Press.

Durkheim, É. ([1912] 1965) *The Elementary Forms of the Religious Life*, translated by J.W. Swain. New York: Free Press.

Durkheim, É. and Mauss, M. ([1901] 1963) *Primitive Classification*, translated by R. Needham. London: Cohen & West.

Elder-Vass, D. (2016) *Profit and Gift in the Digital Economy*. Cambridge: Cambridge University Press.

Elsen, S. and Walk, H. (2016) "Genossenschaften und Zivilgesellschaft: Historische Dynamiken und zukunftsfähige Potenziale einer öko-sozialen Transformation." In *Kapitalismus und Zivilgesellschaft*, edited by F. Adloff and J. Kocka. Special issue of *Forschungsjournal Soziale Bewegungen* 29: 60–72.

Escobar, A. (2011) "Sustainability: Design for the Pluriverse." *Development* 54: 137–40.

Esposito, E. (2017) "Reality of the Future and Future Reality." *The Present of the Future*, edited by S. Witzgall and K. Stakemeier. Zurich: Diaphanes, pp 27–32.

Eze, M.O. (2008) "What Is African Communitarianism? Against Consensus as a Regulative Ideal." *South African Journal of Philosophy* 27: 386–99.

Feenberg, A. (2010) *Between Reason and Experience: Essays in Technology and Modernity*. Cambridge, MA: MIT Press.

Fehr, E. and Gintis, H. (2007) "Human Motivation and Social Cooperation: Experimental and Analytical Foundations." *Annual Review of Sociology* 33: 43–64.

Fehr, E. and Schmidt, K.M. (1999) "A Theory of Fairness, Competition, and Cooperation." *Quarterly Journal of Economics* 114: 817–68.

Felber, C. (2015) *Change Everything: Creating an Economy for the Common Good*, translated by S. Nurmi. London: Zed Books.

Fligstein, N. and Dauter, L. (2007) "The Sociology of Markets." *Annual Review of Sociology* 33: 105–28.

Fluck, W. (1988) "Fiction and Fictionality in Popular Culture: Some Observations on the Aesthetics of Popular Culture." *Journal of Popular Culture* 22: 49–62.

Forum Menschenrechte, Forum Human Rights, Forum on Environment and Development, VENRO, Consortium Civil Peace Service, Amnesty International, Brot für die Welt et al (2016) "Civil Society Threatened All Over the World." Discussion paper. Available at: https://venro.org/fileadmin/user_upload/Dateien/Daten/Publikationen/Diskussionspapiere/Zivilgesellschaftliches_Engagement_weltweit_in_Gefahr_final_ENGLISCH_DIGITAL_01.pdf [Accessed 28 May 2022].

Fourcade, M. and Healy, K. (2007) "Moral Views of Market Society." *Annual Review of Sociology* 33: 286–311.

Fournier, M. (2006) *Marcel Mauss: A Biography*, translated by J.M. Todd. Princeton: Princeton University Press.

Frank, A.G. (1967) *Capitalism and Underdevelopment in Latin America*. New York: Monthly Review Press.

Fromm, E. (1976) *To Have or to Be?* New York: Harper & Row.

Fuchs, T. (2018) *Ecology of the Brain: The Phenomenology and Biology of the Embodied Mind*. Oxford: Oxford University Press.

Gallagher, S. (2005) *How the Body Shapes the Mind*. Oxford: Oxford University Press.

Gallagher, S. and Hutto, D.D. (2008) "Understanding Others through Primary Interaction and Narrative Practice." In *The Shared Mind: Perspectives on Intersubjectivity*, edited by J. Zlatev, T.P. Racine, C. Sinha, and E. Itkonen. Amsterdam: John Benjamins, pp 17–38.

Ganßmann, H. (2012) *Doing Money: Elementary Monetary Theory from a Sociological Standpoint*. London: Routledge.

Garfinkel, H. (1967) *Studies in Ethnomethodology*. Englewood Cliffs, NJ: Prentice-Hall.

Gibson, K., Rose, D.B., and Fincher, R. (2015) *Manifesto for Living in the Anthropocene*. New York: Punctum Books.

Gibson-Graham, J.K. (2014) "Rethinking the Economy with Thick Description and Weak Theory." *Current Anthropology* 55: 147–53.

Godbout, J.T. (1994) "L'état d'endettement mutuel." *Revue du MAUSS* 4: 205–19.

Godbout, J.T. (2000) *Le don, la dette et l'identité: homo donator vs. homo oeconomicus*. Paris: La Découverte.

Godbout, J.T. and Caillé, A. ([1992] 1998) *The World of the Gift*, translated by D. Winkler. Montreal: McGill-Queen's University Press.

Godbout, J.T. and Charbonneau, J. (1993) "La dette positive dans le lien familial." *Revue du MAUSS* 1: 235–56.

Godelier, M. (1999) *The Enigma of the Gift*, translated by N. Scott. London: Polity.

Goffman, E. (1961) *Asylums: Essays on the Condition of the Social Situation of Mental Patients and Other Inmates*. Garden City, NY: Anchor Books.

Goffman, E. (1983) "The Interaction Order: American Sociological Association 1982 Presidential Address." *American Sociological Review* 48: 1–17.

Gouldner, A. (1960) "The Norm of Reciprocity: A Preliminary Statement." *American Sociological Review* 25: 161–78.

Gouldner, A. (1973) *For Sociology: Renewal and Critique in Sociology Today*. New York: Basic Books.

Graeber, D. (2001) *Toward an Anthropological Theory of Value: The False Coin of Our Own Dreams*. New York: Palgrave.

Graeber, D. (2011) *Debt: The First 5,000 Years*. New York: Melville House.

Graeber, D. (2013) "It Is Value That Brings Universes into Being." *HAU: Journal of Ethnographic Theory* 3: 219–43.

Gregory, C.A. (1982) *Gifts and Commodities*. London: Academic Press.

Gudynas, E. (2013) "Debates on Development and Its Alternatives in Latin America: A Brief Heterodox Guide." In *Beyond Development: Alternative Visions from Latin America*, edited by D. Mokrani. Quito: Transnational Institute & Rosa Luxemburg Stiftung.

Guérot, U. (2019) *Why Europe Should Become a Republic: A Political Utopia*, translated by R. Cunningham. Bonn: Dietz.

Guyer, J.I. (2004) *Marginal Gains: Monetary Transactions in Atlantic Africa*. Chicago: University of Chicago Press.

Habermann, F. (2016) *Ecommony: UmCare zum Miteinander*. Sulzbach: Ulrike Helmer Verlag.

Habermas, J. (1971) "Technology and Science as 'Ideology.'" In *Toward a Rational Society: Student Protest, Science, and Politics* by J. Habermas, translated by J.J. Shapiro. Cambridge: Polity, pp 90–5.

Habermas, J. (1984/1987) *The Theory of Communicative Action*, translated by T. McCarthy. Boston: Beacon Press.

Habermas, J. (1996) *Between Facts and Norms: Contributions to a Discourse Theory of Law and Democracy*, translated by W. Rehg. Cambridge, MA: MIT Press.

Habermas, J. (1997) "Die Herausforderung der ökologischen Ethik für eine anthropozentrisch ansetzende Konzeption." In *Naturethik: Grundtexte der gegenwärtigen tier- und ökoethischen Diskussion*, edited by A. Krebs. Frankfurt: Suhrkamp, pp 92–9.

Habermas, J. (2003) *The Future of Human Nature*, translated by W. Rehg, M. Pensky, and H. Beister. Cambridge: Polity.

Habermas, J. (2010) "The Concept of Human Dignity and the Realistic Utopia of Human Rights." *Metaphilosophy* 41: 464–80.

Habermas, J. (2017) *Postmetaphysical Thinking II*, translated by C. Cronin. Cambridge, MA: Polity.

Hann, C. and Hart, K. (2011) *Economic Anthropology: History, Ethnography, Critique*. Cambridge: Polity.

Haraway, D. (2015) "Anthropocene, Capitalocene, Plantationocene, Chthulucene: Making Kin." *Environmental Humanities* 6: 159–65.

Hardin, G. (1968) "The Tragedy of the Commons." *Science* 162: 1243–8.

Hart, K. (1986) "Heads or Tails? Two Sides of the Coin." *Man, New Series* 21: 637–56.

Hart, K. (2005) "Notes towards an Anthropology of Money." *Kritikos* 2. Available at: https://intertheory.org [Accessed 28 May 2022].

Hart, K. (2007) "Marcel Mauss: In Pursuit of the Whole. A Review Essay." *Comparative Studies in Society and History* 49: 473–85.

Hart, K. (2014) "Marcel Mauss's Economic Vision, 1920–25: Anthropology, Politics Journalism." *Journal of Classical Sociology* 14: 34–44.

Hartmann, M. (2003) *Die Kreativität der Gewohnheit: Grundzüge einer pragmatistischen Demokratietheorie*. Frankfurt: Campus.

Harvey, D. (2014) *Seventeen Contradictions and the End of Capitalism*. London: Profile Books.

Hasecke, J.U. (2016) *Soziale Plastik: Die Kunst der Allmende. Ein Essay zum 30. Todestag von Joseph Beuys*. Solingen: self-published.

Hay, C. and Payne, A. (2015) *Civic Capitalism*. Cambridge: Polity.

Healy, K. (2000) "Embedded Altruism: Blood Collection Regimes and the European Union's Donor Population." *American Journal of Sociology* 105: 1633–57.

Healy, K. (2004) "Altruism as an Organizational Problem: The Case of Organ Procurement." *American Sociological Review* 69: 387–404.

Heil, T. (2015) "Conviviality: (Re)Negotiating Minimal Consensus." In *Routledge International Handbook of Diversity Studies*, edited by S. Vertovec. London: Routledge, pp 317–24.

Hénaff, M. (2010) *The Price of the Truth: Gift, Money, Philosophy*, translated by J.-L. Morhange and A.-M. Feenberg-Dibon. Stanford: Stanford University Press.

Henrich, J., Boyd, R., Bowles, S., Camerer, C., Fehr, E., and Gintis, H. et al (2005) "'Economic Man' in Cross-Cultural Perspective: Behavioral Experiments in 15 Small-Scale Societies." *Behavioral and Brain Sciences* 28: 795–815.

Hentschel, I. (2018) "Der Modus der Gabe in Kunst, Theater und Performance." In *Gabe und Tausch: Zeitlichkeit, Aisthetik, Ästhetik*, edited by M. Bies, S. Giacovelli, and A. Langenohl. Hannover: Wehrhahn, pp 105–26.

Herrmann, G. (1997) "Gift or Commodity: What Changes Hands in the U.S. Garage Sale?" *American Anthropologist* 24: 910–30.

Herrmann, U. (2017) "Aus der Krise nichts gelernt: Die Mythen der Mainstream-Ökonomie." *Blätter für deutsche und internationale Politik* 1: 71–82.

Hickel, J. (2017) "The Development Delusion: Foreign Aid and Inequality." *American Affairs* 1. Available at: https://americanaffairsjournal.org [Accessed 28 May 2022].

Hodson, R. (1991) "The Active Worker: Compliance and Autonomy at the Workplace." *Journal of Contemporary Ethnography* 20: 47–78.

Honneth, A. ([1992] 2005) *The Struggle for Recognition: The Moral Grammar of Social Conflicts*, translated by J. Anderson. Cambridge: Polity.

Honneth, A. (2001) "Invisibility: On the Epistemology of Recognition." *The Aristotelian Society: Supplementary Volume* 75: 111–26.

Honneth, A. (2008) *Reification: A New Look at an Old Idea*, edited by M. Jay. Oxford: Oxford University Press.

Honneth, A. (2017) *The Idea of Socialism: Towards a Renewal*, translated by J. Ganahl. Cambridge: Polity.

Horkheimer, M. and Adorno, T.W. ([1944] 1991). *Dialectic of Enlightenment*, translated by J. Cumming. New York: Continuum.

Horn, E. and Bergthaller, H. (2019). *The Anthropocene: Key Issues for the Humanities*. London: Routledge.

Hrdy, S.B. (2009) *Mothers and Others: The Evolutionary Origins of Mutual Understanding*. Cambridge, MA: Belknap Press of Harvard University Press.

Husserl, E. ([1936] 1970) *The Crisis of European Sciences and Transcendental Phenomenology*, translated by D. Carr. Evanston, IL: Northwestern University Press.

Hyde, L. (1983) *The Gift: Imagination and the Erotic Life of Property*. New York: Vintage Books.

Illich, I. (1973) *Tools for Conviviality*. New York: Harper & Row.

The Invisible Committee (2010) *The Coming Insurrection*. South Pasadena: Semiotext(e). Available at: https://theanarchistlibrary.org [Accessed 28 May 2022].

The Invisible Committee (2015) *To Our Friends*, translated by R. Hurley. South Pasadena: Semiotext(e). Available at: https://theanarchistlibrary.org [Accessed 28 May 2022].

The Invisible Committee (2017) *Now*, translated by R. Hurley. South Pasadena: Semiotext(e). Available at: https://theanarchistlibrary.org [Accessed 28 May 2022].

Jackson, T. (2009) *Prosperity without Growth: Economics for a Finite Planet*. Abingdon: Earthscan.

James, W. ([1896] 1979) *The Will to Believe and Other Essays in Popular Philosophy*, edited by F. Burkhardt, F. Bowers, and I.K. Skrupskelis. Cambridge, MA: Harvard University Press.

Jensen, T.E. (2008) "Experimenting with Commodities and Gifts: The Case of an Office Hotel." *Organization* 15: 187–209.

Joas, H. (1996) *The Creativity of Action*, translated by J. Gaines and P. Keast. Chicago: University of Chicago Press.

Joas, H. (2003) *War and Modernity*, translated by R. Livingstone. Cambridge: Polity.

Joas, H. and Adloff, F. (2006) "Milieu Change and Community Spirit: Transformations of German Civil Society." In *Civil Society: Berlin Perspectives*, edited by J. Keane. Cambridge: Cambridge University Press, pp 103–38.

Kallis, G., Demaria, F., and D'Alisa, G. (eds) (2015) *Degrowth: A Vocabulary for a New Era*. London: Routledge.

Kant, I. ([1790] 2007) *Critique of Judgment*, translated by J.C. Meredith, edited by N. Walker. Oxford: Oxford University Press.

Karagiannis, N. (2004) *Avoiding Responsibility: The Politics and Discourse of European Development Policy*. London: Pluto Press.

Kerner, I. (2015) "Konvivialismus und Multikultur: Postkoloniale Reflexionen." In *Konvivialismus: Eine Debatte*, edited by F. Adloff and V. Heins. Bielefeld: transcript, pp 227–36.

Kitcher, P. (2011) "Ethics and Evolution: How to Get Here from There." In *Primates and Philosophers: How Morality Evolved* by F.B.M. de Waal, edited by S. Macedo and J. Ober. Princeton: Princeton University Press, pp 120–39.

Kitcher, P. (2012) *Preludes to Pragmatism: Toward a Reconstruction of Philosophy*. Oxford: Oxford University Press.

Klein, N. (2017) *No Is Not Enough: Resisting Trump's Shock Politics and Winning the World We Need*. Chicago: Haymarket Books.

Knorr-Cetina, K. (2009) "The Synthetic Situation: Interactionism for a Global World." *Symbolic Interaction* 32: 61–87.

Kocka, J. (2003) "Zivilgesellschaft in historischer Perspektive." *Forschungsjournal Soziale Bewegungen* 16: 29–37.

Kothari, A. (2016) "Radical Ecological Democracy: Reflections from the South on Degrowth." Available at: https://degrowth.info [Accessed 28 May 2022].

Krebs, A. (1997) "Einleitung." In *Naturethik: Grundtexte der gegenwärtigen tier- und ökoethischen Diskussion*, edited by A. Krebs. Frankfurt: Suhrkamp, pp 7–12.

Kühl, S. (2016) *Ordinary Organizations: Why Normal Men Carried Out the Holocaust*, translated by J. Spengler. Cambridge: Polity.

Kunstmuseum Liechtenstein (2017) "Who Pays? 10.2.—21.5.2017." Available at: https://kunstmuseum.li [Accessed 28 May 2022].

Langenohl, A. (2018) "Die Frist: Konstitution der Gabe und Konstitution von Wert." In *Gabe und Tausch: Zeitlichkeit, Aisthetik, Ästhetik*, edited by M. Bies, S. Giacovelli, and A. Langenohl. Hannover: Wehrhahn, pp 47–63.

Lanier, J. (2013) *Who Owns the Future?* London: Allen Lane.

Latouche, S. (2009) *Farewell to Growth*, translated by D. Macey. Cambridge: Polity.

Latouche, S. (2014) *Essays on Frugal Abundance*. Melbourne: Simplicity Institute. Available at: https://degrowth.info [Accessed 28 May 2022].

Latour, B. (1993) *We Have Never Been Modern*, translated by C. Porter. Cambridge, MA: Harvard University Press.

Latour, B. (1994) "On Technical Mediation: Philosophy, Sociology, Genealogy." *Common Knowledge* 3: 29–64.

Latour, B. (2004) *Politics of Nature: How to Bring the Sciences into Democracy*, translated by C. Porter. Cambridge, MA: Harvard University Press.

Latour, B. (2005) *Reassembling the Social: An Introduction to Actor-Network Theory*. New York: Oxford University Press.

Latour, B. (2010) "An Attempt at a 'Compositionist Manifesto.'" *New Literary History* 41: 471–90.

Latour, B. (2011) "Waiting for Gaia: Composing the Common World through Arts and Politics. A Lecture at the French Institute, London, November 2011." Available at: https://runo-latour.fr [Accessed 28 May 2022].

Latour, B. (2017) *Facing Gaia: Eight Lectures on the New Climatic Regime*, translated by C. Porter. Cambridge: Polity.

Latour, B. (2018) *Down to Earth: Politics in the New Climatic Regime*, translated by C. Porter. Cambridge: Polity.

Laum, B. ([1924] 2006) *Heiliges Geld: eine historische Untersuchung über den sakralen Ursprung des Geldes*. Berlin: Semele-Verlag.

Laurier, E. and Philo, C. (2006) "Cold Shoulders and Napkins Handed: Gestures of Responsibility." *Transactions of the Institute of British Geographers* 31: 193–207.

Lefort, C. (1988) *Democracy and Political Theory*, translated by D. Macey. Minneapolis: University of Minnesota Press.

Leggewie, C. (2011) "Sea and Sun for Europe: A New Project for the Next Generation." *Eurozine* 2 November 2011. Available at: www.eurozine.com [Accessed 28 May 2022].

Leggewie, C. (2015) "Konvivialismus als neuer Internationalismus." In *Konvivialismus: Eine Debatte*, edited by F. Adloff and V. Heins. Bielefeld: transcript, pp 237–47.

Leopold, A. ([1949] 1989) *A Sand County Almanac, and Sketches Here and There*. New York: Oxford University Press.

Les Convivialistes (2014) *Convivialist Manifesto: A Declaration of Interdependence*, translated by M. Clarke. Duisburg: Centre for Global Cooperation Research. Available at: www.gcr21.org [Accessed 28 May 2022].

Lessenich, S. (2019) *Living Well at Others' Expense: The Hidden Costs of Western Prosperity*. Cambridge: Polity.

Lessenich, S. and Mau, S. (2005) "Reziprozität und Wohlfahrtsstaat." In *Vom Geben und Nehmen: Zur Soziologie der Reziprozität*, edited by F. Adloff and S. Mau. Frankfurt: Campus, pp 257–76.

Lichterman, P. and Eliasoph, N. (2014) "Civic Action." *American Journal of Sociology* 120: 798–863.

Liebersohn, H. (2011) *The Return of the Gift: European History of a Global Idea*. New York: Cambridge University Press.

Luhmann, N. ([1984] 1995) *Social Systems*, translated by J. Bednarz Jr. and D. Baecker. Stanford: Stanford University Press.

Luhmann, N. ([1997] 2012) *Theory of Society*, translated by R. Barrett. Stanford: Stanford University Press.

Luxemburg, R. ([1913] 2003) *The Accumulation of Capital*, translated by A. Schwarzschild. London: Routledge.

MacIntyre, A. (1999) *Dependent Rational Animals: Why Human Beings Need the Virtues*. Chicago: Open Court.

Malinowski, B. (1922) *Argonauts of the Western Pacific: An Account of Native Enterprise and Adventure in the Archipelagoes of Melanesian New Guinea*. London: Routledge.

Mallard, G. (2011) "*The Gift* Revisited: Marcel Mauss on War, Debt, and the Politics of Reparations." *Sociological Theory* 29: 225–47.

Maraniello, G., Risaliti, S., and Somaini, A. (eds) (2001) *Il dono: Offerta ospitalità insidia/The Gift: Generous Offerings Threatening Hospitality*. Milan: Charta.

Marchart, O. (2007) *Post-Foundational Political Thought: Political Difference in Nancy, Lefort, Badiou and Laclau*. Edinburgh: Edinburgh University Press.

Marcuse, H. ([1964] 2012) *One-Dimensional Man: Studies in the Ideology of Advanced Industrial Society*. Boston: Beacon Press.

Margulis, L. (1998) *Symbiotic Planet: A New Look at Evolution*. New York: Basic Books.

Marion, J.-L. ([1997] 2002) *Being Given: Toward a Phenomenology of Givenness*, translated by J.L. Kosky. Stanford: Stanford University Press.

Marx, K. ([1867] 2019) *Capital: Volume One. A Critique of Political Economy*, translated by S. Moore and E. Aveling, edited by F. Engels. Mineola, NY: Dover Editions.

Mason, P. (2015) *Postcapitalism: A Guide to Our Future*. London: Allen Lane.

Maturana, H. and Varela, F. (1980) *Autopoiesis and Cognition: The Realization of the Living*. Dordrecht: Reidel.

Mauss, M. (1914) "Les origines de la notion de monnaie." *L'Anthropologie* 2: 14–19.

Mauss, M. ([1920] 1969) "La nation." In *Cohésion sociale et divisions de la sociologie*, edited by V. Karady. Paris: Les Éditions de Minuit.

Mauss, M. ([1924] 1992) "A Sociological Assessment of Bolshevism." In *The Radical Sociology of Durkheim and Mauss*, edited by M. Gane. London: Routledge, pp 165–211.

Mauss, M. ([1925] 1990) *The Gift: The Form and Reason for Exchange in Archaic Societies*, translated by W.D. Halls. London: Routledge.

Mauss, M. ([1947] 2007) *Manual of Ethnography*, edited by N.J. Schlanger. New York: Durkheim Press/Berghahn Press.

Mauss, M. (1997) *Écrits politiques*, edited by M. Fournier. Paris: Fayard.

Mauss, M. (2006) *Techniques, Technology, and Civilization*, edited by N.J. Schlanger. New York: Durkheim Press/Berghahn Books.

Mauss, M. and Hubert, H. ([1898] 1964) *Sacrifice: Its Nature and Function*, translated by W.D. Halls. London: Cohen & West.

Mauss, M. and Hubert, H. ([1902] 1975) *A General Theory of Magic*, translated by R. Brain. New York: Norton.

McCarthy, T. (2009) *Race, Empire, and the Idea of Human Development*. Cambridge: Cambridge University Press.

Meadows, D.H., Meadows, D.L., Randers, J., and Behrens, W.W. II. (1972) *The Limits to Growth: A Report for the Club of Rome's Project on the Predicament of Mankind*. New York: Universal Books.

Menke, C. (2013) *Die Kraft der Kunst*. Berlin: Suhrkamp.

Menke, C. (2020) *Critique of Rights*, translated by C. Turner. Cambridge: Polity.

Messner, D., Guarín, A., and Haun, D. (2013) *The Behavioural Dimensions of International Cooperation*. Duisburg: Centre for Global Cooperation Research.

Michéa, J.-C. (2009) *The Realm of Lesser Evil: An Essay on Liberal Civilization*, translated by D. Fernbach. Cambridge: Polity.

Mignolo, W.D. (2011) *The Darker Side of Western Modernity: Global Futures, Decolonial Options*. Durham, NC: Duke University Press.

Mills, C.W. (1940) "Situated Actions and Vocabularies of Motive." *American Sociological Review* 5: 904–13.

Mishra, P. (2017) "What Is Great about Ourselves." *London Review of Books* 39. Available at: www.lrb.co.uk [Accessed 28 May 2022].

Moebius, S. (2006) *Marcel Mauss*. Konstanz: UVK.

Molm, L. (2003) "Theoretical Comparisons of Forms of Exchange." *Sociological Theory* 21: 1–17.

Molm, L. (2010) "The Structure of Reciprocity." *Social Psychology Quarterly* 73: 119–31.

Monroe, K.R. (1994) "A Fat Lady in a Corset: Altruism and Social Theory." *American Journal of Political Science* 38: 861–93.

Münkler, H. (1998) "Civil Society and Civic Virtue: Do Democratically Constituted Communities Require a Socio-Moral Foundation?" *International Review of Sociology* 8: 425–38.

Muraca, B. (2012) "Towards a Fair Degrowth Society: Justice and the Right to a 'Good Life' beyond Growth." *Futures* 44: 535–45.

Nachtwey, O. (2018) *Germany's Hidden Crisis: Social Decline in the Heart of Europe*, translated by D. Fernbach and L. Balhorn. London: Verso.

Neuhäußer, C. (2018) *Reichtum als moralisches Problem*. Berlin: Suhrkamp.

Neumann, M. and Winker, G. (2020) "Care Revolution: Care Work. The Core of the Economy." In C. Burkhart, M. Schmelzer and N. Treu (eds) *Degrowth in Movement(s): Exploring Pathways for Transformation*. Winchester: Zero Books, pp 100–13.

Nietzsche, F. ([1887] 2017) *"On the Genealogy of Morality" and Other Writings*, translated by C. Diethe, edited by K. Ansell-Pearson. Cambridge: Cambridge University Press.

Noë, A. (2010) *Out of Our Heads: Why You Are Not Your Brain, and Other Lessons from the Biology of Consciousness*. New York: Hill and Wang.

Nowicka, M. and Vertovec, S. (2014) "Comparing Convivialities: Dreams and Realities of Living-with-difference." *European Journal of Cultural Studies* 17: 341–56.

Nussbaum, M.C. (2001) *Upheavals of Thought: The Intelligence of Emotions*. Cambridge: Cambridge University Press.

Oberthür, J. and Schulz, P. (2016) "Nach dem Maschinensturm: Überlegungen zu einer Erweiterung von Technologiekritik in der Postwachstumsdebatte." In *Wachstum—Krise und Kritik: Die Grenzen der kapitalistisch-industriellen Lebensweise*, edited by A.K. Postwachstum. Frankfurt: Campus, pp 159–76.

Offe, C. (2016) *Europe Entrapped*. Cambridge: Polity.

Oliner, S.P. and Oliner, P.M. (1988) *The Altruistic Personality: Rescuers of Jews in Nazi Europe*. New York: Free Press.

Osterhammel, J. (1997) *Colonialism: A Theoretical Overview*, translated by S.L. Frisch. Princeton: Wiener.

Ostrom, E. (2010) "Beyond Markets and States: Polycentric Governance of Complex Economic Systems." *American Economic Review* 100: 641–72.

Parry, J. (1986) "The Gift, the Indian Gift and the 'Indian Gift.'" *Man* 21: 453–73.

Parry, J. and Bloch, M. (1989) "Introduction: Money and the Morality of Exchange." In *Money and the Morality of Exchange*, edited by J. Parry and M. Bloch. Cambridge: Cambridge University Press, pp 1–32.

Parsons, T. (1968) "On the Concept of Value-Commitments." *Sociological Inquiry* 38: 135–60.

Parsons, T. (1977) *Social Systems and the Evolution of Action Theory*. New York: Free Press.

Parsons, T. and Platt, G.M. (1973) *The American University*. Cambridge, MA: Harvard University Press.

Perra, L. (2020) "Tradition Can Save the Future of Nature: A Biocentric View of Law." In *Environment, Social Justice, and the Media in the Age of the Anthropocene*, edited by E.G. Dobbins, M.L. Piga, and L. Manca. Lanham, MD: Lexington Books, pp 339–54.

Piketty, T. (2020) *Capital* and *Ideology*, translated by A. Goldhammer. Cambridge, MA: Harvard University Press.

Piliavin, J.A. and Charng, H.-W. (1990) "Altruism: A Review of Recent Theory and Research." *Annual Review of Sociology* 16: 27–65.

Polanyi, K. ([1944] 2001) *The Great Transformation: The Political and Economic Origins of Our Time*. Boston: Beacon Press.

Polanyi, K. (1957) "The Economy as an Instituted Process." In *Trade and Market in the Early Empires: Economies in History and Theory*, edited by K. Polanyi, C.M. Arensberg, and H.W. Pearson. Chicago: Henry Regnery, pp 243–70.

Polanyi, K. (1968) *Primitive, Archaic, and Modern Economies: Essays of Karl Polanyi*, edited by G. Dalton. Garden City, NY: Doubleday.

Portmann, A. (1960). *Neue Wege der Biologie*. Munich: Piper.

Preston, S.D. and de Waal, F.B.M. (2002) "Empathy: Its Ultimate and Proximate Bases." *Behavioral and Brain Sciences* 25: 1–20.

Purves, T. (2005) *What We Want Is Free*. New York: SUNY Press.

Putnam, H. (1992) *Renewing Philosophy*. Cambridge, MA: Harvard University Press.

Putnam, H. (2002) *The Collapse of the Fact/Value Dichotomy; and Other Essays*. Cambridge, MA: Harvard University Press.

Putnam, R. (1993) *Making Democracy Work: Civic Traditions in Modern Italy*. Princeton: Princeton University Press.

Putnam, R. (2000) *Bowling Alone: The Collapse and Revival of American Community*. New York: Simon & Schuster.

Rawls, A.W. (1987) "The Interaction Order Sui Generis: Goffman's Contribution to Social Theory." *Sociological Theory* 5: 136–49.

Rawls, A.W. (1990) "Emergent Sociality: A Dialectic of Commitment and Order." *Symbolic Interaction* 13: 63–82.

Rawls, A.W. (2012) "Durkheim's Theory of Modernity: Self-Regulating Practices as Constitutive Orders of Social and Moral Facts." *Journal of Classical Sociology* 12: 479–512.

Rawls, A.W. and David, G. (2005) "Accountably Other: Trust, Reciprocity and Exclusion in a Context of Situated Practice." *Human Studies* 28: 469–97.

Reichardt, S. (2014) *Authentizität und Gemeinschaft: Linksalternatives Leben in den siebziger und achtziger Jahren*. Berlin: Suhrkamp.

Ricœur, P. (1995) *Figuring the Sacred: Religion, Narrative, and Imagination*, translated by D. Pellauer, edited by M.I. Wallace. Minneapolis: Fortress Press, pp 315–29.

Ricœur, P. (2005) *The Course of Recognition*, translated by D. Pellauer. Cambridge, MA: Harvard University Press.

Ricœur, P. (2006) *Memory, History, Forgetting*, translated by K. Blamey and D. Pellauer. Chicago: University of Chicago Press.

Rifkin, J. (2014) *The Zero Marginal Cost Society*. Basingstoke: Palgrave Macmillan.

Rockström, J., Steffen, W., Noone, K., Persson, A., Stuart Chapin III, F., Lambin, E.F., et al (2009) "A Safe Operating Space for Humanity." *Nature* 461: 472–5.

Rödel, U. (1990) "Einleitung." In *Autonome Gesellschaft und libertäre Demokratie*, edited by U. Rödel. Frankfurt: Suhrkamp, pp 7–29.

Rosa, H. (2019) *Resonance: A Sociology of the Relationship to the World*, translated by J.C. Wagner. Cambridge, MA: Polity.

Rosanvallon, P. (2013) *The Society of Equals*, translated by A. Goldhammer. Cambridge, MA: Harvard University Press.

Rothschild, J. (2016) "The Logic of a Co-operative Economy and Democracy 2.0: Recovering the Possibilities for Autonomy, Creativity, Solidarity, and Common Purpose." *Sociological Quarterly* 57: 7–35.

Rushton, J.P. (1984) "The Altruistic Personality: Evidence from Laboratory, Naturalistic, and Self-Report Perspectives." In *Development and Maintenance of Prosocial Behavior: International Perspectives on Positive Morality*, edited by E. Staub, D. Bar-Tal, J. Karylowski, and J. Reykowski. New York: Springer, pp 271–90.

Safranski, R. (2004) *Friedrich Schiller oder Die Erfindung des Deutschen Idealismus*. Munich: Carl Hanser.

Sahlins, M. (1972) *Stone Age Economics*. Chicago: Aldine.

Sahr, A. (2017) *Keystroke-Kapitalismus: Ungleichheit auf Knopfdruck*. Hamburg: Hamburger Edition.

Santos, B. de S. (2014) *Epistemologies of the South: Justice against Epistemicide*. London: Routledge.

Santos, B. de S. (2017) "A New Vision of Europe: Learning from the South." In *European Cosmopolitanism: Colonial Histories and Postcolonial Societies*, edited by G.K. Bhambra and J. Narayan. London: Routledge, pp 172–84.

Sassen, S. (2014) *Expulsions: Brutality and Complexity in the Global Economy*. Cambridge, MA: Belknap Press of Harvard University Press.

Schatzki, T. (2015) "Spaces of Practices and of Large Social Phenomena." 24 March 2015. Available at: www.espacestemps.net/en/ [Accessed 28 May 2022].

Schiller, F. ([1793] 1971) *Kallias oder Über die Schönheit*, edited by K.L. Berghahn. Stuttgart: Reclam.

Schmitz, L. (ed) (2015) *Artivismus: Kunst und Aktion im Alltag der Stadt*. Bielefeld: transcript.

Schneidewind, U., Singer-Brodowski, M., Augenstein, K., and Stelzer, F. (2016) *Pledge for a Transformative Science: A Conceptual Framework*. Wuppertal: Wuppertal Institute for Climate, Environment and Energy.

Schütz, A. (1972) "On Multiple Realities." *The Problem of Social Reality* by Schütz, edited by M. Natanson. Dordrecht: Springer, pp 207–59.

Shils, E. (1991) "The Virtue of Civil Society." *Government and Opposition* 26: 3–20.

Simmel, G. ([1896] 1991) "Money in Modern Culture." *Theory, Culture & Society* 8: 17–31.

Simmel, G. ([1900] 2011) *The Philosophy of Money*. London: Routledge.

Simmel, G. ([1908] 1950) *The Sociology of Georg Simmel*, edited by K.H. Wolff. New York: Free Press.

Singer, P. (2011) "Morality, Reason, and the Rights of Animals." In *Primates and Philosophers: How Morality Evolved* by F.B.M. de Waal, edited by S. Macedo and J. Ober. Princeton: Princeton University Press, pp 140–58.

Smith, A. ([1776] 1957) *Selections from The Wealth of Nations*, edited by G.J. Stigler. Wheeling, IL: Harlan Davidson.

Solomon, R.C. (1988) "On Emotions as Judgments." *American Philosophical Quarterly* 25: 183–91.

Sorel, G. ([1908] 1999) *Reflections on Violence*, translated by T.E. Hulme, edited by J. Jennings. Cambridge: Cambridge University Press.

Steffen, W., Broadgate, W., Deutsch, L., Gaffney, O., and Ludwig, C. (2015) "The Trajectory of the Anthropocene: The Great Acceleration." *The Anthropocene Review* 2: 81–98.

Steiner, P. (2019) "Altruism, Sociology and the History of Economic Thought." *European Journal of the History of Economic Thought* 26: 1252–74.

Stern, D. (1977) *The First Relationship: Infant and Mother*. Cambridge, MA: Harvard University Press.

Stern, D. (1985) *The Interpersonal World of the Infant: A View from Psychoanalysis and Developmental Psychology*. New York: Basic Books.

Stowasser, H. (2006) *Anarchie! Idee—Geschichte—Perspektiven*. Hamburg: Edition Nautilus.

Tenbruck, F.H. (1989) "The Cultural Foundations of Society." In *Social Structure and Culture*, edited by H. Haferkamp. Berlin: De Gruyter, pp 15–35.

Thomas, W.I. and Thomas, D.S. (1928) *The Child in America: Behavior Problems and Programs*. New York: Knopf.

Titmuss, R.M. (1970). *The Gift Relationship: From Human Blood to Social Policy*. London: Allen & Unwin.

Tomasello, M. (1999) *Why We Cooperate*. Cambridge, MA: MIT Press.

Tomasello, M. (2014) "The Ultra-Social Animal." *European Journal of Social Psychology* 44: 187–94. Available at: www.ncbi.nlm.nih.gov [Accessed 28 May 2022].

Toulmin, S. (1990) *Cosmopolis: The Hidden Agenda of Modernity*. New York: Free Press.

Tsing, A.L. (2015) *The Mushroom at the End of the World: On the Possibility of Life in Capitalist Ruins*. Princeton: Princeton University Press.

Turner, J.H. (1987) "Toward a Sociological Theory of Motivation." *American Sociological Review* 52: 15–27.

Turner, J.H. (2002) *Face to Face: Toward a Sociological Theory of Interpersonal Behavior*. Stanford: Stanford University Press.

Ullrich, W. (2018) "Gefährliche Schönheit: Die Ästhetik der Überwältigung." *Blätter für deutsche und internationale Politik* 2: 109–20.

Ulrich, B. (2015) "Muslime: Das Ende der Arroganz." *DIE ZEIT* 19 November 2015. Available at: www.zeit.de [Accessed 28 May 2022].

van Dooren, T., Kirksey, E., and Münster, U. (2016) "Multispecies Studies: Cultivating Arts of Attentiveness." *Environmental Humanities* 8: 1–23.

Vaneigem, R. ([1967] 2012) *The Revolution of Everyday Life*, translated by D. Nicholson-Smith. Oakland: PM Press.

Varela, F. (1988) *Connaitre: les sciences cognitives, tendences et perspectives*. Paris: Éditions du Seuil.

Varela, F., Thompson, E., and Rosch, E. (1991) *The Embodied Mind: Cognitive Science and Human Experience*. Cambridge, MA: MIT Press.

Varga, S. and Gallagher, S. (2011) "Critical Social Philosophy, Honneth and the Role of Primary Intersubjectivity." *European Journal of Social Theory* 12: 243–60.

Vetter, A. and Best, B. (2015) "Konvivialität und Degrowth." In *Konvivialismus: Eine Debatte*, edited by F. Adloff and V. Heins. Bielefeld: transcript, pp 101–12.

Victor, P. (2008) *Managing without Growth: Slower by Design, not Disaster*. Cheltenham: Edward Elgar.

Viveret, P. (2011) "Stratégies de transition vers le bien-vivre face aux démesures dominantes." In *De la convivialité: Dialogues sur la société conviviale à venir*, edited by A. Caillé, M. Humbert, S. Latouche, and P. Viveret. Paris: Éditions La Découverte, pp 25–41.

von Hagen, J. and Welker, M. (eds) (2014) *Money as God? The Monetization of Markets and Its Impact on Religion, Politics, Law, and Ethics*. Cambridge: Cambridge University Press.

Waldenfels, B. (2012) *Hyperphänomene: Modi hyperbolischer Erfahrung*. Berlin: Suhrkamp.

Walk, H. (2015) "Kubanische Genossenschaften zwischen Sozialismus und Marktwirtschaft." *Konvivialismus: Eine Debatte*, edited by F. Adloff and V. Heins. Bielefeld: transcript, pp 121–32.

Wallace-Wells, D. (2019) *The Uninhabitable Earth: A Story of the Future*. London: Penguin.

Weber, A. (2013) *Enlivenment: Towards a Fundamental Shift in the Concepts of Nature, Culture and Politics*. Berlin: Heinrich Böll Foundation.

Weber, M. ([1905] 1930) *The Protestant Ethic and the Spirit of Capitalism*, translated by T. Parsons. London: Allen & Unwin.

Weber, M. ([1915] 1951) *The Religion of China: Confucianism and Taoism*, translated by H.H. Gerth. New York: Free Press.

Weber, M. ([1920] 1963) *The Sociology of Religion*, translated by E. Fischoff. Boston: Beacon Press.

Weber, M. ([1921] 2019) *Economy and Society*, translated and edited by K. Tribe. Cambridge, MA: Harvard University Press.

Wenzel, H. (2005) "Social Order and Communication: Parsons's Theory on the Move from Moral Consensus to Trust." In *After Parsons: A Theory of Social Action for the Twenty-First Century*, edited by R.C. Fox, V.M. Lidz, and H.J. Bershady. New York: Russell Sage Foundation, pp 66–82.

Wessendorf, S. (2014) "'Being open, but sometimes closed': Conviviality in a Super-Diverse London Neighborhood." *European Journal of Cultural Studies* 17: 392–405.

Wheeler, W. (2006) *The Whole Creature: Complexity, Biosemiotics and the Evolution of Culture*. London: Lawrence & Wishart.

Widlok, T. (2013) "Sharing: Allowing Others to Take What Is Valued." *HAU: Journal of Ethnographic Theory* 3: 11–31.

Wikan, U. (2012) *Resonance: Beyond the Words*. Chicago: Chicago University Press.

Windelband, W. (1894) "Geschichte und Naturwissenschaft: Rede zum Antritt des Rektorats der Kaiser-Wilhelm-Universität Strassburg." Available at: https://edoc.hu-berlin.de [Accessed 28 May 2022].

Wright, E.O. (2010) *Envisioning Real Utopias*. London: Verso.

Wright, E.O. (2016) "How to Think about (and Win) Socialism." *Jacobin* 27 April 2016. Available at: https://jacobinmag.com [Accessed 28 May 2022].

Wulf, A. (2015) *The Invention of Nature: Alexander von Humboldt's New World*. New York: Knopf.

Zelizer, V.A. (1996) "Payments and Social Ties." *Sociological Forum* 11: 481–95.

Zelizer, V.A. (2012) "How I Became a Relational Economic Sociologist and What Does That Mean?" *Politics & Society* 40: 145–74.

Index

Reference to endnotes show both the page number and the note number (159n3).

A

activism 8, 40, 70, 71, 78, 121, 127, 136, 139, 141, 148
advertising 76, 84, 137
aesthetics 72, 105, 131–40
Africa 1, 4, 89, 90, 103, 142, 147
agonistic 28–36, 42, 55–7, 73, 76, 85, 94, 116, 121, 135
agriculture 48, 108–9, 113
AIDS 104
altruism 13–21, 44–6
Amazonia 103, 146
Amnesty International 23
analogism 103
anarchism 73, 44, 127, 137, 139
ancestor 45, 61, 87, 138
animal rights 105, 110–15
animism 103, 105, 115
Anthropocene 108–9, 117–18, 156, 160n2
anthropology 6–8, 28, 38–43, 44–9, 64, 81, 82, 102–3
apes 43–5
a priori 39, 100
Aristotle 119
art 9, 34, 105, 133–40
asymmetry 4, 7, 14, 17, 29, 30–7, 55, 62, 68, 76, 87, 93–5, 132–5, 149–52, 156
attachment 6, 20, 34, 43, 56, 82, 86–8, 159n2
Australia 29, 103, 110
Austria 2, 78, 131

B

bank 92–4, 142, 150
Barad, Karen 110–11, 133
beauty 132–4
Beck, Ulrich 77
Bellah, Robert 6, 120
beneficence 15
Big Data 76
billionaire 1
biodiversity 103, 108, 118, 146, 156
biology 38, 42, 64, 111, 115, 144

biosemiotics 111–13
Bitcoin 93
Blau, Peter 16–17
bolshevism 27, 30, 71, 73
Booth, William James 82
Bourdieu, Pierre 15–16, 22, 34
Braidotti, Rosi 110–11
Brazil 4, 155

C

Caillé, Alain 2, 3, 5, 8, 33–5, 64, 66, 86, 115, 121–5, 146, 157
Callon, Michel 35, 109
Camus, Albert 142
capitalism 1–8, 26, 30, 61, 70–9, 83–8, 99, 107–10, 118, 126, 127, 136, 141–2, 148, 151–6, 160n4
capitalocentric 79
caregiver 41, 50, 159n2
Cartesian dualism 39
Castoriadis, Cornelius 87–8, 92, 122, 134, 160n1
Catholic Church 23
charity 15, 30, 114
childhood *see* children
children 15, 23, 40, 44–5, 50, 64, 67, 83–5, 90, 114, 159n2
China 89, 99, 103, 141
Christianity 20, 32, 75, 125
see also Catholic Church, Protestantism
Civil Rights Movement 22, 121–2, 144
civil society 9, 23, 33, 71–5, 77–80, 91, 119–28, 152–3
climate crisis 156, 158
coexistence 5–9, 59, 125, 157
Cold War 1
colonialism 9, 102–3, 138, 141–8, 150, 152, 159n3
see also post-colonialism
colonization 95, 143–5, 150
communism 35, 36, 57, 73, 74, 87, 94, 121, 125, 138–40, 141, 157, 159n6

182

INDEX

computer 17, 62
Comte, Auguste 20
Confucianism 99
consciousness 72, 102, 109, 115
consumerism 5, 78, 101, 124, 125, 136–7
convivialism 2–5, 7, 9, 114, 121–4, 141, 146, 150, 157
Convivialist Manifesto 2, 33, 35, 121, 123, 126, 154, 155
cosmology 103, 104, 145, 146
COVID-19 9, 154–7
culturalism 38, 102, 144

D

da Vinci, Leonardo 101
death 30, 105, 112
debt 1, 14, 29, 34–6, 86–9, 91, 93, 94, 142, 151, 156
deconstructivism 31
  see also Derrida, Jacques 31
décroissance 3, 77–8
degrowth theory 3
democracy 1, 3, 8, 46–8, 72, 75, 77, 79, 80, 104, 121, 122, 126, 128, 140, 146, 147, 155
depression 39, 42, 68
Derrida, Jacques 31, 32, 34, 94
Descartes, René 100
Descola, Philippe 36, 102–5, 114
Detroit 59
de Waal, Frans 43–5
Dewey, John 8, 38–40, 46–51, 64, 74, 104, 112–13, 120, 125, 128, 132, 135
DNA 4, 43, 111
Durkheim, Émile 20, 26–9, 67, 71, 72, 157

E

eBay 84
economics 5, 6, 13, 18, 19, 34, 81, 90, 100, 131
Economy for the Common Good 78, 80
  see also GWÖ
eco-village 75
education 20, 23, 35, 71, 76, 79, 85, 91, 146, 148, 152, 156, 157
egalitarianism 58, 62, 87, 107, 121
elderly 92, 114
election 80, 122, 154
emissions 77, 78, 108
emotion 38–46, 49, 50, 68, 100, 134
Enlightenment 114, 119, 120, 145
environmentalism 105
ethnomethodology 57
Euro 15, 91
European Union (EU) 4, 21, 142, 151, 153
evil 6, 101, 124
experimentalism 124, 125, 128, 156

F

Facebook 76, 77, 84
fair trade 125, 143
family 20, 26, 28, 34, 60, 120, 159n6
Fanon, Frantz 139, 149–50
feminism 79, 110, 112, 149
fishing 1, 19
flood 4, 117, 156
food 44, 45, 90, 110, 113
foreign aid 143
forest 19, 75, 103, 114, 118, 160n2
  see also rain forest
France 2, 19, 21, 26, 28, 31–5, 71, 72, 75, 78, 102, 137, 142, 150, 152
  see also Paris
Frankfurt School 94, 101
freedom 4, 8, 9, 14, 19, 25, 57, 62, 64–9, 105, 107, 131–40, 145, 153, 155
Freigeld 92
French Section of the Workers' International (SFIO) 71
Fridays for Future 154–5
  see also Thunberg, Greta
friendship 35, 86, 124
Fromm, Erich 2, 81, 100

G

G20 summit 139
Gaia 9, 106, 116–18, 138, 149
Galileo 101
game theory 17
Garfinkel, Harold 57–8, 68
gender 78, 84, 156
Germany 1, 23, 71–5, 78, 94, 103, 142, 150–5
Gesell, Silvio 92
  see also Freigeld
gift
  agonistic 28, 30–6, 55, 56, 73, 76, 85, 86, 94, 135
  counter- 14–16, 28, 33, 36
  economy 15, 16
  exchange 15–17, 159n2
  extraordinary 8, 55–7, 60, 65, 72, 149, 159n1
  non-agonistic 30–6, 76, 85, 86, 94
globalization 33, 59, 102, 141, 156
Global North 1, 4, 9, 79, 149, 150
Global South 3, 4, 7, 75, 79, 141–3
global warming 1, 78, 80, 116–17, 142
God 89, 91, 93, 94, 99, 100, 118, 139
Godbout, Jacques 33, 61, 78, 86, 159n5
Goffman, Erving 58, 62
Golden Rule 22, 32
Google 76
Gorz, André 2, 77
Greece 86, 89, 142, 150, 151
Greenpeace 23
growthism 3, 5, 77, 78, 149, 151, 155
GWÖ 78–9

183

H

Habermas, Jürgen 48–9, 66–7, 87, 101, 102, 106, 115
habits 39, 40, 45, 50, 73, 144
Hardin, Garrett 19
health care 150, 156
Hegel, Georg Wilhelm Friedrich 33, 35, 119
Hénaff, Marcel 34, 70
hierarchy 17, 31, 68, 81, 95, 99, 106, 121, 126
Hobbes, Thomas 6, 20, 25, 47, 119, 159n2
Holocaust 20, 152
Holocene 108, 118
homo donator 7, 8, 38–51, 124, 156, 159n5
homo oeconomicus 3, 7, 18, 30, 34, 74, 81, 159n5
homo sapiens 43–4, 48, 51
homo sociologicus 18
Honneth, Axel 33, 35, 50, 60
householding 81
humanism 100, 101, 144, 151
human rights 1, 142, 144, 147, 154
Hungary 81, 155
Hinduism 60, 61, 109
Hyde, Lewis 131–2

I

Illich, Ivan 2, 3, 9, 81, 107
immigration 38, 77, 142, 144
indebtedness 14, 28, 36, 86, 95
India 31, 103, 147, 155
industrialization 38, 103, 148
inequality 1, 3, 4, 29, 77, 88, 144, 145, 148, 155–7
insurrection 138, 140
interactionism 24
interculturality 36, 55, 56, 59–60, 102, 145, 159n1
International Geological Congress 108
intersubjectivity 8, 40–1, 51, 60
Invisible Committee 9, 137–40
Islam 59, 60, 61, 125, 150
isolation 1, 4, 6, 40, 44, 72
Italy 7, 21, 22, 78, 142

J

James, William 38, 49
journalism 70, 76
Judaism 20, 26, 28, 59, 71, 99, 125

K

Kant, Immanuel 34, 46, 103, 132, 133
Klein, Naomi 141

L

labor 23, 29, 30, 62, 72, 77–87, 91–2, 101, 114, 126, 141, 152, 153, 160n1
language 3, 6, 44, 58, 66–7, 102, 110, 113, 115, 134–9, 155–6

Latin America 4, 106, 138, 148
Latouche, Serge 3, 78
law 14, 28–30, 78, 80, 87, 99, 101, 103, 118, 124, 128, 135, 155
liberalism 26, 124–5
see also neoliberalism
Linux 75
Local Exchange Trading Systems (LETS) 92
logic 5–6, 31–2, 42, 50, 61–3, 73–9, 80, 83–8, 92, 95, 100, 102, 121, 124, 126, 133–9, 150, 155
Luhmann, Niklas 66
Luxembourg 21

M

Marxism 35, 74, 79, 83–5, 120, 122, 126–8, 137, 148
Marx, Karl *see* Marxism
Mauss, Marcel 5, 8, 24, 25–37, 38, 49, 56, 67, 70–4, 81, 84, 88–94, 127, 141, 152–3, 159n1
Mead, George Herbert 8, 38, 39, 46, 47, 49, 67
media 18, 66–7, 132
see also journalism
memory 28, 42, 82, 91, 138, 141, 142
Menke, Christoph 87, 134–5
Merkel, Angela 143
Michéa, Jean-Claude 124–5
Middle East 142, 150
military 63
model of motivations 64, 66
modernity 9, 25, 31, 78, 82, 90, 99, 100, 104–5, 118–20, 124, 144, 149–50, 156, 157
money 8, 14, 18, 44, 66–8, 77, 80, 81–91, 93–5, 121, 139, 146, 158
Montesquieu 119–20
morality 9, 20, 35, 43, 46–7, 87, 124, 144–5
mother 18, 23, 45, 86
Mother Earth 116, 117
Mouvement socialiste, Le 71
mutualité 36, 74

N

nationalism 9, 73, 118, 142–4, 152–4
nation state 117–18, 151–5, 157
naturalism 9, 38, 46, 47, 102–5
naturalistic fallacy 46
nature-culture divide 103–5, 110, 112, 116, 118, 145, 149
neoclassical 5, 77, 79–81
neoliberalism 18, 34, 71, 75, 122, 148, 151, 153
Nestlé 4
New Guinea 28
Nietzsche, Friedrich 20
Nobel Prize 19
normativism 7, 47, 60, 124, 135
nuclear 107, 142

O

Occupy 93
  Freicoin 93
ocean 75, 108, 114, 118
Oliner, Pearl and Samuel 20
Open Access 75
Orwell, George 124
Ostrom, Elinor 19
Ottoman Empire 89
Oxfam 1

P

Palestine 143
pandemic *see* COVID-19
Paris 26, 27, 33, 137
  Climate Agreement 154
Parsons, Talcott 68, 159n2
phenomenology 32, 104
Peirce, Charles Sanders 38, 112
pluriversalism 9, 141–9, 153
poetic 9, 137–40
Polanyi, Karl 8, 81–4, 90
Populaire 72
positivism 26
post-colonialism 142, 149, 152
potlatch 28, 159n2
poverty 4, 131, 142, 146, 148
pragmatism 8, 38–40, 46–9, 64, 112
prejudice 142–3
profit 3–5, 16, 18, 23, 48, 64, 72, 75–9, 80–4, 93, 94, 100–1, 121, 126, 142–3, 155
profitability 79
proletariat 73–4
prosociality 8, 19, 22–5, 38, 42–5, 55
Protestantism 99–100
public sector 80
Pulcini, Elena 7
Puritanism 99
Putnam, Robert 22–3, 47, 120
psychology 19–21, 27, 38, 40, 43, 49–50, 64, 100, 102, 124

R

racism 59, 118, 143–5, 150, 154
Radical Ecological Democracy 147
rain forest 75, 103, 118
Rawls, John 57–60, 68
Realpolitik 150
reciprocity 8, 14–18, 22, 23, 28, 30–6, 43, 56, 58–60, 62, 63, 79, 81–2, 86, 92, 121, 135, 159n2
resonance 60, 61, 133, 135
resources 16, 19, 29, 50, 71, 75–8, 80, 86–90, 100, 107, 116, 118, 121, 138, 141–3, 148–57
renewable energy 75, 80
Ricœur, Paul 32, 33, 57
Rifkin, Jeremy 76
right-wing 1, 151, 155

ritual 27–9, 42, 67, 159n2
Russia 119, 155, 158

S

sanctions 19, 25, 33, 60, 62, 67
Sarkozy, Nicolas 143
science 9, 19, 20, 38, 40, 47, 70, 77, 78, 99, 100–9, 111–17, 126, 132, 156–7, 160n1
self-expression 58, 67, 110, 111
self-fulfilling prophecy 6, 124
self-interest 2, 6, 8, 13, 24, 25, 34, 35, 39, 61, 64, 66, 69, 82, 84, 94, 116, 119, 123, 126, 150, 152
self-realization 6, 48, 79, 133, 138
self-reflection 23, 49, 74
self-verification 64
sequentiality 59
Simmel, Georg 14, 16, 85, 88–9
situationism 136–7
slavery 90, 151
Smith, Adam 13, 25, 47, 119
socialism 3, 8, 26–30, 70–9, 122–8, 137, 149, 152, 157
socialization 13, 35, 44, 45, 51, 61, 134
social media 76
  see also Facebook
sociology 6, 16–17, 25–33, 65–6, 79, 82, 99, 102, 103, 146, 147, 159n1
Spain 78–9, 125, 142
Spinoza, Baruch 109–10
stereotype 1, 23, 38, 59–60, 126
Switzerland 94, 111
Syria 1, 142

T

tax 78, 86, 127, 155
technology 2, 9, 99–109, 122, 107, 146
terrorism 126, 137, 150
theater 135
third way 26, 33, 71, 128
Thunberg, Greta 154
  see also Fridays for Future
time bank 92
Tomasello, Michael 43–6
totalitarianism 122–4, 126, 134
totemism 29, 103
Trotskyism 122
Trump, Donald 154
Turkey 119, 155

U

Überfremdung 1
ultra-sociality 46, 51
unemployment 3, 18, 30, 127, 156
United Nations (UN) 149
universal basic income 30
universalism 144–6
utilitarianism 2–8, 14, 16, 19–24, 25, 30–6, 55, 64, 73, 74, 81, 90, 100, 107, 124, 126, 153

see also Blau, Peter
utopia 7, 9, 74, 78, 119–27, 136, 153

V

veganism 105
vegetarianism 105
violence 42, 73, 128, 139–40
Viveret, Patrick 3

W

wealth 1, 3, 23, 28, 29, 80, 93, 123, 131, 141, 146, 155, 158
Weber, Andreas 111–12

Weber, Max 65, 99, 100–5, 118, 133, 159n6
welfare 20, 30, 38, 44, 77, 80, 119, 141, 151
  queens 18
well-being 4, 6, 34, 93, 117, 147
Wenzel, Harald 68
Wikipedia 75–6, 125
Wittgenstein, Ludwig 57
women 7, 21, 59, 84, 90, 141
World War I 27, 38, 71, 72
World War II 71, 108, 143

Z

Zola, Émile 71

www.ingramcontent.com/pod-product-compliance
Lightning Source LLC
Chambersburg PA
CBHW051547020426

42333CB00016B/2145